THE NEW
GOD-IMAGE

Other books by Edward F. Edinger

Ego and Archetype
Melville's Moby Dick
The Creation of Consciousness
Anatomy of the Psyche
Encounter with the Self
The Bible and the Psyche
The Christian Archetype
Goethe's Faust
The Living Psyche
Transformation of the God-Image
The Eternal Drama
The Mystery of the Coniunctio
The Mysterium Lectures
The Aion Lectures

THE NEW GOD-IMAGE

A STUDY OF JUNG'S KEY LETTERS CONCERNING THE EVOLUTION OF THE WESTERN GOD-IMAGE

EDWARD F. EDINGER

EDITED BY DIANNE D. CORDIC
AND CHARLES YATES, M.D.

CHIRON PUBLICATIONS • WILMETTE, ILLINOIS

Grateful acknowledgment is made for the following permissions:

The Collected Works of C. G. Jung, trans. R. F. C. Hull, Bollingen Series XX, Vol. 18. Copyright © 1976 by Princeton University Press. Excerpts, cited passim, are reprinted by permission of Princeton University Press.

C. G. Jung: Letters, ed. Gerhard Adler and Aniela Jaffé, trans. R. F. C. Hull, Bollingen Series XCV, Vol. 2: 1951–1961. Copyright © 1973, renewed 1975 by Princeton University Press. Letters reprinted by permission of Princeton University Press.

Memories, Dreams, Reflections by C. G. Jung, trans. Richard and Clara Winston. Copyright © 1961, 1962, 1963, renewed 1989, 1990, 1991 by Random House, Inc. Excerpts reprinted by permission of Pantheon Books, a division of Random House, Inc.

Library of Congress Catalog Card Number: 95-51642

Printed in the United States of America.
Copyedited by Andrew C. Baker.
Book design by Vivian Bradbury.
Jacket design by D. J. Hyde.

Library of Congress Cataloging-in-Publication Data:

Edinger, Edward, F.
    The new God-image : a study of Jung's key letters concerning the evolution of the western God-image / Edward F. Edinger : edited by Dianne D. Cordic and Charles Yates.
        p.   cm.
    "A lecture series given in 1991 at the C. G. Jung Institute of Los Angeles."
    Includes bibliographical references and index.
    ISBN 0-933029-98-5 (pbk.)
    1. Jungian psychology—Congresses.   2. Image of God—Congresses.   3. Psychoanalysis and religion—Congresses.
    I. Cordic, Dianne D.   II. Yates, Charles.   III. Title.
    BL53.E29   1996
    211—dc20   95-51642
                                                                         CIP

ISBN 0-933029-98-5

CONTENTS

AUTHOR'S NOTE   *vii*

EDITORS' NOTE   *ix*

INTRODUCTION   *xi*

PART ONE
EPISTEMOLOGICAL PREMISES

Chapter One   3
Chapter Two   15
Chapter Three   27
Chapter Four   35

PART TWO
THE PARADOXICAL GOD

Chapter Five   51
Chapter Six   63

PART THREE
CONTINUING INCARNATION

Chapter Seven   77
Chapter Eight   91
Chapter Nine   109

APPENDIX
SELECTIONS FROM JUNG'S LETTERS

Bernhard Lang, June 1957   123

Pastor Walter Bernet, 13 June 1955   128

Valentine Brooke, 16 November 1959   135

Robert C. Smith, 29 June 1960   138

Pastor Tanner, 12 February 1959   141

Father Victor White, 24 November 1953   147

Father Victor White, 10 April 1954   153

Erich Neumann, 10 March 1959   159

Frau N., 28 June 1956   162

Elined Kotschnig, 30 June 1956   164

Reverend Morton T. Kelsey, 3 May 1958   169

Père William Lachat, 27 March 1954   172

Reverend David Cox, 25 September 1957   183

Reverend David Cox, 12 November 1957   191

WORKS CITED   197

INDEX   00

Author's Note

I warmly thank the editors, Dianne D. Cordic and Charles Yates, M.D., for their efforts and devotion in editing this manuscript.

Edward F. Edinger

Editors' Note

This book follows the text of a lecture series on Jung's *Letters* given by Edward F. Edinger. The lectures were given during a ten-week period in the Fall of 1991 at the C. G. Jung Institute of Los Angeles, as part of the Analysts' Training Program.

Charles Yates, M.D., prepared this text from an audiotape of those lectures. In making this record, we have tried to keep to Dr. Yates's transcript as closely as possible. We did so to preserve the colloquial format of Dr. Edinger's lectures and to avoid changing his intended and implied meaning. Therefore, we have used square brackets [ ] to indicate words that were not on the tape, but which we inserted to provide continuity. Occasionally, Dr. Edinger spoke within a quotation; we have therefore used double-barred square brackets [[ ]] to differentiate his own words from the text of the quotation he was reading.

References to the Bible are to the King James Version, unless otherwise noted.

Dianne D. Cordic
Charles Yates, M.D.

INTRODUCTION

. . . dem langen Entwicklungswege eines Göttlichen Dramas.

C. G. Jung, CW 11, par. 560

THE HISTORY OF WESTERN MAN CAN BE VIEWED AS A HISTORY OF ITS GOD-IMAGES, THE primary formulations of how mankind orients itself to the basic questions of life, its mysteries. It was Jung's phenomenological discovery that the Western God-image has undergone a whole series of transformations in the course of its evolutionary and historical development, and that we are now on the verge of another such evolutionary leap in the development of the God-image. We are right on the verge of witnessing the birth of a new God-image as a result of Jung's work. It is an idea Jung developed most explicitly in his book *Answer to Job*.

The very first sentence of *Answer to Job* reads as follows: "The Book of Job is a landmark in the long historical development of a divine drama"(Jung 1952, par. 560). That is the way Hull translates it, but that translation is not exactly right. What Hull translates as "historical development" is *Entwicklungswege*. *Entwicklungswege* denotes nothing about history. The word means development or, alternatively, evolution, so that it is a term that has a biological connotation, as well as a more general connotation. A more accurate translation of that sentence would be, "The Book of Job is a landmark in the long evolutionary pathway of a divine drama." To be specific, Jung is explicitly stating that the development of the God-image is not just a cultural process but is also an evolutionary process, something which has a biological substrate.

The remarkable idea in the sentence is the phrase *divine drama*, referring to a dynamic process. The God-image is not a static entity. The archetype of the God-image—what we live by whether we know it or not—is part of a dynamic process. It means that in the course of the evolution of the human species and in the historical-cultural development of the human species, the God-image is a living entity, a living process that moves, that unfolds, that develops and undergoes transformations.

That transformation process is also evident if one makes a historical examination of the facts of the collective psyche.

The God-image is a synonym for the Self in Jungian terms. The term God-image should not be confused with the term God. To speak of the God-image asserts nothing about God. As Jung states:

> [N]o man can know God. Knowing means seeing a thing in such a way that all can know it, and for me it means absolutely nothing if I profess a knowledge which I alone possess. (1975a, 377)

More specifically, the term God-image is synonymous with a particular aspect of the Self—what would be called the collective Self. In other words, it is a transpersonal center shared by a whole body of humanity and may have more than an individual reference (Jung 1969a, par. 757). One way of looking at it is charted below.

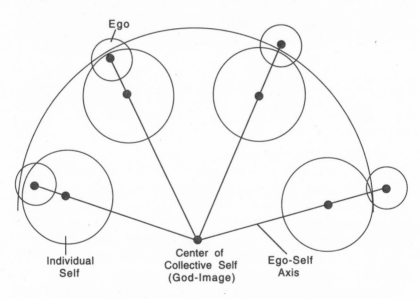

The Great Circle and the Collective Self

The great arc of the great circle refers to the collective Self. The intermediate-sized circles refer to the individual Self. The smallest circles refer to the individual ego. Notice that different individual egos have greater or lesser areas outside the great collective circle, indicating greater or lesser degrees of consciousness (Edinger 1987b, 67f.). The basic point is that—it is not just hypothesis, it is not just philosophical theorizing—there is evidence to support the idea that there is a collective Self, as contrasted with just an individual Self. It is approximately synonymous with what is termed the God-image.

Before examining what Jung has to say in his *Letters* about the transformation of the God-image that is occurring today, it might be worthwhile to review the series of transformations the Western God-image has gone through, as far as it is visible, in the course of recorded history, very briefly. As with all schematic presentations, it must not be taken too literally. What schematic thinking does is make certain points clear, but at the price of concrete reality.

All God-images are modes of expression of humanity's experience and understanding of the autonomous psyche—a very modern formulation. Such a formulation was not psychologically possible before Jung. But now we can understand all manifestations of the God-image as descriptive stages of humanity's experience of the autonomous aspect of the psyche. There is evidence to indicate that the stages of psychological development do tend to go through these historically represented stations. Commonplace in embryology is the phrase, "ontogeny recapitulates phylogeny," meaning the development of the individual recapitulates the development of the species. For example, a human embryo in its early development has gill slits—anatomical structures found in the fish. Vestiges of evolutionary development are repeated in the human embryo in the course of its own embryological development. There is reason to believe that something similar happens in the development of the psyche. Looking back on one's own psychological history, it is not so hard to see that in oneself. All those stages do exist; however, in the maximally integrated person—in someone like Jung— they are integrated in a unified way. They are experienced not so much as separate compartments, but as an harmonic whole. [6 states]

For descriptive purposes, there are six major stages in the evolution of the Western God-image. These are the following: animism, in which the God-image is an animistic one; matriarchy; hierarchical polytheism; tribal monotheism; universal monotheism; and number six, the discovery of the psyche, individuation. These stages form an historical sequence. At the same time, these historical stages are also layers of the collective unconscious in the individual psyche. It means that if we had some method at our disposal by which we could peel away various layers of the collective God-image, starting with our most modern mentality, we could work our way (theoretically) through these historical layers down to the most elemental one. It is not just a historical exercise. History is not the primary interest of the analyst; the individual psyche is the primary interest. In the course of studying the phenomena of the collective unconscious, as manifest in the individual psyche, we are obligated to look into historical parallels, because history has deposited its vestiges, its residues, so to speak, in the collective unconscious of humanity. These stages will be looked at in turn, starting from the bottom, remembering that if one is involved in an individual analysis, one starts from the top and works down; but with a historical survey, one starts from the bottom and works up. If one is destined to reach the level of psychological development called individuation—the psychic level, level number six—and if development proceeds without serious obstacle, then in an approximate way, one will have gone through these various stations.

1) *Animism*

In the initial stage of animism, the autonomous objective psyche is experienced in a diffuse way. The primitive psyche experiences autonomous spirits everywhere: in animals, in trees, in places, in rivers. The whole surrounding environment is animated, which is why it is called animism. It is animated with what we moderns would call a projection of the autonomous objective psyche. But projection is not the right word, because that would imply a rather differentiated psychology capable of projection; whereas an elemental psychology is immersed in its environment and surroundings, and therefore it experiences that immersion as an animistic activation of its surroundings. The easiest way to illustrate this situation for the modern is to refer to the poets, who have the chance to dip into the depths and bring up more primitive formulations. Shakespeare, for instance, formulates the animistic experience in *As You Like It* in this way, speaking about the Arden woods:

> And this our life, exempt from public haunt,
> Finds tongues in trees, books in the running brooks,
> Sermons in stones, and good in everything.
> (2.1.15–17)

One gets the same animistic approach in a remark that Jung makes in the late pages of his memoirs, speaking about how he is feeling in his very old age. He says:

Yet there is so much that fills me: plants, animals, clouds, day and night, and the eternal in man. (1963b, 359)

When he was alone in his Bollingen retreat, he would talk to his pots and pans; they were animated. He was in touch with the animistic level of the psyche along with all the other levels at the same time. He also encountered, in more conscious and differentiated form, the raw, animistic layer of the psyche activated in overt psychosis. (For example, ideas of reference, the delusional experience that objects and events are conveying a personal message to the patient, derive from the animistic level of the psyche).

2) *Matriarchy*
The animism phase historically belongs to the hunting and gathering traits of humanity. As soon as agriculture is discovered, hunting and gathering become less important, and the more settled community that tills the earth takes on primary importance. We then get the matriarchal stage of the God-image, in which the great, nourishing earth-mother is the primary factor. This development is associated with agriculture, with vegetation symbolism, with fertility rites, with the death and rebirth imagery of the annual cycle of the vegetation spirit. In this setting the masculine principle has not yet taken on an independent status of its own, but is still subordinate to the great-mother earth principle, indicated by the characteristic myth of this stage, the Attis-Cybele myth and its variants: the great mother and her son-lover, who is castrated and dies young, is mourned the way the vegetation is mourned and is then reborn again the following year. This stage is described quite fully by Erich Neumann, particularly in chapter 2 of *The Origins and History of Consciousness*. Symbolically, the great mother has a son-lover who is castrated or dismembered, or killed by a boar or something of that sort, but then is reborn again. The myth represents, on the one hand, the dying and reborn vegetation. More fundamentally, it represents the feeble state of human consciousness at this stage, which is still under the domination of nature and the earth principle, and hence is born but does not achieve full maturity, dies young and

goes through the cycle repetitively. This stage is found primarily in the settled, agricultural communities.

3) *Hierarchical Polytheism*
Sufficient produce and resources have now been acquired by the community so that cities can start to develop. There is the emergence of urban society. At this stage the masculine principle begins to supersede the feminine principle. A family of deities begins to emerge, with a patriarchal sky-god as the head of the family. The powers of the various deities are organized in a hierarchical way with the sky-god father as the king. Simultaneously, kingship is born. The polytheism of Mesopotamia, Egypt, and Greece are all examples of this third stage, as is the mythology of Norse and Germanic peoples. One sees the emergence of the city-state and the kingship required to govern it. The result is that a rather rigid organization is imposed on the new social structure. Accompanying developments are metallurgy, technology, and writing. Earlier cultures have no writing, and therefore no scriptures exist to illustrate the stages of animism or matriarchy. Written scriptures are illustrative and exemplary of this polytheistic stage. For the West the classical scripture would be, for example, Homer's *Iliad*.

It is quite interesting to read Homer's *Iliad* from the standpoint of modern psychology. A good bit of the *Iliad* is made up of battle scenes. You have the Trojans on one side and the Greeks or Achaeans on the other side, and you have the heroic personalities who are participating in the battle. Then, right in the midst of the furor of battle, deities appear: Mars, [Ares], Athena, Aphrodite helping their particular champions. It is astonishing to read from a modern standpoint, because it is evident that the level of experience referred to indicates a kind of psychological condition in which the autonomous factors of the psyche in times of crisis were living presences. Achilles, for instance, would go to battle, something would happen and he would be filled with a divine energy, so that a pathway on the battlefield would open up. No one would dare confront him; they would flee this individual filled with divine *furor bellicus*. It was described as the presence of Ares, the war god, who manifested himself on the battlefield. These deities were experienced as living presences by the Homeric heroes. The *Iliad* can be viewed as a description of the phenomenology of the psychology of that stage of psychological development, the polytheistic phase. These deities were not abstractions; they were experiential realities, not just poetic constructs. If the modern poet looked at it that way, it would be a poetic construct. These were expressions of a living psychic reality.

4) Tribal Monotheism

This stage was discovered or created by the ancient Hebrews. The fact I put it both ways is significant. The question always arises—the question comes just from examining this chart: what is responsible for the transformation of the God-image? On the one hand, the God-image has within it a latent dynamic tendency to evolve and develop. On the other hand, there is evidence to indicate its development and dynamism results from the feedback it receives from conscious egos.

Referring to the chart, the lines drawn between the individual egos and the center of the collective Self are two-way streets, not just one-way. If the transformation of the God-image took place just through an innate dynamic, then a new God-image would be discovered. But if the new God-image is encouraged into transformation by conscious behaviors or reactions of individual egos, then the transformation is created. Both are true.

Out of the many deities of the ancient Near East, Yahweh emerged as the single, all-encompassing One for this little tribe of nomads, the ancient Hebrews. The emergence of this new God-image, called Yahweh, was linked to this chosen people, who owed their existence to Yahweh, on the one hand; and correspondingly, one could say that Yahweh owed His existence to them—a two-way street. The difference between the Hebrew Yahweh and Zeus, the father-god of Greek pantheism, is considerable. Jung speaks about this difference in *Answer to Job*.

> His jealous and irritable nature, prying mistrustfully into the faithless hearts of men and exploring their secret thoughts, compelled a personal relationship between himself and man, who could not help but feel personally called by him. That was the essential difference between Yahweh and the all-ruling Father Zeus, who in a benevolent and somewhat detached manner allowed the economy of the universe to roll along on its accustomed courses and punished only those who were disorderly. He did not moralize but ruled purely instinctively. He did not demand anything more *from* human beings than the sacrifices due to him; he did not want to do anything *with* human beings because he had no plans for them. Father Zeus is certainly a figure but

not a personality. Yahweh, on the other hand, was interested in man. Human beings were a matter of first-rate importance to him. He needed them as they needed him, urgently and personally. (1952, par. 568)

You see Yahweh's first requirement was that He be the only God.

Hear, O Israel: the Lord our God is one Lord.
(Deut. 6:4)[1]

Not many, but One: that is the announcement that separates Yahweh from ancient Near East polytheism. At this stage, although one God is insisted upon, and although He is creator of the universe and governor of all, nevertheless He has personal relations with the chosen people only, connecting Him directly with this small tribe of the elect, hence the term tribal monotheism. Even though the singleness of God is proclaimed, He does not control everything, because He does have enemies both among and outside his chosen people. Many of His chosen people did not do what He said, so they were His enemies. Also there were external enemies like the Amalekites. All goes to indicate there is a latent dualism in the God-image, even though monotheism is consciously insisted upon.

5) *Universal Monotheism*
With the emergence of Christianity, the tribal monotheism of ancient Israel was universalized. It became available to the nations. One of the major features of early Christianity was that Yahweh's promise to the tribe Israel was disseminated to everyone. It was stolen from the Jews, so to speak, and given to the gentiles, to the *gentes*, to the nations.[2] The monotheism of one tribe becomes available to all tribes, all *gentes*.

The other feature of this new God-image was that it split into two—in the course of becoming all good. You see, Israel's Yahweh is a Father-God, and Christianity's God-image is a Son-God. However, as Jung has elaborated, Yahweh had two sons: Christ and Satan. In order for Yahweh to turn into the all-good Christ-Son, he had to split off the

---

[1]See also Exod. 3:14; also extensive literature on the names of the Deity.
[2]From *gens, gentes*—clan, people, tribe, nation.

all-bad Satan-Son, who nevertheless remained lurking around to be dealt with sooner or later (Jung 1951, par. 68 ff.). The latent dualism that was within the monotheistic God-image becomes even more overt in Christian symbolism, even though that fact has been assiduously disregarded. As Jung has demonstrated in *Aion*, this antithesis then lived itself out in the Christian aeon. The first half of the aeon was under the aegis of Christ, the first fish, and then the second half of the aeon was under the aegis of Satan, the second fish (Jung 1951, par. 127ff.).

Another feature of the transformation of the God-image from tribal monotheism to universal monotheism at the beginning of our era is what might be called the Marcion problem. Since we are living in the time of a new transformation of the God-image, it is very instructive for us to look back two thousand years and examine the phenomena which happened the last time there was a transformation. Marcion, a good example of one aspect of the problem, lived from about A.D. 90–160. He was a Christian heretic, who maintained that the God of love as revealed by Christ had nothing to do with Yahweh, the God of law. According to Marcion, they were totally separate deities; thus he rejected the whole Old Testament and a good bit of the New Testament too. Yahweh was the just God; the Christian God was the good God (Jung 1951, par. 89; 1969a, par. 408).

The emerging church rejected that heresy. Had Marcion prevailed, there would have been no continuity. There would have been a total split in the historical sequence, so that what we witness would not be a progressive evolution of the God-image, which keeps the psyche connected to its roots; but instead, there would be a dissociation from the source. Jung has something to say about that in *Mysterium Coniunctionis*:

> Any renewal not deeply rooted in the best spiritual tradition is ephemeral; but the dominant that grows from historical roots act[s] like a living being within the ego-bound man. He does not possess it, it possesses him. (1955, par. 521)

Obviously the issue is relevant to modern man also.

6) *Individuation*

Individuation, the discovery of the psyche, refers to the psychological level which understands religious imagery as the phenomenology of the objective psyche. On this subject Jung wrote *Answer to Job* and *Aion* in 1951. At that time he still had ten years to live. The second volume of the *Letters*, from 1951 to 1961, covers his last ten years, and includes a whole series of remarkable letters concerning the nature of the God-image and the transformation it is undergoing for modern man *via* the individuation process.

Out of this larger number of letters, fourteen have been chosen to illustrate Jung's discovery. As selected, three main themes or subjects leaped out of the contents of the letters themselves. First is Jung's *epistemological premise*, the subject of part 1 [of this book]. The second subject is the *paradoxical God*, which is to be found in part 2. The third subject is the *continuing incarnation*, which will be emphasized particularly in part 3. These subjects exist throughout, but the order is arranged purposefully for the sequence to stand out.

Three steps are involved in understanding what Jung is talking about in his material concerning the new God-image. The first step is the ability to perceive the new God-image, which requires that one master the epistemological premises that enable one to recognize the reality of the psyche. The second step then follows from the seeing of the new God-image Jung is talking about. He is not imposing it by fiat; rather, he is teaching us how to perceive for ourselves what he is talking about. It is not a matter of accepting this idea on faith. Quite the contrary—it is a matter of perceiving for yourself. Then the third step, after seeing the reality of this new God-image, as it lives itself out in one's own individual psychology, as well as in the psychology of the collective, is an awareness of what the individual can do to help the process of transformation of this God-image. That is what is meant by the process of continuing incarnation.

In many respects these letters offer a clearer expression of Jung's views than are found in his more formal writings. In any case, the *Letters* supplements the more formal presentations of the *Collected Works* in a helpful way, because they spell out for us a new God-image which is destined to inaugurate a whole new aeon of human cultural history.

Part One

Epistemological Premises

... Here that threshold which separates two epochs plays the principal role. I mean by that threshold the theory of knowledge whose starting-point is Kant. On that threshold minds go their separate ways: those that have understood Kant, and the others that cannot follow him.

C. G. Jung, *Letters II*, 375

ONE

IN JUNE 1957, JUNG WROTE A LETTER TO BERNARD LANG, WHICH BEGINS AS follows:

> Many thanks for your friendly letter, which shows that the Buber-Jung controversy is a serious matter for you. And so indeed it is, for here that threshold which separates two epochs plays the principal role. I mean by that threshold the theory of knowledge whose starting-point is Kant. On that threshold minds go their separate ways: those that have understood Kant, and the others that cannot follow him. I will not enter here into the *Critique of Pure Reason*, but will try to make things clear to you from a different, more human standpoint. (1975a, 375)

He speaks of "that threshold the theory of knowledge whose starting-point is Kant." The theory of knowledge is the definition of epistemology, a word which is derived from two Greek words: *episteme*, meaning knowledge and *logos*, meaning word or reason. Epistemology is the study of the process of knowing. It asks such questions as what do we know for certain and how do we know it? It is a concern with the study, origin, nature, and validity of knowledge. Put in psychological terms, epistemology refers to the nature and function of consciousness.

In ancient times, epistemology was concerned with what could be known objectively. Human subjectivity, the beginning of modern consciousness, began about the year 1500, a crucial date in the Christian aeon, the time when the spring point moved over into the second fish in the astrological constellation of Pisces. Jung makes quite a point of what took place in human history right around 1500: the ego took a giant leap forward in its hubristic efforts, and the God-image fell out of heaven and into the psyche of man. The awareness of human subjectivity was born (Jung 1951, par. 149).

3

One of the major starting points in the change in humanity's awareness of itself was Copernicus' discovery that the sun did not revolve around the earth: the earth revolved around the sun. Kant himself (1965) later described his own discoveries as a Copernican revolution in philosophy. And indeed it is a different standpoint. What Copernicus did was to "dis-identify" himself from subjective experience, and, as a result, was able to take an objective attitude toward human perception, thus separating out subjectivity, an attitude never before available. From all ordinary (subjective) experience, it is obvious that the sun revolves around the earth, as the earth stands still. Only a fool would think otherwise. It is perfectly obvious. One's (subjective) experience teaches that irrefutably. Right at this period of human history, Copernicus and the others who followed him, who were able to recognize the validity of what he said, were able to begin to "dis-identify" with that subjectivity and to view experience as though it were from an Archimedean standpoint some distance from oneself. The result was a whole new view about the nature of man's place in the universe. Modern epistemology began. Copernicus' discovery is an example of a new discovery in epistemology, because he was able to challenge what was assumed to be objective knowledge and demonstrate it was not true knowledge.

The philosopher Descartes (1966) carried this development further. He begins his inquiry with the question: How do I know anything for certain? He is concerned with epistemology—How do I know? He says:

> As far as I know, it is perfectly possible that the entire outer world, everything that I perceive, including my own body, could be an hallucination or a delusion generated by some diabolical creator.

One cannot know for certain. He reached the conclusion that the only thing he did know for certain is that he exists and that he perceives himself as a questioner, somebody who is asking the question: "What do I know?" Then out of that came his famous formulation, "*Cogito ergo sum*"—"I think, therefore I am," perhaps better translated: "I am conscious, therefore I am." It is not a matter of thinking, as opposed to feeling or perceiving. The fact that he is conscious of his own functioning is the bedrock upon which he builds all the rest of his epistemology. It is the beginning of the new subjective standpoint. The basis of certain knowledge for Descartes was subjective experience.

Alfred North Whitehead (1956, 141)[1] speaks of how crucial the change of viewpoint was at this time.

Modern philosophy is tinged with subjectivism, as against the objective attitude of the ancients. The same change is to be seen in religion. In the early history of the Christian Church, the theological interest centered in discussions on the nature of God, on the meaning of the Incarnation. . . .

. . . At the Reformation, the Church was torn asunder by dissension as to the individual experiences of believers in respect to justification. The individual subject of experience had been substituted for the total drama of all reality. Luther asked, "How am I justified?"; modern philosophers have asked, "How do I have knowledge?" The emphasis lies upon the subject of experience. The ancient world takes its stand upon the drama of the universe, the modern world upon the inward drama of the soul. Descartes, in his *Meditations*, expressly grounds the existence of this inward drama upon the possibility of error. There may be no correspondence with objective fact, and thus there must be a soul with activities whose reality is purely derivative from itself. . . . "But it will be said that these presentations are false, and that I am dreaming. Let it be so. At all events it is certain that I seem to see light, hear a noise and feel heat. This cannot be false, and this is what in me is properly called perceiving which is nothing else than thinking. From this I begin to know what I am." ". . . as I before remarked, although the things which I perceive or imagine are perhaps nothing at all apart from me, I am nevertheless assured that those modes of consciousness which I call perceptions and imaginations, in as far only as they are modes of consciousness, exist in me."

Descartes had a very interesting argument to prove the existence of God. In essence, the argument stated that since man has the idea of an omnipotent, perfect Creator, therefore He must exist. It is faulty reasoning, but, as with so many of the great philosophers, Descartes is doing more than expounding a logical, rational, systematic theory. What he is saying here is that because man has an image of God, therefore God exists. Although that does not stand up to scrutiny, nevertheless, Descartes' basing God's existence on the fact that there is an inner, psychological

---

[1]See also Cassirer, 1948.

God-image is an expression of the fact that modern psychological man has been born, as indicated by the fact that he is even thinking in such terms. As Whitehead said, the ancient and medieval world did not think in those terms at all. It is the modern way of thinking.

What he is describing is a unique vision of reality. All the great philosophers are visionaries. Descartes' career started with a mystical experience of a great dream. Von Franz talks about that dream, too extensively to include here, in her essay on "The Dream of Descartes" (1991, 107ff.). Descartes describes his state of mind directed toward subjective experience:

> After I had spent some years thus studying in the book of the world and in trying to acquire some experience, I one day made the resolution to study *within myself also*, and to use all the powers of my mind for the choosing of the paths that I ought to follow; in the which I succeeded far better, so it seems to me, than if I had never left my country or my books. (von Franz 1991, 112)

Kant takes the next decisive step, the more radical step, toward elaborating the nature of the reality of psychic subjectivity. Here again his basic discoveries are not so much philosophy as revelation. They are visions. He saw more deeply than anyone previously.

Kant's basic discovery is that of the *a priori* forms and categories. According to Kant, perceptions of outer reality are structured and ordered by means of innate, built-in forms of perception. These forms of perception are space and time. Space and time do not exist in the outer world. They are forms of perception that the human mind imposes on the flux of sensory data to order it. Furthermore, our understanding of what we perceive, our ability to grasp and conceptualize what we perceive, is brought about by a number of innate categories of understanding—categories such as quantity, quality, cause and effect, and relation. His discovery, then, is that the human mind, the human psyche, pours into sensory data the forms of perception and the categories of understanding which create our total view of the world.

Once the basic premise is recognized, one can then distinguish three levels of reality. There is the phenomenal world, which is the world of appearances, the world outside of us. There is the world of the understanding, which is composed of the forms of perception and the categories of understanding that structure the phenomenal world. Then there is ultimate reality itself, the thing in itself, which is assumed to exist beyond the subjective sensations it sends out but which is totally unknowable. Ultimate reality, the thing in itself, is unknowable because the knower is imprisoned in the box of the categories of understanding and the forms of perception. By analogy, it is as though one were looking out through various peepholes in an enclosed room, peepholes composed of stained glass that have certain structures superimposed on them and with various images and colors imposed on them. Everything that reaches the inside from the outside must go through these little windows. All one can see is what the window lets through in the form it lets it through. What is on the other side is ultimate reality. One cannot know it without breaking the window. Since the window is the organic structure of one's being, it is impossible as a living organism to break that window to find out. Therefore, the thing in itself is essentially unknowable. Logically then, metaphysics is impossible. There is no such thing as metaphysics according to Kant, because metaphysics assumes one has some *entré* into the transpersonal world. Neither the metaphysics of external reality nor of spiritual reality is possible, because one cannot break out of the limitations or containment of one's organic being.

Although Kant did not formulate it psychologically, as psychology had not reached that level yet, it means that all experience is psychic experience. All experience has a subjective substrate. It means we can never perceive the archetype, as such, in itself. The archetype is a thing in itself, a metaphysical entity. We assume it exists because we can experience the effects of it, but the effects can be experienced psychologically only.

Kant distinguishes the terms *phenomenon* and *noumenon*. *Phenomenon* means appearance, phenomenal reality, the world of appearances (from *phanein*—to show, reveal). *Noumenon* is the thing in itself which is unknown, which is postulated to exist. The only reference to it is the mental construct that the mind creates for it. (From *nous*—mind). The word *fantasy* derives from *phanein* also. Fantasies are one's inner phenomena. They are what relate us to the unknown object, to the noumenon, which is postulated. The fantasy corresponds internally to the phenomenological object in the outer world. Any presumption to such absolute knowledge as metaphysics or knowledge of the thing in itself is just that, a presumption. It is a psychological sin, an inflation. Regarding numinous images, Jung says:

The tremendous effectiveness (mana) of these images is such that they not only give one the feeling of pointing to the *Ens realissimum*, but make one convinced that they actually express it and establish it as a fact. This makes discussion uncommonly difficult, if not impossible. It is, in fact, impossible to demonstrate God's reality to oneself except by using images which have arisen spontaneously or are sanctified by tradition, and whose psychic nature and effects the naïve-minded person has never separated from their unknowable metaphysical background. He instantly equates the effective image with the transcendental X to which it points. . . .[I]t must be remembered that the image and the statement are psychic processes which are different from their transcendental object; they do not posit it, they merely point to it. (1952, par. 558)

In his youth Jung revered Kant. In his *Zofingia Lectures*, which he gave to his fraternity in medical school, there are many examples of extravagant praise of Kant. For example:

I would like to introduce my talk tonight with these divine words of Immanuel Kant. (1983, 23)

. . . the consecrated ground of Kantian philosophy. (1983, 33)

Kant, the greatest of all sages ever born on German soil . . . (1983, 34)

Kant was the turning point for the modern psyche. Although not a philosopher, Jung may be seen in a psychological sense as a successor to Kant. Jung's epistemological premise has its starting point in Kant, as may be seen in the Lang letter:

And so indeed it is, for here that threshold which separates two epochs plays the principal role. I mean by that threshold the theory of knowledge whose starting-point is Kant. On that threshold minds go their separate ways: those that have understood Kant, and the others that cannot follow him. (1975a, 375)

Kant, by differentiating subjective factors from objective ones, established the basis for the scientific approach to the psyche. As Jung says:

Although I have often been called a philosopher, I am an empiricist and adhere as such to the phenomenological standpoint. I trust that it does not conflict with the principles of scientific empiricism if one occasionally makes certain reflections which go beyond a mere accumulation and classification of experience. As a matter of fact I believe that experience is not even possible without reflection, because "experience" is a process of assimilation without which there could be no understanding. As this statement indicates, I approach psychological matters from a scientific and not from a philosophical standpoint. Inasmuch as religion has a very important psychological aspect, I deal with it from a purely empirical point of view, that is, I restrict myself to the observation of phenomena and I eschew any metaphysical or philosophical considerations. I do not deny the validity of these other considerations, but I cannot claim to be competent to apply them correctly. (1969a, par. 2)

Jung's epistemology obviously corresponds to Kant's epistemology. Jung recognizes Kant's position is the "threshold which separates two epochs." It is a statement which, like lightning, lights up a whole landscape. Before Kant, in spite of the beginning efforts of Copernicus and Descartes and others, humanity had been identified with its subjective experience. After Kant, if one is able to see what he points out, one is no longer able to be identified with his subjective experience; one is now conscious of the subjectivity of the experience and therefore no longer can grant it metaphysical validity. All experience is a subjective, psychological experience. It is an experience of the soul, because there is nothing else to be experienced except the psyche. For the individual this is either a self-evident perception or it is a ridiculous presumption. Either one sees it as a fact—"Yes, of course, it is a self-evident truth"— or one does not. There are those that follow Kant and those that cannot. It is not a philosophical issue. It is an issue of the perception of the nature of human experience. It is a question of vision, of seeing. It is not a matter of volition. Either it is seen or it is not.
As Jung says:

My human limitation does not permit me to assert that I know God, hence I cannot but regard all assertions about God as relative because subjectively conditioned—and this out of respect for my brothers, whose other conceptions and beliefs have as much to justify them as mine. If I am a psychologist I shall try to take these differences seriously and to understand them. But under no circumstances shall I assume that if the other person doesn't share my opinion it is due to a deformity or lack of an organ. . . . Though I am sure of my subjective experience, I must impose on myself every conceivable restriction in interpreting it. I must guard against identifying with my subjective experience. I consider all such identifications as serious psychological mistakes. (1975a, 376)

It is a very important formula: *do not identify with your subjective experience.* It is crucial for anyone wanting to do Jungian analysis. To the extent one is contained in a metaphysical belief, one is identified with one's subjective experience, and one gives universal validity to an experience which is only individually valid.

To the extent one is contained in such a situation, one cannot conduct a depth analysis. Analysis does not take place in such a setting. What happens instead, no matter how well intentioned the individual, [is that] the so-called analysis becomes a process of indoctrination. It applies to any analyst. All analysts have belief systems of one kind or another to serve as a boat to keep one afloat on the sea of the collective unconscious. One must have a boat. These belief systems are based on one's subjective experience; we have no other basis for them. Either they derive from past experience taken over from someone else— which is still our subjective experience—or from our own individual experience. Such a boat is absolutely necessary, but one should be aware it is one's own boat and should not assume the same boat will keep someone else afloat. One must guard diligently against identifying with subjective experience. When one really understands that, then one can do depth analysis and not indoctrination. Such an understanding will allow one to follow the patient's psychic experience wherever it goes without imposing one's own presuppositions.

Jung says:

Knowing means seeing a thing in such a way that all can know it, and for me it means absolutely nothing if I profess a knowledge which I alone possess. . . . I therefore regard the proposition that belief is knowledge as absolutely misleading. What has happened to these people is that they have been overpowered by an inner experience. Take as an example our national saint Nicholas von der Flüe: he sees an overwhelmingly terrifying face which he involuntarily interprets as God and then twiddles it around until it turns into the image of the Trinity, which still hangs today in the church at Sachseln. This image has nothing to do with the original experience, but represents the Summum Bonum and divine love, which are miles away from God's Yahwistic terrors or the "wrath fire" of Boehme. Actually after this vision Nicholas should have preached: "God is terrible." But he believed his own interpretation instead of the immediate experience. This is a typical phenomenon of belief. (1975a, 377f.)

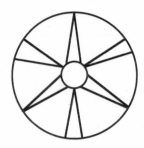

Vision of Nicholas of Flüe (von Franz, n.d.)

Nicholas of Flüe had this terrifying experience of a countenance of extreme wrath (Jung 1969a, par. 477; 1988, 883). It had such a terrible effect on him that those in his surroundings could not look upon his face; his face was so shattered. It took him years to come to terms with it. He ended up by deciding that it was a vision of the Trinity. His version (see above) is an elaborate idea of the Trinity that works in two different directions simultaneously. It is going outward and inward at the same time. This image was concocted to get rid of the terror.

Jung further says:

> Interpretation by faith seeks to represent the experienced content of a vision, for instance, as the visible manifestation of a transcendental Being, and it invariably does so in terms of a traditional system and then asserts that this representation is the absolute truth. Opposed to this is my view, which also interprets, in a sense. It interprets by comparing *all* traditional assumptions and does not assert that Transcendence itself has been perceived; it insists only on the reality of the fact that an experience has taken place, and that this is exactly the form it took. I compare this experience with all other experiences of the kind and conclude that a process is going on in the unconscious

amplification

which expresses itself in various forms. I am aware that this process is going on, but I do not know what its nature is, whether it is psychic, whether it comes from an angel or from God himself. We must leave these questions open, and no belief will help us over the hurdle, for we do not know and can never know. (1975a, 379)

What Jung says here is that he uses the method of amplification. Rather than setting the particular subjective experience into a preestablished context, amplification instead compares the experience with a myth here, a folktale there, a religious observance here. Whenever we follow the method of amplification, which of course is the hallmark of Jungian analysis, it is important as much as possible to choose the amplifications from many different contexts. There is then a better opportunity for the patient's own subjective experience to be able to say, "Aha, that is the one that fits."

For the sake of completeness, there were four figures subsequent to Kant who assisted in developing psychological empiricism and who influenced Jung. Kant discovered the forms and categories of the mind, of subjectivity, that serve to structure experience, and established the fact that it is impossible to know the nature of the thing in itself. All we can know is the psychic representation. These subsequent figures further develop epistemology toward a phenomenology of the psyche, without yet recognizing the unconscious as an entity or yet having a notion of an empirical method as *entré* to the unconscious.

Schopenhauer, following Kant, applied his [Kant's] ideas, but thought he discovered the thing in itself. His major work was entitled *The World as Will and Representation*. His idea was that the individual human being could know the thing in itself by virtue of his own inner experience. It was Schopenhauer's conclusion that the thing in itself was Will, a dynamic towards existence. It would be a kind of philosophical version of libido, unconscious libido. For Schopenhauer, all the representations which go to make up the inner and outer world, with which we are familiar, are representations of the will; the cosmic Will (Jung 1971, par. 233 et al.; 1966, par. 229; 1963b, 69).

Eduard von Hartmann developed this idea further in his work, *The Philosophy of the Unconscious*. He postulated a "universal will" that was purposeful. Schopenhauer was ambiguous about how purposeful the will was. Hartmann carried the idea further (Jung 1971, par. 279). Nietzsche elaborated the same idea in terms of the "will to power." He

12

had the unique distinction, not just of conceptualizing and theorizing, but of falling into a living experience of the unconscious, and coming to a tragic end in the process (Jung 1971, several pars.; 1969a, par. 141f.; 1963b, 189).

The fourth figure, Carl Gustav Carus, was not a philosopher. He was a physician and a student of animal psychology. He was approximately a contemporary of Schopenhauer. His book, *Psyche*, defined psychology as the science of the soul's development, going from the unconscious to the conscious. His book was published in German in 1846 (Jung 1969a, par. 141f.; 1970, par. 791).[2] Carus is a significant figure, to whom Jung alludes several times. Hartmann got many of his ideas from Carus, as well as from Schopenhauer. These four are significant precursors of Jungian psychology.

[2]A good summary can be found in Ellenberger 1970.

TWO

In a letter dated June 13, 1955, Jung replied to a book that the author, Pastor Walter Bernet, had sent to him.[1] In it, Jung himself gives a lengthy discourse on religious realities. He begins talking about his own religious experience as follows:

> It was the tragedy of my youth to see my father cracking up before my eyes on the problem of his faith and dying an early death. (Jung 1975a, 257; 1963b, 91–96ff.)

That is a strong statement: "the tragedy of my youth." It is a very important remark on Jung's part, not only because of the personal reference of its effect on him as a child, but also, more importantly, because he realized he was witnessing in his father's experience a collective phenomenon.

The problem was not only personal but universal. Western society in the latter half of the nineteenth century was cracking up over the problem of its faith. It was exactly at this time Nietzsche had arrived at the realization that "God is dead."[2] It was exactly at this time that Matthew Arnold speaks in lachrymose terms in his poem "Dover Beach" about the ebbing of the sea of faith. At this time also, Arnold wrote a poem that puts it all in a nutshell. The title of the poem is "Stanzas from the Grand Chartreuse." The Grand Chartreuse is a famous monastery in France. Matthew Arnold had visited the monastery. He speaks to modern, secular rationalists, rhetorically:

---

[1] Walter Bernet's book was *Inhalt und Grenze der religiösen Erfahrung*. It is translated as *The Content and Boundaries of Religious Experience*.
[2] First mentioned in Nietzsche 1982, Book 3, sec. 125, *The Gay Science*; cf. also Nietzsche 1964, Prologue, sec. 3, *Thus Spake Zarathustra*.

Forgive me, masters of the mind!
At whose behest I long ago
So much unlearnt, so much resign'd—
I come not here to be your foe!
I seek these anchorites, not in ruth,
To curse and to deny your truth;

Not as their friend, or child, I speak!
But as, on some far northern strand,
Thinking of his own Gods, a Greek
In pity and mournful awe might stand
Before some fallen Runic stone—
For both were faiths, and both are gone.

Wandering between two worlds, one dead,
The other powerless to be born,
With nowhere yet to rest my head,
Like these, on earth, I wait forlorn.
Their faith, my tears, the world deride—
I come to shed them at their side.
                    (Arnold 1965, 305f.)

It is a funeral ode to the lost God-image. It is the state of mind of
humanity waiting for the birth of the new God-image. Jung's personal
experience with his father connected him simultaneously with its collective equivalent and obliged him to find the answer, which he did:

> I was thrown back on experience alone. Always Paul's experience on
> the road to Damascus hovered before me, and I asked myself how his
> fate would have fallen out but for his vision. Yet this experience came
> upon him while he was blindly pursuing his own way. As a young
> man I drew the conclusion that you must obviously fulfill your des-
> tiny in order to get to the point where a *donum gratiae* might happen
> along. But I was far from certain, and always kept the possibility in
> mind that on this road I might end up in a black hole. I have re-
> mained true to this attitude all my life.
>
> From this you can easily see the origin of my psychology: only by
> going my own way, integrating my capacities headlong (like Paul),
> and thus creating a foundation for myself, could something be
> vouchsafed to me or built upon it. (Jung 1975a, 257f.)

There is a lot of evidence that the apostle Paul was a very important figure to Jung. In the Index to the *Letters* alone, there are twenty-five references to Paul just in the two volumes of the *Letters*. There are a lot of references in the *Collected Works* as well. Paul's "going his own way" led to his numinous experience on the road to Damascus. He describes in *Acts*:

> As for me, I once thought it was my duty to use every means to oppose the name of Jesus the Nazarene. This I did in Jerusalem. I myself threw many of the saints into prison, acting on authority from the chief priests, and when they were sentenced to death I cast my vote against them. I often went around the synagogues inflicting penalties, trying in this way to force them to renounce their faith; my fury against them was so extreme that I even pursued them into foreign cities.
>
> On one such expedition I was going to Damascus, armed with full powers and a commission from the chief priests, and at midday as I was on my way . . . I saw a light brighter than the sun come down from heaven. It shone brilliantly around me and my fellow travelers. We all fell to the ground, and I heard a voice saying to me in Hebrew, "Saul, Saul, why are you persecuting me? It is hard for you, kicking like this against the goad." Then I said: Who are you Lord? And the Lord answered, "I am Jesus, and you are persecuting me. But get up and stand on your feet, for I have appeared to you for this reason: to appoint you as my servant and as witness of this vision in which you have seen me, and of others in which I shall appear to you. I shall deliver you from the people and from the pagans, to whom I am sending you to open their eyes, so that they may turn from darkness to light." (Acts 26:9–18 Jerusalem Bible)

Taking this example seriously, Jung expresses a basic idea: *follow your libido wherever it takes you.* Paul's libido took him into a hatred of the Christians. He poured himself into his task with everything that he had. Jung decided he would do the same—follow his libido—because the example implied to him that grace was possible in no other way and that nature would correct a wrong course. It is a matter requiring not a little faith. The idea is that even if one gets into trouble by following one's libido with all the conviction at one's disposal, it will still be your trouble, not someone else's trouble. It will be your experience; it will belong to your reality. It is a dangerous doctrine, but that is what he is saying:

The only way open to me was the experience of religious realities which I had to accept without regard to their truth. [He probably means without regard to their theoretical truth]. In this matter I have no criterion except the fact that they seem meaningful to me. (Jung 1975a, 258)

Religious realities in Jungian terms have their basis in one's subjective experience, as phenomenological expressions of the archetypal psyche. Jung's discovery of the archetypal unconscious and of the subjectivity of religious realities appears to have occurred at the age of eleven, in 1886. The description of it occupies six pages of his memoirs, which indicates how important he took it to be.

One fine summer day that same year I came out of school at noon and went to the cathedral square. [[The Basel Cathedral.]] The sky was gloriously blue, the day one of radiant sunshine. The roof of the cathedral glittered, the sun sparkling from the new, brightly glazed tiles. I was overwhelmed by the beauty of the sight, and thought: "The world is beautiful and the church is beautiful, and God made all this and sits above it far away in the blue sky on a golden throne and . . ." Here came a great hole in my thoughts, and a choking sensation. I felt numbed, and knew only: "Don't go on thinking now! Something terrible is coming, something I do not want to think, something I dare not even approach . . . I would be committing the most frightful of sins. . . . The most terrible sin is the sin against the Holy Ghost, which cannot be forgiven." (Jung 1963b, 36)

That agony went on for three days and three nights, and several pages, until it comes to this passage:

"God knows I cannot resist much longer, and He does not help me. . . . He could easily lift this compulsion from me, but evidently He is not going to. . . ."
I thought it over again and arrived at the same conclusion. "Obviously God also desires me to show courage," I thought. "If that is so and I go through with it, then He will give me His grace and illumination."
I gathered all my courage, as though I were about to leap forthwith into hell-fire, and let the thought come. I saw before me the cathedral, the blue sky. God sits on His golden throne, high above the world—and from under the throne an enormous turd falls upon

the sparkling new roof, shatters it, and breaks the walls of the cathedral asunder. (1963b, 39)

That was the terrible image, welling up from the collective psyche. It refers not just to Jung personally, but to the state of Christendom as a whole. Jung continues:

So that was it! I felt an enormous, an indescribable relief. Instead of the expected damnation, grace had come upon me, and with it an unutterable bliss such as I had never known. I wept for happiness and gratitude . . . I had experienced an illumination. A great many things I had not previously understood became clear to me . . . what my father had not understood . . . he had failed to experience the will of God, had opposed it for the best reasons and out of the deepest faith. And that was why he had never experienced the miracle of grace which heals all and makes all comprehensible. . . . If one fulfills the will of God one can be sure of going the right way. . . . From that moment on, when I experienced grace, my true responsibility began . . . then came a dim understanding that God could be something terrible. I had experienced a dark and terrible secret. It overshadowed my whole life, and I became deeply pensive. (1963b, 40)

It is an example of a religious reality, the phenomenological experience of a religious reality. How many people, let alone how many eleven-year-olds, would set that experience in a religious framework (1963b, 39)? Very few. Certainly adults would set it in a psychopathological framework. Jung's genius is that, like Job, he never questioned the fact that his immediate perceptions—which are the foundation of one's psychological experience—had a transpersonal basis. It was something immediately evident to him. It is something you cannot prove; you either see it or not see it. It is like whether or not you are color-blind. His awareness led him to the conclusion that the compulsion came from God.

Jung gives another example in the Terry lectures (1969a, pars. 15ff., and esp. 24–25). A patient had an imaginary cancer. No matter how much reassurance he got from medical doctors that he was physically fine, he would acknowledge it, but add, "I know I do not have cancer but I think I have cancer." Jung says about this, that it would be demoralizing to interpret this in such a fashion as to indicate that he is imagining that he has cancer. He is doing no such thing. He is not imagining it. *He does not choose to have such an idea, the idea is forced upon him.* Therefore, Jung says:

> [I]t is better for him to understand that his complex is an autonomous power directed against his conscious personality. (1969a, par. 26)

There was a psychiatric case, presented in grand rounds when I was in medical school in the 1940s. The patient was a young man who had been admitted to the psychiatric institute associated with the university with a compulsion. Whenever he got into company, he was obliged, very shortly, to yell out the word, "fuck." He was brought into the amphitheater; and not long after, out it came. Well, that meant a little more in the '40s than it does today. None of the psychiatrists discussing that case mentioned that the compulsion might have come from God.

These experiences come from the God-image, just as the cathedral vision of the eleven-year-old Jung came from God. The psyche can and does function autonomously. These religious realities are the inner and outer experiences that astound or contradict the ego. They may be positive experiences, in which one feels he is bathed in divine grace, or they may be negative experiences that contradict all of one's dearest plans and intentions and have even a diabolical quality to them. The word *diabolical* is used purposefully, because it derives from the Greek word for devil, *diabolos*, which means to throw across, to accuse. The devil is one who throws something across one's path to make one stumble or to arrest one's movement (Jung 1988, 1320–25; 1969a, pars. 248–49).

We experience religious realities all the time, if only our eyes are open to the fact. A light is constantly showing through events, both inner events and outer events, that serves a guiding function, if one can see it. One will be pushed toward certain things and away from other things, if one is alert to perceive the guidance. They are all examples of religious realities.

[At this point in the lecture, Dr. Edinger accidentally knocked over the cup of water on the side table.]

Ohh—that's a religious reality right there. You see? I've just spilled the water. That is a religious reality. I did not intend to do that: this is a living example of "speak of the devil." This is a living example of it. I hope you're impressed. I mean that most seriously. You see, it's a serious matter; it is really a serious matter. When something like this happens, it's trivial in itself, but it underlines what's being talked about. It's desperately serious, because little mistakes can cost one his life you know: you step in the wrong place at the wrong time, that's all it takes.

The modern ego is so conditioned to take personal responsibility for everything that happens to it that it is hard for modern man to recognize *religious realities* even when hit over the head with them. *Religious realities* mean realities which are derived from an inner, purposeful, non-ego origin. It was a major discovery of Jung's that these religious realities, which he had realized as a child, derive from the archetypal psyche and, furthermore, that honoring one's own subjective (psychic) experience is in the empirical tradition. It is not a matter of autism or psychopathology or speculation.

> It is, to my mind, a fatal mistake to regard the human psyche as a purely personal affair and to explain it exclusively from a personal point of view. Such a mode of explanation is only applicable to the individual in his ordinary everyday occupations and relationships. If, however, some slight trouble occurs, perhaps in the form of an unforeseen and somewhat unusual event, instantly instinctual forces are called up, forces which appear to be wholly unexpected, new and strange. They can no longer be explained in terms of personal motives, being comparable rather to certain primitive occurrences. (Jung 1969a, par. 24)

As Jung says in the Bernet letter:

> I don't know whether the archetype is "true" or not. I only know that it lives and that I have not made it. (1975a, 258)

He goes on to say that he gradually developed "the conviction that what is experienced is an endless approximation":

> The goal of this approximation seems to be anticipated by archetypal symbols which represent something like the circumambulation of a centre. With increasing approximation to the centre there is a corresponding depotentiation of the ego in favour of the influence of the "empty" centre, which is certainly not identical with the archetype but is the thing the archetype points to. As the Chinese would say,

[handwritten marginal note: image as circum-ambulation of an "empty" centre which points to the archetype]

the archetype is only the *name* of Tao, not Tao itself. Just as the Jesuits translated Tao as "God," so we can describe the "emptiness" of
the centre as "God." Emptiness in this sense doesn't mean "absence"
or "vacancy," but something unknowable which is endowed with the
highest intensity. (1975a, 258)

The experience of the *"empty centre"* is what one encounters following the crackup of the containment in a traditional religious belief. As
long as one is contained in a functioning religious myth, the center of
his mandala will be occupied by the particular God-image of that traditional creed, whatever it is. But if that center is "empty," it exposes
that individual to direct experience of the autonomous psyche without
the benefit of the buffering effect of a traditional image, as Nicholas of
Flüe experienced. His terrifying experience of the image of God's
countenance in a state of terrible wrath took him years to recover from,
and only then by constructing a screen between himself and that
image. The screen was the image of the Trinity. When he got that
screen over the image, then he had assimilated it. It was probably appropriate for the particular stage of psychological development of his
time (Jung 1975a, 258; see also Jung 1950a, 1950b).

I once had a dream where I saw a one-celled creature, something
like an amoeba. As a boy I was quite interested in microscopy and en-
joyed examining one-celled protozoa and such things, so they were
very familiar items to me. In my dream I saw such a creature. It was
much enlarged, as though it were being seen under a microscope. Such
creatures have as their central life-source a nucleus. Every cell has a nucleus as its center of life. This organism, in place of the nucleus, had an
empty hole, and looking through it, I could see a blue sky beyond. It
is an image of the empty center. The center becomes a window that
looks out on another dimension of reality. When the center is filled up
with a traditional God-image, it is a more comfortable state of affairs,
but then it is not a window anymore.

The whole course of individuation is dialectical, and the so-called
"end" is the confrontation of the ego with the "emptiness" of the centre. Here the limit of possible experience is reached: the ego dissolves as the reference-point of cognition. It cannot coincide with
the centre, otherwise we would be insensible; that is to say, the ex-

tinction of the ego is at best an endless approximation. But if the ego usurps the centre it loses its object (inflation!).

. . . The ego has to acknowledge many gods before it attains the centre where no god helps it any longer against another god. (Jung 1975a, 259)

It is a dialectical process. Consciousness is based on the process of a dialectic. *Dialectic* derives from two Greek words: *dia*, meaning across and *legein*, meaning to speak. Dialectic means speaking across, between two things. It requires a twoness to take place. If the ego usurps the center, it loses its object. There is a tendency for the modern mind, if it finds an empty center, to rush in and fill it up, because nature abhors a vacuum. If the center is unoccupied, the ego moves in, just like an army patrol. If the territory is not occupied, the army moves in and occupies it. That is what has happened to the modern mind and, as Jung says in the parenthesis, it is inflation. For the modern mind it can be quite a subtle, intellectual form of inflation. The result is that, as Jung says, the ego loses its object. What is its object? What he means is that the ego loses its internal object. It loses the realization that there is an inner center that stands over and against the ego as something separate from it. Then, if the ego usurps the empty center, it feels the way Jung describes picturesquely in another place, just like the Creator all alone with His creation. The ego usurps the prerogatives of the center and assumes it is the creator of its own being.

[T]he archetype is increasingly detached from its dynamic background and gradually turned into a purely intellectual formula. In this way it is neutralized, and you can then say "one can live with it quite well." (Jung 1975a, 259)

Jung is evidently referring to something Bernet had said in his book. One then reaches this conclusion: when the ego has usurped the center, then the archetypal reality that stands over and against the ego turns into a purely intellectual formula and is neutralized. An example of this abstraction process is what has happened to the original Homeric experience. In the Homeric world of the *Iliad*, the deities on the battlefield were experienced as immediate reality. They were living religious realities. Not just Homer's poetic constructs, those figures accurately depicted the way the early Greeks experienced existence. If the modern poet did it, it would be poetic license, but not for those primitive Greeks. Those experiences, which were originally recognized as being associated with the living presence of the deities, have in the modern mind been interpreted as nothing but the emotions of the warriors who happened to be engaged in battle. The modern mind abstracts the experience to coincide with modern orientation: the concept of a personal emotion, an abstraction, which neutralizes the experience of divinity. It happens throughout all areas of human experience. That is what the modern mind does with all the living presences that the primitive perceives as immediately engaging him. It is not to say that this development was not necessary, because it brought about an enormous ego development, allowing the archetypal realities to be experienced on an entirely different level. Nonetheless, it is just as Jung says: the archetype is increasingly detached from its dynamic background and is gradually turned into a purely intellectual formula. In this way it is neutralized. Then you can live with it quite well. But you would not say that, if you had the deities nudging you in the ribs on a daily basis.

Jung goes on to say:

> In the individuation process the ego is brought face to face with an unknown superior power which is likely to cut the ground from under its feet and blow consciousness to bits. The archetype is not just the formal condition for mythological statements but an overwhelming force comparable to nothing I know. . . . All talk of this opponent is mythology. All statements about and beyond the "ultimate" are anthropomorphisms and, if anyone should think that when he says "God" he has also predicated God, he is endowing his words with *magical power*. Like a primitive, he is incapable of distinguishing the verbal image from reality. . . .
>
> However interesting or enthralling metaphysical statements may be, I must still criticize them as anthropomorphisms. But here the theologian button-holes me, asseverating that his anthropomorphism is God and damning anyone who criticizes any anthropomorphic weaknesses, defects, and contradictions in it as a blasphemer. (1975a, 260–61)

The word anthropomorphism derives from two Greek words: *anthropos*, meaning man, and *morphe*, meaning form. So the term anthropomorphism means in human form, in the form of mankind. Jung's point is that all psychic representations are necessarily anthropomorphic, because humans can function only with human forms. As some ancient author once said, if horses had a conception of God, it would be in the form of a horse, because that would be the only way they could conceive of it.

Bernet raises the issue in criticizing Jung for blasphemy in *Answer to Job*. Jung's response was as follows:

> The very fact that you consider this critique of anthropomorphisms worthy of condemnation proves how strongly you are bound to these psychic products by word-magic. If theologians think that whenever they say "God" then God is, they are deifying anthropomorphisms, psychic structures and myths. This is exactly what I don't do . . . I speak exclusively of the *God-image*. (1975a, 261)

It is a fundamental point. After Yahweh revealed himself to Job out of the whirlwind, He boasted about his greatness. He put the whole grand universe on display as a manifestation of his creative power and then He brought out his brutal creations, Behemoth and Leviathan, to demonstrate his great power. Regarding that account in the Book of Job, Jung makes this observation, which might be subject to the criticism of blasphemy by theological critics:

> Yahweh's allocutions have the unthinking yet none the less transparent purpose of showing Job the brutal power of the demiurge. (1969a, par. 605)

God is saying, in effect:

> "This is I, the creator of all the ungovernable, ruthless forces of Nature, which are not subject to any ethical laws. I, too, am an amoral force of Nature, a purely phenomenal personality that cannot see its own back." (1969a, par. 605)

While such a statement might very well be considered to be blasphemy by orthodox critics, it is however an accurate description of how Yahweh behaves towards Job in the Book of Job, if Yahweh is considered as though he were a man. In other words, in terms of anthropomorphic imagery, it is an accurate description of what the Book of Job describes. Indeed, it is how the Book of Job and the whole Old

Testament describe Yahweh, as if he were a man—because there is no other way to describe him other than mythologically.

According to Jung's epistemology, one cannot speak in any other terms except those categories and forms of perception and representation that are an innate part of our understanding process, as Kant demonstrated. It is all one can know. The nature of the anthropomorphic God-image, that we experience and that the unconscious presents us with, our scriptures and mythological formulations, all of which were born out of the psyche, all reveal themselves only through anthropomorphic imagery.

THREE

Jung received a letter from Valentine Brooke concerning the "Face to Face" television interview that was broadcast on the BBC. Jung replied November 6, 1959. A footnote to the Brooke letter tells the circumstances of the letter:

> In the course of the interview Freeman asked: "Do you believe in God" to which Jung answered after a long pause: "I don't need to believe, I know." These words gave rise to considerable argument. (Jung 1975a, 521 n.1)

Brooke then sent Jung a letter asking him to elaborate on what he meant by that cryptic statement. The dialogue ran like this in the "Face to Face" interview:

> FREEMAN. What sort of religious upbringing did your father give you?
> JUNG. Oh, we were Swiss Reformed.
> FREEMAN. And did he make you attend church regularly?
> JUNG. Oh, well, that was quite natural, everybody went to church on Sunday.
> FREEMAN. And did you believe in God?
> JUNG. Oh yes.
> FREEMAN. Do you now believe in God?
> JUNG. Now? [Pause.] Difficult to answer. I know. I don't need to believe, I know.[1]

In the Brooke letter, Jung sets down the epistemological basis for the statement, "I don't need to believe, I know." He reiterates that all acts of apperception are influenced by preexisting patterns:

---

[1]See *Psychological Perspectives* 7.3 (Fall 1976): 155ff.

Whatever I perceive from without or within is a representation or image, a psychic entity caused, as I rightly or wrongly assume, by a corresponding "real" object. But I have to admit that my subjective image is only *grosso modo* identical with the object. . . . The difference between image and real object shows that the psyche, apperceiving an object, alters it by adding or excluding certain details. The image therefore is not entirely caused by the object; it is also influenced by certain pre-existent psychic conditions which we can correct only partially . . . we know from experience that all acts of apperception are influenced by preexistent patterns of perceiving objects (f.i., the premise of causality), particularly obvious in pathological cases (being exaggerations or distortions of so-called "normal" behavior). They are presuppositions pertaining to the whole of humanity. The history of the human mind offers no end of examples (f.i., folklore, fairy tales, religious symbolism, etc.) . . . I call them archetypes, i.e., instinctual forms of mental functioning. *They are not inherited ideas, but mentally expressed instincts*, forms and not contents. (1975a, 521)

One can take the reference to causality as an example of a preexistent archetypal pattern. Kant first demonstrated that causality was one of the categories of understanding. But Kant did not have the notion of the reality of the objective psyche. Causality is the principle whereby an event is understood to be a necessary consequence of a prior event, thereby producing a sense of orderly, meaningful sequence to a chain of circumstances. For example, a cause may be either mechanical or intentional. In Aristotelian terms it would be either an efficient cause or a final cause. If one pushes a switch, the lights will go off. The mechanical or efficient cause would be that the circuit is broken by pushing the switch. The intentional or final cause would be that I am going home and I do not want to leave the lights on. These are basically two different modes of causality. Jung speaks of causality as a preexistent pattern in the psyche. It means that the psyche is so constructed that all events it encounters must be conceived as meaningful. Causality has at its root the supposition of meaning. In other words, events are not arbitrary, random or disconnected. Every occurrence must have a reason to exist, according to the archetypal preexistent pattern of causality built into the psyche.

Consider, for example, a sickness that occurs in tropical climates that is characterized by the symptoms of cyclical episodes of chills and fever. This disease entity has been observed since the earliest of times.

Primitives having, in keeping with all human beings, causality built in, sought a cause for this illness, which they attributed to possession by an evil spirit. The ancients put it in terms consistent with more accurate observation. They noticed that this disease occurred after people visited dank, swampy regions of bad air, so they called it bad air disease, in other words, malaria. Moderns, with the aid of the microscope and scientific method, have discovered that this disease is caused by a plasmodium, a pathogenic protozoa carried by mosquitoes, to which we attribute the cause of the disease. It is probably not the end of the matter. There will be other causes and meanings discovered to take into account the reality of the psyche. No matter the stage of psychological development humanity may be in, the innate, preexistent archetypal pattern of causality by necessity manifests itself in the human's attempt to understand his surroundings.

To carry it a step further, Jung mentions the fact that the premise of causality is particularly evident in pathological cases. We see it in delusional, psychotic thinking, for example. As an actual example, a patient in a mental hospital I was able to observe one day watched some sparrows fluttering around outside the ward window. He asked himself what was causing them to be fluttering around like that. Perhaps someone had thrown some grain out, but he did not follow up that possibility. He decided that God was trying to talk to him through the movements of the sparrows. As he looked at them, he thought he could understand the message, which was that God had appointed him the new messiah. His interpretation was causality operating. He looks at a phenomenon. He is not content with the idea that it is random or meaningless; he then assumes it has to have a meaning, so a meaning is imposed on it.

In ancient Rome that very procedure was built into the collective operations of the State. Official augurs were required to examine the movement of birds and take the auspices every time some major event was anticipated. They would not declare war, for instance, without having the augurs take the auspices under formal, religious circumstances. The movement of birds would be observed, and it would be determined whether the omens were auspicious or inauspicious. If it were too ominous, they would put off the whole undertaking.

One does the same thing in consulting the *I Ching*. There again one is looking for the intentional cause of a particular mood or situation, for its meaning. The basic idea is that the psyche, by necessity of its very structure, must impute meaning to its experience. This fact is why, as Jung teaches, man cannot live a meaningless life. If his conscious attitude has become disconnected from the roots of the objective psyche, out of which he has come, then he is not a viable organism anymore, because meaning is a requirement built into our structure. This explanation is part of the basis of his remark, "I don't have to believe, I know."

The letter written to M. Leonard on December 5, 1959, only weeks after the Brooke letter, reiterates the same message:

> Mr. Freeman in his characteristic manner fired the question you alluded to at me in a somewhat surprising way, so I was perplexed and had to say the next thing which came into my mind. As soon as the answer had left the "edge of my teeth" I knew I had said something controversial, puzzling, or even ambiguous. I was therefore just waiting for letters like yours. Mind you I didn't say "there is a God." I said: "I don't need to believe in God, I know." Which does not mean: I do know a certain God (Zeus, Yahweh, Allah, the Trinitarian God, etc.) but rather: I do know that I am obviously confronted with a factor unknown in itself, which I call "God" *in consensu omnium (quod semper, quod ubique, quod ab omnibus creditur).*[2] I remember Him, I evoke Him, whenever I use His name, overcome by anger or by fear, whenever I involuntarily say: "Oh God." That happens when I meet somebody or something stronger than myself. It is an apt name given to all overpowering emotions in my own psychic system, subduing my own conscious will and usurping control over myself. This is the name by which I designate all things which cross my wilful path violently and recklessly, all things which upset my subjective views, plans, and intentions and change the course of my life for better or worse. (Jung 1975a, 525)

His remark, whenever we are gripped "by anger or by fear" we exclaim, "Oh God," was vividly demonstrated some months ago. There was a television account of a subway accident in New York City. The camera recorded people coming out of the car, looking back and seeing what had happened. What they saw was a mass of tangled wreckage, dead and bleeding bodies. As they came out of the train to that

---

[2]Which quote means, in translation "which in the consensus of all, always, everywhere and by everyone is believed."

shocking view, each said, "Oh God," "Oh God," over and over again. It was very impressive to see. It is an example of what Jung is referring to here. The psyche itself, at such moments, exclaims spontaneously: this is a manifestation of God. It is an example of the indisputable evidence on which we base our empirical understanding of the God-image. These psychic events are indisputable. Humankind does behave this way.

The Smith letter was written slightly later, in June 1960. Robert Smith had raised some questions about Jung's controversy with Martin Buber, which serves as a good example of a general, widespread attitude that criticizes Jungian psychology and which illustrates another aspect of Jung's epistemology. In February 1952, the Jewish religious philosopher Martin Buber published an article entitled "Religion and Modern Thinking" in the European journal *Mercury*. The same article was later published in a chapter in Buber's book *Eclipse of God*. In it, Buber discusses three modern thinkers: Sartre, Heidegger, and Jung—all of whom, according to Buber, although reaching somewhat different conclusions, based their work on Nietzsche's announcement that "God is dead." The section concerning Jung criticized Jung for replacing God with the human psyche, which he does, if you put it in its simplest terms. According to Buber:

> Jung . . . oversteps with sovereign license the boundaries of psychology. (1952, 78)

He criticizes Jung's statement that religion is a:

> living relation to psychical events which do not depend upon consciousness but instead take place on the other side of it in the darkness of the psychical hinterland. (Buber 1952, 79)[3]

According to Buber, Jung is placing psychic processes in place of a transcendent being. He thinks Jung considers God to be "an autonomous psychic content," not existing apart from man. [To Jung, Buber feels] God is just a representation in the psyche of man, which he considers a metaphysical statement "according to which God does

---

[3]Buber's source is Jung and Kerényi 1963a, 102, *Essays on a Science of Mythology*.

not exist 'absolutely,' that is, independent of the human subject and beyond all human conditions" (Buber 1952, 80f.; cf. Jung 1966, par. 402). Buber accuses Jung of saying:

> [P]sychology becomes here the only admissible metaphysic. . . . Although the new psychology protests that it is "no world-view but a science". . . It proclaims the new religion, the only one which can still be true, the religion of pure psychic immanence. (1952, 83f. and 1933, 217)

Finally, Buber refers to a statement Jung made in *Two Essays* which disturbed him:

> [M]ankind is, essentially, psychologically still in a state of childhood— a stage that cannot be skipped. The vast majority needs authority, guidance, law. This fact cannot be overlooked. The Pauline overcoming of the law falls only to the man who knows how to put his soul in the place of conscience. Very few are capable of this ("Many are called, but few are chosen.") And these few tread this path only from inner necessity, not to say suffering, for it is sharp as the edge of a razor. (Jung 1966, par. 401)

Buber's reaction was especially to the statement, "only to those persons who know how to set the soul in the place of conscience," which, Buber says, leads to the question of the positive function of evil. The implication is that Jung is neglecting moral values (Buber 1952, 87f.).

This type of criticism one encounters all the time from the philosophically or the theologically educated. These criticisms are inevitable if one is dealing with a person for whom the reality of the objective psyche still resides in metaphysical containment, an example of which is Buber's telling remark:

> [Psychology] proclaims the new religion, the only one which can still be true, the religion of pure psychic immanence. (1952, 83)

It reminds me of a remark that a philosopher once made about Jung's psychology. He was quite offended in his perception that Jung subsumed the whole history of philosophy under the rubric of its being data for his psychological theory. That is, however, what he does. Jungian psychology is a Copernican revolution, which, for the first time, allows mankind to see the autonomous psyche objectively and to see the way it has manifested itself in history. It has manifested itself in myth, in religion, in philosophy, in art and much, much more. As long as one is in an identification with the objective psyche, of course, it is not visible. One has to find that Archimedean point outside of it before he can see it, similar to Copernicus, who had to transport himself off the earth before he could discover the fact that the sun did not revolve around the earth. An example is an instructive story from Eastern Buddhism or Zen. The question is asked: "Who discovered water?" The answer to the question is: "I do not know who discovered it, but I know who did not discover it—the fish."

Jung goes on to explain the fact that Buber does not understand him at all. Having done his best, he is finally a little irritated. Jung says:

> My empirical standpoint is so disappointingly simple that it needs only an average intelligence and a bit of common sense to understand it, but it needs an uncommon amount of prejudice or even ill-will to misunderstand it, as it seems to me. (1975a, 573)

Is it "so disappointingly simple that it needs only an average intelligence and a bit of common sense to understand it"? It doesn't need a lot of intelligence, but it does need a level of consciousness that is very rare; therefore, the reason for the fish story. A bunch of fish listening to a lecture on the nature of water are not going to get it. It would be very unusual for someone to come out of the water "naturally" without a pretty good stint of personal analysis. That does not mean to say there are not a few. Currently, a personal analysis must be considered a prerequisite for understanding what Jung is talking about, for achieving an awareness of the psyche as an objective entity. The ego is analogous to a fish swimming around in the psyche. It cannot perceive the psyche as an object. One has to be separated from a given object before one can perceive it to be an object. It pertains to the whole phenomenon of containment.

The ego almost always is contained in the objective psyche in an invisible way. There are different ways it can take place. There is religious, metaphysical containment, for instance, in which a religious creed or a philosophical creed or a political creed or an ideological creed is the containing agent. In that case one can recognize the fact of the containment by the individual's being a perfectly reasonable and responsible person, who is willing to engage in thoughtful interchange, until one touches the containing medium. Then one hits a stone wall, and all reason and decent human interchange ends, because what one is hitting is an expression of the transpersonal value that the individual lives by. His psychic existence, being contained in that value, stands or falls on its validity, so it cannot exist as an object. It exists as a containing medium, which is immediately visible.

FOUR

THE LETTER TO PASTOR TANNER, DATED FEBRUARY 12, 1959, IS ON THE *nature of religion*. This topic is an absolutely central topic for Jungian psychology, for the reason that Jung considers the essential nature of the human psyche to be religious. It requires us to have some understanding of what we mean by the terms *religion* and *religious*, terms which have various connotations. In this letter Jung presents with great clarity exactly what he means by religion and by the religious function of the psyche.

In antiquity and in church history, the word religion has been given two different etymologies from Latin, depending on whether one traces the word back to *religare* or to *religere*. Traced back to the word *religare*, one follows the etymology that Saint Augustine used. *Religare* breaks down to two stem words: *re* meaning back and *ligare* meaning to tie or to bind. A ligature, for instance, is a tie that derives from the Latin *ligare*. From that etymology the word religion means to tie oneself back to some prior state of existence, to an earlier source of being, so to speak.

The other etymology has more ancient roots. It was the etymology used by the classic ancients. They derived the word from *religere*, which means to take into careful account. Unfortunately, there is no neat, single verb to apply, so one must use the rather cumbersome phrase: to take into careful account. One way to remember the significance of the word *religere* is to remember that it signifies the opposite of what our word neglect means. Neglect is a negative term that has as its root the same source as *religere*, so neglect means not to take into careful account.

In this letter Jung expresses his preference for the second, earlier etymology. He then goes ahead to make some very interesting remarks concerning the historical stages of Western religion, which he breaks down into three different stages. He speaks of the religions of antiquity, of ancient Judaism and of Christianity. Antiquity is associated

3 5

with what is in modern terms superstitious observances or omens. Ancient Judaism is associated primarily with the image of a legal contract, a covenant. Christianity is largely associated with the idea of a love relationship, and the faith and loyalty that is attached to such a relationship. Each of these stages corresponds to a different aspect of the ego's relation to the Self.

Starting with antiquity, here is what Jung says:

> [I]n pagan antiquity: the gods are exalted men and embodiments of ever-present powers whose will and whose moods must be complied with. Their *numina* must be carefully studied, they must be propitiated by sacrifices just as the favour of archaic princes is won by gifts. Here religion means a watchful, wary, thoughtful, careful, prudent, expedient, and calculating attitude towards the powers-that-be, with not a trace of that legal and emotional contract which can be broken like a marriage [[a reference to ancient Judaism and Christianity]]. (1975a, 483)

The major collective religious operation of antiquity that epitomizes the nature of that early relation to the Self is the ceremony of taking the auspices. In ancient Rome all the way up into the fifth century, there existed what was called a College of Augurs. At first it was a small group, about six men. Later it was enlarged to nine, and eventually to fifteen or sixteen. It had many similarities to our modern Supreme Court. The Augurs were appointed for life. They formed a priestly college and were attributed great dignity in society. Whenever any sizeable state enterprise was to be initiated, the College of the Augurs was requested to take a reading of the auspices to determine whether it was auspicious to proceed with the undertaking or not. Going to war, of course, would be the biggest undertaking. There was an elaborate, formal procedure to take the auspices. The top of a particular hill was marked out and a specific area was set up. A little tent was set up, and the Augurs took their places in this square tent with its entrance looking southward. The Augurs sat down and asked the gods for a sign. They sat and waited and watched the birds. There were complicated rules about how to read the movements of the birds: birds moving in certain directions, at certain times, in certain ways meant certain things. Just the appearance of special kinds of numinous birds was an auspicious event in itself. They took the reading of the birds and then gave their report to the government. The report would be either "the birds allow it," so you may proceed with what you are supposed to do, or the report would be "on another day," which meant the birds do not allow it. It was a major religious ritual of a collective nature in ancient Rome, which illustrates very well the etymology of *religere*, meaning to take into careful account.

One does something like that on a more conscious level in consulting the *I Ching* before embarking on some uncertain enterprise. I find myself taking the auspices all the time to be on the alert for what events will occur if I take a certain course of action. I remember, for instance, some time back, I ventured to put a certain project in the hands of somebody who required me to drive to his house and deliver it in person. In the process of that trip, although I am a fairly careful driver, I found myself driving the wrong way on a one-way street. I knew then I was doing something wrong. I took those auspices right on the spot. It is an illustration of the attitude of the auspices. I had already delivered the project, so it was too late, but I knew what was going to happen; and it did.

The second phase that Jung speaks about is that of ancient Judaism, in which the ego-Self relation is expressed in the form of a legal contract—a covenant. The basic texts to illustrate this particular mode are found in Genesis 17 and Exodus 24. In Genesis 17, Yahweh announces to Abraham that He is going to make a covenant with him. Abraham, who up to that time had no children, was to have a progeny as many as the stars. The other text is Exodus 24, where Moses acts out the ritual of establishing a covenant between Yahweh and the Israelites. He sacrifices an animal, collects the blood and divides it into two portions. One portion is thrown onto Yahweh's altar, signifying the presence of Yahweh; the other portion of the blood is thrown onto the Israelites, thus setting up a blood covenant. The idea is the two parties have been united by the glue of blood that was shed. They are now committed to fulfilling the contract that they had agreed to. The contract was that the Israelites would obey Yahweh's laws, and He would take care of them in return.

The third one is Christianity, which according to Jung emphasizes a love relation. In ancient Judaism, marriage was one of the images used to describe the relation between the whole nation of Israel and Yahweh. Israel was considered to be the wife of Yahweh. This relationship was differentiated further in Christian elaboration so that it applied more to individuals than to the collective. Also it elaborated the love aspect of the relationship between the ego and the Self. One gets the most extreme version in the First Letter of John, which Jung refers to in the latter part of *Answer to Job* (1969a, par. 729). The extreme form of it is in First John, chapter 4, verses 7–12:

> Beloved, let us love one another: for love is of God; and everyone that loveth is born of God, and knoweth God.
> He that loveth not knoweth not God; for God is love.
> In this was manifested the love of God toward us, because that God sent his only begotten Son into the world, that we might live through him.
> Herein is love, not that we loved God, but that he loved us and sent his Son to be the propitiation for our sins.
> Beloved, if God so loved us, we ought also to love one another.
> . . . If we love one another, God dwelleth in us, and his love is perfected in us.

It is all love, which links up with what has become the operative term for the Christian ego-Self relation: *faith*. Faith is a confusing term, because it developed in two different directions. It developed, on the one hand, to refer to belief and, on the other hand, to refer to loyalty, to a value that one loves. The distinction is clearer when you consider the opposites of those two terms. The opposite of belief is doubt; and the opposite of loyalty is treason. They are distinctly different notions. The aspect of belief is the one Jung expresses himself so forcefully about. He says to the effect that whenever there is an excess of conscious belief, doubt will be generated in the unconscious (1975a, 484). Of course, the same can be said of loyalty. Whenever there is a totally dependent, one-sided notion of loyalty for a given value, treason can be generated in the unconscious. The important point is that the idea of faith is associated with love in the ego-Self relation.

These three stages of religious development could be characterized with three different words. In antiquity the word is *omen*. In ancient Judaism the operative word is *law*. In Christianity the word is *faith*. Going onto the fourth phase, the psychological phase, the operative word would be *experience*. Now each of these has a psychological equivalent. The superstitious phase will refer to an openness to the unconscious on the part of a weak and undeveloped ego. It is something one would find in childhood, the apotropaic [acts] of childhood: "Don't step on a crack, you'll break your mother's back." The lurking of witches and things like that would correspond to the superstitious phase on the unconscious level. The legal phase corresponds to a condition in which the ego relates to the transpersonal authority with great emphasis on rules and precepts, maybe even compulsive preoccupation with correct behavior, even to the extreme of informing on those who violate the rules. *Law* (and rule) is the ·operative term. For those for whom the ego-Self relation is largely determined by love or *faith*, a feeling of attachment to an ideal, a principle or a beloved model of some kind will dominate. Then there is the fourth phase, the psychological phase, in which there is a living experience of the psyche and its transpersonal center, which in a certain sense involves a return to number one.

> [T]he original form of *religio* is, without question, aptly characterized by the implications of *relegere* [[or *religere*]]. I prefer this interpretation of *religio* because it is in better accord with the general psychological findings. (Jung 1975a, 483)

Jung describes the attitude involved very clearly: "religion means a watchful, wary, thoughtful, careful, prudent, expedient and calculated attitude towards the powers-that-be" (1975a, 483). He is describing the attitude one ought to have toward the unconscious. The religious function of the psyche requires the proper attitude; it is not just a matter of faith:

> "Faith without religion" could therefore be translated as "(nondenominational) religion without creed," manifestly an unorganized, non-collective, entirely individual exercise of the "religious function." (By the latter I mean the allegiance, surrender, or submission to a supraordinate factor or to a "con-vincing" [= overpowering!] principle: *religio erga principium*.) (1975a, 484)

The proper attitude involves the "allegiance, surrender, or submission to a supraordinate factor." In the Lang letter, Jung said, "I am loyal to my inner experience and have *pistis* in the Pauline sense." *Pistis* is a Greek word that is translated as faith, but with a special nuance of loyalty. Jung describes these matters with great clarity in his Terry

39

Lectures. These passages amplify what Jung says in the letter about the religious function:

> Religion appears to me to be a peculiar attitude of mind which could be formulated in accordance with the original use of the word *religio*, which means a careful consideration and observation of certain dynamic factors that are conceived as "powers": spirits, daemons, gods, laws, ideas, ideals, or whatever name man has given to such factors. (Jung 1969a, par. 8)

> It is, however, true that every creed is originally based on the one hand upon the experience of the *numinosum* and on the other hand upon *pistis*, that is to say, trust or loyalty, faith and confidence in a certain experience of a numinous nature and in the change of consciousness that ensues. . . . We might say, then, that the term "religion" designates the attitude peculiar to a consciousness which has been changed by experience of the *numinosum*. (1969a, par. 9)

As did Kant, Jung differentiates empiricism—a trait of the modern psyche—from faith or belief:

> I can also confirm that I regard all declarations of faith . . . as an object of psychological research . . . since they are subjective human statements about actual experiences whose real nature cannot be fathomed by man in any case. These experiences contain a real mystery, but the statements made about them don't. (Jung 1975a, 378)

In many places Jung speaks of faith as a *donum spiritus sancti*, as a gift of the Holy Spirit. It means a living faith is a consequence of an encounter with the *numinosum*. If one has a living faith, it gives one a connection with the transpersonal dimension. Such a connection can be a precious thing. Faith in that sense is not the same thing as belief. Belief is more a cramp of the will. It tries to achieve a connection to the transpersonal by sidestepping a certain aspect of reality.

One should not necessarily apply a strictly empirical approach to all patients. If the patient makes a declaration of religious faith, it should not be analyzed unless the dreams clearly require it. As long as a faith is intact, it should not be questioned. As long as it is functional, it serves as a safe container for the archetypal psyche. If one has such a favorable setup, one does not throw that away lightly. If the patient is forcibly dumped out of a functional container into the sea of the collective unconscious, there can be dangerous consequences.

> Interpretation by faith seeks to represent the experienced content of a vision, for instance, as the visible manifestation of a transcendental Being, and it invariably does so in terms of a traditional system and then asserts that this representation is the absolute truth. (Jung 1975a, 379)

The same thing can take place if one is operating out of a theoretical framework instead of religious dogma. A theoretical framework can operate the same way, by your interpretation being grounded on your faith in the theory that you are using.

In this letter Tanner apparently asked Jung about his reaction to Bultmann. Jung replies to clarify the issue of faith,

> [T]he tenets of belief have to be purified, or made easier, by being relieved of their principal encumbrances, which for the rationalist are their particularly obnoxious "mythological" components. Bultmann's endeavors are obviously intended to serve this purpose. Where they should or could stop is highly questionable. Christ as "Redeemer," for instance, is a mythologem of the first order, and so too is the "Son of God," the "Son of Man," the "Son of the Virgin," etc. "Faith without religion" or "religion without creed" is simply a logical consequence which has got out of Bultmann's control. (1975a, 484)

Jung is referring to a major notion of Bultmann's, namely: Bultmann thought that modern Christianity, in order to be palatable to the rationalism of moderns, must be demythologized. Bultmann, a New Testament scholar and theologian, in later work was concerned with the idea of demythologizing the New Testament. He concluded that the whole framework of early Christian preaching, which the New Testament illustrates, presupposed an obsolete conception of the universe and that all these mythological elements needed to be removed or reinterpreted, so that the issue could become meaningful to modern man. So, Bultmann:

> The cosmology of the New Testament is essentially mythical in character. The world is a three storied structure: earth in the center, heaven above and the underworld below. . . . It is the scene of the

supernatural activity of God and his angels and Satan and his demons. . . . [[This proclamation]] is incredible to modern man, for he is convinced that the mythical view of the world is obsolete. . . . Theology must understand the task of stripping the [[proclamation]] from its mythical framework, of "demythologizing" it. (1953, 1ff.)

Before Bultmann, Matthew Arnold had come to believe a similar idea. Matthew Arnold was a poet only in his romantic youth. When he got older he became preoccupied with the whole question of how religion could be rescued from its demise. He came to the idea it could be approached as literature or poetry, which demythologizes it also. He gave us the very anemic definition that religion is morality tinged with emotion.

Jung writes:

> But if the believer without religion now thinks that he has got rid of mythology, he is deceiving himself: he cannot get by without "myth." *Religio* is by its very nature always an *erga*, a "towards," no matter whether the following accusative be "God," "Redeemer," a philosophical idea or an ethical principle; it is always a "mythic" or transcendental statement. (1975a, 484)

Jung can say that because he discovered the archetypes. A person who has not yet discovered the archetypes cannot be aware that the particular principle that he is deifying, in effect, has at its core an archetypal content.

Matter, too, can be a numinous mythological object, as Jung goes on to say:

> This is naturally also the case when the ultimate principle is called "matter." Only the totally naïve think this is the opposite of "myth." *Materia* is in the end simply a chthonic mother goddess, and the late Pope seems to have had an inkling of this. (Cf. the second Encyclical to the dogma of the Assumption!) (1975a, 485)

Matter also can be a numinous mythological object, an orientation which became widespread beginning about A.D. 1500. The numinosum fell out of heaven and fell into the psyche, to be immediately projected into matter, either in terms of extraverted activity or of introverted activity. What took Columbus across the ocean? a projection of the numinosum on the other side. What gave the newly emerging scientists their impetus? a projection of the numinosum into matter. Matter became fascinating. Alchemy had prepared the way for it. For the alchemists the numinosum already had been projected into matter, which gave them their indefatigable energy to pursue this impossible quest for a lifetime. The image of the philosophers' stone shining through matter beckoned them on their religious quest. The alchemists' studies, psychologically, were very much the precursors of modern science. Scientific research, up until it became a government project, was a religious quest, basically. I know the projection of the numinosum into matter to be a fact, because I experienced it in my own boyhood in an intense fascination with chemistry. I feel I really had a sense of what the alchemists were experiencing.

For many moderns, religion has been replaced by a surrogate—if not matter in the form of science, then by some form of materialism:

> For many religious people today even this concession to myth is dropped and they content themselves with a bashfully veiled theism which has a minimum of the traditional mythic encumbrances. Beyond that there are only surrogates like exotic theosophical ideas or other regressive -isms, all of which culminate in materialism, where one succumbs to the illusion of having finally escaped each and every mythological bugbear. (Jung 1975a, 485–86)

Jung made a number of pronouncements about regressive "isms." Some examples come from one essay:

> In the majority of cases they [unconscious contents] are not repressed contents, but simply contents that are *not yet conscious* and have not been subjectively realized, like the demons and gods of the primitives or the "isms" so fanatically believed in by modern man. (1969b, par. 366)

> With more foreboding than real knowledge, most people feel afraid of the menacing power that lies fettered in each of us, only waiting for the magic word to release it from the spell. This magic word, which always ends in "ism," works most successfully with those who have the least access to their interior selves and have strayed the furthest from their instinctual roots into the truly chaotic world of *collective consciousness*. (1969b, par. 405)

And the more highly charged the collective consciousness, the more the ego forfeits its practical importance. It is, as it were, absorbed by the opinions and tendencies of collective consciousness, and the result of that is the mass man, the ever-ready victim of some wretched "ism." (1969b, par. 425)

But once Mother Church and her motherly Eros fall into abeyance, the individual is at the mercy of any passing collectivism in the attendant mass psyche. He succumbs to social or national inflation, and the tragedy is that he does so with the same psychic attitude which had once bound him to a church. (1969b, par. 426)

But if he is independent enough to recognize the bigotedness of the social "ism," he may then be threatened with subjective inflation [[as opposed to social inflation]]. (1969b, par. 427)

These phenomena are seen everywhere today, and I do not even dare to give you specific examples of the "isms" that are flourishing.

When a containing universal myth is breaking down and a new myth is in the process of formation, one is more likely to encounter what I referred to in the introduction as the Marcion phenomenon. In this case the new formulation, as a symptom of hubris, denies all meaning and validity to the previous myth and thus dissociates humanity from its roots. One of the main values of Jungian psychology is that it consciously and methodically seeks to link current psychic phenomena with collective antecedents, so that one's operative myth is a living current flowing in the stream of humanity. Those movements which seek to sever the psyche from its roots are not only psychologically dangerous but do not survive. Marcion, who thought the God of the New Testament had nothing to do with the God of the Old Testament, wanted to split off Christianity from its roots, which would have been a dangerous dissociation. In the period of time of change from one age to another, there is a danger of that happening. Jung was concerned about that happening in our time. To demythologize everything is to lose the connection to meaning, the connection to our roots.

I went through this sequence in my own evolving development. I went through a period of time in my life when I considered religion and all its manifestations as just the archaic, superstitious and ignorant prelude to rational consciousness. On that ground I could not understand why people would spend their time doing scholarly studies of these ancient religious mythologies. The same thing applied to ancient philosophy. So far as I could see, the ancient philosophers were just groping around in the dark, making largely ignorant efforts to picture their surrounding reality, when more modern developments revealed such groping just to be ignorant mistakes.

In this regard Jungian psychology is a redemptive power. Not only did Jung redeem alchemy, he also redeemed ancient philosophy, mythology and all of the more primitive aspects of existence by virtue of demonstrating that they are manifestations of the psyche—not just the past psyche, but the permanent, eternal, ever-living psyche that we can be in touch with right now. For me Jung's work has been a vast redemptive process.

Now if I had been of a different temperament, I might have gotten that redemption in a different way. I could have discovered poetry, let's say, and discovered some of the charm of some of those early ignorant mistakes. That might redeem them somewhat. For the thinker, redemption has to take place on his own level. Jung supplied that. Of course, the Marcion phenomenon was the one I was caught in earlier: the previous gods were to be totally superseded and discarded. One cannot live a whole life that way because it splits you right down the middle.

Such a process might not be true for everyone. Some individuals have no inner imperative for achieving a highly differentiated psychology. It is certainly true that many of our analysands will not find individuation relevant to their immediate analytic process; however, it is my conviction that the nature and the extent of the analytic process is determined very largely by the depth of consciousness of the individual analyst. If the individual analyst has some groping notion of what we are dealing with here—and that is all we can expect, that is all I've got, a very groping notion—if these issues of the new aeon have touched the psyche of the analyst, that is going to affect the analytic process between the analyst and the patient, inductively. It is not something to be pushed on the individual if it is not appropriate. Providing the analyst is conscious enough about it, he will not impose religious and transpersonal considerations, if the material does not dictate it. But for certain individuals, the awareness of that transpersonal and transhistorical dimension by the analyst allows for an unfolding of the analytic process in a way that would not otherwise be possible.

These modern possibilities started with Jung. Jung exemplifies a whole quantum leap in human consciousness. He is occupying that new place all by himself. He knew that. He expressed that fact in one of his lugubrious letters. He bemoaned the fact that he is all alone: "a few [[people]] understand this and that, but almost nobody sees the whole."[1] That is the fate of the person who is ahead of his time, whose life therefore is largely a posthumous life. He recognized that about himself. He used that phrase concerning himself: his "life is a posthumous one." The question relevant for us to ask is—what does this have to do with everyday psychotherapy?

Jungian psychology, by preserving a living myth which connects both the individual and society to its roots, has redemptive powers for society also:

> Myth is pre-eminently a social phenomenon: it is told by the many and heard by the many. It gives the ultimately unimaginable religious experience an image, a form in which to express itself, and thus makes community life possible. (Jung 1975a, 486)

A generally accepted myth "makes community life possible." The implications of that psychological fact are immense. I believe the evidence is very clear that every organic community, including the largest communities—namely, whole civilizations—exist as organic entities because [they are] contained within a common myth, which provides all the members of that community a common basis of connection to the transpersonal. What we are witnessing today is a profound breakdown of our collective myth. The result is that there is a fragmentation of the body social. It is breaking up into fragments of wretched "isms," which are at war against each other. We see the same thing happening in Yugoslavia, and other places that are released from the imposition of unity from above. With no containing myth to unify them from within or from below, they disintegrate into wretched, regressive "isms." That is the vast panorama we witness everywhere today.

Each of the stages mentioned earlier had a containing myth. Even today various myths exist concurrently, depending on the advancement of culture and the individual. Antiquity was the phase of polytheism, and ancient Judaism was the beginning of monotheism. Monotheism was associated with the establishment of a specific rela-

---

[1]*Psychological Perspectives*, 6.1 (Spring 1975): 14. From a letter to Eugene Rolfe dated 13 Nov. 1960, reproduced in entirety in Rolfe 1989.

tionship between God and man. There was no such personal relationship in polytheism, which makes all of antiquity essentially tragic. There is no redemption to be had in antiquity, with the exception of initiation into the Eleusinian Mysteries, because, although there were various devices like the augurs and the omens to read certain messages from the divine realm, there was no living connection of concern between man and the divine. That means that antiquity hovered between heroism and despair. The heroic was accomplished in spite of the tragic, futile state of humanity. The central wisdom of antiquity was enunciated by Sophocles: "Best for man never to have been born at all, and next best to die young."[2] That was the pinnacle of ancient wisdom, the consequence of that stage of relation between the ego and the Self. That all changes with the emergence of monotheism and with the personal relationship connection between the ego and the Self.

---

[2]Sophocles 1954, l.1224, *Oedipus at Colonus*.

PART TWO

THE PARADOXICAL GOD

Man's suffering does not derive from his sins but from the maker of his imperfections, the paradoxical God.

C. G. Jung, *CW* 18, par. 1681

FIVE

JUNG'S TWO LETTERS OF INTEREST TO FATHER VICTOR WHITE ARE DATED November 24, 1953, and April 10, 1954. Chapter 3 elaborates Jung's response to issues raised by Martin Buber, a Jewish religious philosopher. Chapter 4 follows with Jung's response to Rudolf Bultmann, a Protestant New Testament theologian. In these letters to Victor White, one has a response to a Catholic priest.

Father Victor White was a priest of the Dominican Order. He was English. He taught in a seminary as a Catholic theologian and he was a friend of Jung. At one stage of their friendship, he spent some time with Jung at Bollingen. Their friendship waned in later years, because White was offended by Jung's *Answer to Job*. He could not swallow it and he wrote a very negative review of it, which Jung responded to in a later letter. One can find this matter discussed in *The Creation of Consciousness* (Edinger 1984, 77ff.). Their friendship soured about five years after the letters were written. Jung was still hoping to get his point across at the time these letters were written. Unfortunately, White's God-image remained embedded in metaphysics, so he was unable to get Jung's fundamental point. What we have is a noble effort on Jung's part. The letters will serve us, even if they did not serve Victor White. Jung writes:

> *Christ as a symbol is far from being invalid*, although he is one side of the self and the devil the other. This pair of opposites is contained in the creator as his right and left hand, as Clemens Romanus says. From the psychological standpoint the experience of God the creator is the perception of an overpowering impulse issuing from the sphere of the unconscious. We do not know whether this influence or compulsion deserves to be called good or evil, although we cannot prevent ourselves from welcoming or cursing it, giving it a bad or a good name, according to our subjective condition. (1975a, 133)

51

The reason for the reference to Clement of Rome is that it is a rare example of a theologian actually foreshadowing or anticipating the paradoxical God-image Jung has presented to us. The actual reference was called the pseudo-Clementine literature. Clement of Rome was one of the early Bishops of Rome, perhaps the third Bishop after St. Peter, about A.D. 100. In the second century A.D., a sizeable amount of literature grew up attributed to Clement. It is a composite of Christian, Gnostic, and pagan elements. It clearly does not derive from Clement of Rome, so it is called pseudo-Clementine. In *Aion*, Jung makes this interesting remark about the God-image of the Clementine Homilies:

> Yahweh and Allah are unreflected God-images, whereas in the Clementine Homilies there is a psychological and reflective spirit at work. (1951, 54n.)

It is a rather high compliment for Jung to pay one of the early authors, because a psychological and reflective spirit is what Jung considers one of the greatest virtues. An example of the Clementine God-image follows in a passage from the New Testament Apocrypha:

> Now that he might bring men to the true knowledge of all things, God, who himself is a single person, made a clear separation by way of pairs of opposites, in that he, who from the beginning was the one and only God, made heaven and earth, day and night, life and death. Among these he has gifted free will to men alone so that they may be just or unjust. For them he has also permuted the appearing of the pairs of opposites, in that he had set before their eyes first the small and then the great, first the world and then eternity, this world being transitory, but the one to come eternal. . . .
> . . . As God, who is one person, in the beginning made first the heaven and then the earth, as it were on the right hand and on the left, he has also in the course of time established all the pairs of opposites. . . . Thus directly from Adam, who was made in the image of God, there issued as the first son the unrighteous Cain and as the second the righteous Abel. And in the same way from the man who amongst you is called Deucalion, [[that's the Greek Noah]] two symbols of the Spirit, the unclean and the clean, were sent out, the black raven and after it the white dove. And also from Abraham, the progenitor of our people, there issued two sons, the older Ishmael and

then Isaac, who was blessed by God. And from this same Isaac there sprang two sons, the godless Esau and the godly Jacob. . . .

And thereafter in the end Antichrist must first come again, and only afterwards must Jesus, our actual Christ, appear. (Schneemelcher 1964, 5.2.545)

This is a quite striking expression of the opposites that reside in God, yet while maintaining the oneness of God: that is the paradoxical God. Jung makes a point of drawing attention to it to show he is not pulling this material out of the air.

Jung identified the split, which occurred at the time of the incarnation of Christ. As Jung says, Christ and Satan were born together at the same time; however, Christ's manifestation as the totally good God required that he separate himself from the shadow. What we have in the New Testament is the statement of the fact that at the same time that Christ fell out of heaven into Mary's womb, so to speak, and was born out of that womb as man, Satan fell out of heaven. In Luke 10:18, Christ announces, "I beheld Satan as lightning fall from heaven." You see, the process of incarnation involves, at the same time, a split in the Godhead: the Self splits into opposites, which is what occurs when it is perceived by ego-consciousness.

The incarnation is a symbolic expression of the fact that the Godhead is now available for conscious reflection. It becomes a <u>reflected image</u>, whereas at an earlier time, as mentioned from *Aion*, Yahweh was previously an unreflected image. When He becomes a reflected image, He splits into the opposites. This event of the splitting of the Self into opposites on the archetypal realm, so to speak, corresponds on the earthly realm to Christ's encounter with the two manifestations of the Holy Spirit, the good and the evil manifestation during the episode of the temptation, which occurred immediately following His baptism.

I think that the great split in those days was by no means a mistake but a very important collective fact of synchronistic correspondence with the then new aeon of Pisces. . . .

. . . When Christ withstood Satan's temptation, that was the fatal moment when the shadow was cut off. Yet it had to be cut off in order to enable man to become morally conscious. If the moral opposites could be united at all, they would be suspended altogether and there could be no morality at all. (Jung 1975a, 165f.)

Jung refers to the occasion of Christ's temptation by Satan. I discuss this symbolism in some detail in my book, *The Christian Archetype* (Edinger 1987a, 47ff.). The event is described in Matthew, from 3:16 to 4:10. I will read some of it—a description of the great split, as it happened on the earthly level. On the heavenly level it had occurred by Yahweh being split into a positive son and a negative son. On the earthly level it takes place at the baptism of Christ. He [Christ] submits to being baptized by John the Baptist. Just as he is being submerged in the River Jordan and then brought up, we read as follows:

> And Jesus, when he was baptized, went up straightway out of the water: and, lo, the heavens were opened unto him, and he saw the Spirit of God descending like a dove, and lighting upon Him:
> And lo a voice from heaven, saying, This is my beloved Son, in whom I am well pleased. (Matt. 3:16–17)

That represents the good side of God. But then the very next words that follow are these:

> Then was Jesus led up of the Spirit into the wilderness to be tempted of the Devil.
> And when he had fasted forty days and forty nights, he was afterward an hungred.
> And when the tempter came to him, [[and there were the three temptations]] he said, If thou be the Son of God, command that these stones be made bread.
> But he answered and said, It is written, Man shall not live by bread alone, but by every word that proceedeth out of the mouth of God. (Matt. 4:1–4)

Then the second temptation: he took him on a high pinnacle of the temple and said:

> If thou be the Son of God, cast thyself down: for it is written, He shall give his angels charge concerning thee. . . .
> Jesus said unto him, It is written again, Thou shalt not tempt the Lord thy God. (Matt. 4:6–7)

Finally, the third time:

> Again, the devil taketh him up into an exceeding high mountain, and showeth him all the kingdoms of the world, and the glory of them;
> And saith unto him, All these things will I give thee, if thou wilt fall down and worship me.
> Then saith Jesus unto him, Get thee hence Satan. . . .
> Then the devil leaveth him, and, behold, angels came and ministered unto him. (Matt. 4:8–11)

On the earthly level, Christ split himself off from the Devil, which is what Jung is referring to here. Two things are happening. One is that Christ sees Satan for what he is—the raw power motive—and he rejects it. He splits himself off from it. The other thing that happens *at the same time* is that Yahweh splits into two, as is expressed in Christ's experience of the double nature of the baptism. As he is baptized, the good, benevolent Yahweh looks down on him with favor and—in the apocryphal material—a brilliant light shines, so that it is a time of great light. Immediately afterward, the divine Spirit turns dark and evil and becomes a tempting Spirit. This is precisely what the Clementine God-image describes: the double nature of God who has a dark left side and a bright right side, which is precisely what Christ experienced at the time of his baptism, one side right after the other.

Jung refers to this basic phenomenon of divine light followed by divine darkness in the letter:

> It is a historical fact that the real devil only came into existence together with Christ. Though Christ was God, as Man he was detached from God and he watched the devil falling out of heaven, removed from God as he (Christ) was separated from God inasmuch as he was human. In his utter helplessness on the cross, he even confessed that God had forsaken him. The Deus Pater would leave him to his fate as he always "strafes" those whom he had filled before with this abundance by breaking his promise. This is exactly what S. Joannes à cruce describes as the "dark night of the soul." It is the reign of darkness, which is also God, but an ordeal for Man. The Godhead has a double aspect. (1975a, 134)

This pattern occurs not only in mythological material, of course, but in individual experience.

When a patient in our days is about to emerge from an unconscious condition, he is instantly confronted with his *shadow* and he
has to decide for the good, otherwise he goes down the drain. *Nolens
volens* [willing or unwilling] he "imitates" Christ and follows his example. The first step on the way to individuation consists in the discrimination between himself and the shadow.

In this stage the Good is the goal of individuation, and consequently Christ represents the self.

The next step is the *problem of the shadow*: in dealing with darkness,
you have got to cling to the Good, otherwise the devil devours you.
You need every bit of your goodness in dealing with Evil and just
there. To keep the light alive in the darkness, that's the point, and
only there your candle makes sense. (1975a, 135)

The operative phrase there is "in dealing with darkness, you have got
to cling to the Good." In a later letter, the Kotschnig letter, Jung says:

His goodness means grace and light and His dark side the terrible
temptation of power. (1975a, 316)

The issue of the temptation of power comes up whenever the Self
is experienced, in big ways or small. To give a small, personal example,
which illustrates the point, I recall a patient I once worked with, who
developed quite an intense transference, which could be called a Self-
projection. I was carrying the Self to a significant degree. She hung on
every word. The consequence was that it gave what I said and did a
God-like effect on her, whether I liked it or not, for good or ill. She
was quite a meek woman, who was very much identified with the archetypal victim. In that situation I tried consciously to embody the understanding, good side for her. I did my best to dispense the grace and
light that is the positive side of the God-image. But on at least one or
two occasions, after particular sessions, I realized that her identification with the victim role, and her projection on me of God-like power,
had the effect of causing me to bully her.

In other words, I was experiencing the very pair of opposites Jung
speaks of in the letter: "God's goodness means grace and light and His
dark side the terrible temptation of power." To a certain extent, I had
fallen unwittingly into the temptation of power and had bullied her.
People who are identified with the victim ask for it, of course, but that
is no excuse for giving it to them. As soon as I realized it, I had to cling

to the good, as Jung directs us to do, by immediately confessing my error and apologizing for it, even though she never knew it had happened. Darkness is most likely to get a "hold" when you think you are safely settled in the good and righteous position, where nothing can assail you. When you are absolutely right is the most dangerous position of all, because, most probably, the devil has already got you by the throat.

> As a matter of fact, our society has not even begun to face its shadow or to develop those Christian virtues so badly needed in dealing with the powers of darkness. Our society cannot afford the luxury of cutting itself loose from the *imitatio Christi*, even if it should know that the *conflict with the shadow*, i.e., Christ versus Satan, is only the first step on the way to the far-away goal of the unity of the self in God.
>
> It is true, however, that the *imitatio Christi* leads you into your own very real and *Christ-like* conflict with darkness, and the more you are engaged in this war and in these attempts at peacemaking helped by the anima, the more you begin to look forward beyond the Christian aeon to the *Oneness of the Holy Spirit*. (Jung 1975a, 135)

[handwritten margin note: attempt @ peace-making helped by the anima]

Regarding the imitation of Christ, the *imitatio Christi*, one should keep in mind there are two imitations of Christ: the traditional, conventional one and the psychological one. They are quite different. The traditional imitation of Christ got its classic, comprehensive formulation from a medieval monk, Thomas à Kempis, who wrote a devotional volume entitled *The Imitation of Christ*, an example of which follows:

> "He that followeth Me, walketh not in darkness," saith the Lord. These are the words of Christ, by which we are taught to imitate His life and manners, if we would be truly enlightened, and be delivered from all blindness of heart. Let therefore our chief endeavor be to meditate upon the life of Jesus Christ.
>
> Whosoever then would fully and feelingly understand the words of Christ, must endeavor to conform his life wholly to the life of Christ.
>
> What will it avail thee to be engaged in profound reasonings concerning the Trinity, if thou be void of humility and art thereby displeasing to the Trinity.
>
> Surely great words do not make a man holy and just; but a virtuous life maketh him dear to God. I would rather feel compunction

than know its definition. Vanity of vanities, all is vanity except to love God and serve Him. This is the highest wisdom.

It is vanity therefore to seek after riches which must perish and to trust in them. It is vanity to be ambitious of honors and to raise oneself to a high station. It is vanity to follow the lusts of the flesh and to desire that for which thou afterwards must be grievously punished. It is vanity to wish for a long life and to take little care of leading the good life. (1894, 9f.)

The conventional imitation of Christ doctrine preaches separation from the shadow. It implores one to imitate Christ in saying "get thee behind me, Satan," in order to build up the Christian virtues. This message corresponds to stage one of the *coniunctio*, the so-called *unio mentalis* (Jung 1955).

The psychological imitation of Christ is quite different, as Jung spells out in *Mysterium Coniunctionis*:

> If the adept [[meaning the alchemist]] experiences his own self, the "true man," in his work, then . . . he encounters the analogy of the true man—Christ—in new and direct form, and he recognizes in the transformation in which he himself is involved a similarity to the Passion. It is not an "imitation of Christ" but its exact opposite: an assimilation of the Christ-image to his own self, which is the "true man." It is no longer an effort, an intentional straining after imitation, but rather an involuntary experience of the reality represented by the sacred legend. . . . The Passion *happens to* the adept, not in its classic form—otherwise he would be consciously performing spiritual exercises—but in the form expressed by the alchemical myth. . . . Nor does it originate in contemplation of Christ's Passion; it is the real experience of a man who has got involved in the compensatory contents of the unconscious by investigating the unknown, seriously and to the point of self-sacrifice. (1955, par. 492)

The psychological *imitatio* is a doctrine of wholeness, rather than a doctrine of perfection. This psychological imitation of Christ corresponds to the second stage of the coniunctio in which the *unio mentalis* is joined to the body. It involves the enduring of opposites. It involves the assimilation of the shadow rather than separation from the shadow—radically different psychological operations. As Jung says, certainly as a collective accomplishment, this step is still a "far-away goal," the accomplishment of which is the achievement of the Holy Spirit.

> The state of the Holy Spirit means a restitution of the original one-ness of the unconscious on the level of consciousness. (1975a, 135)

In Jung's essay on "The Psychological Approach to the Dogma of the Trinity," the psychological meaning of the three Trinitarian ages are described. The age of the Father corresponds to a state of original one-ness before consciousness, before the God-image has undergone a state of reflection. The age of the Son corresponds to the great split we have just been talking about, in which the opposites come into view. The age of the Son is a period of conflict and doubt and doubleness. The age of the Holy Spirit represents, psychologically, a restitution of the state of original oneness on a conscious level (Jung 1969a, pars. 129ff.). Jung goes on to say:

> The symbolic history of the Christ's life shows, as the essential teleological tendency, the crucifixion, viz., the union of Christ with the symbol of the tree. It is no longer a matter of an impossible reconciliation of Good and Evil, but of man with his vegetative (= unconscious) life. In the case of the Christian symbol the tree how-ever is dead and man upon the Cross is going to die, i.e., the solution of the problem takes place after death. That is so far as Christian truth goes. But it is possible [[that it can have another reference]]. . . . In this case the post-mortal solution would be symbolic of an entirely new psychological status . . . which is certainly a oneness, presumably that of the Anthropos [[which would appear]]. (1975a, 167)

Symbol of Christ on cross

The image of Christ on the cross carries a reference beyond itself. Since it happens on the post-mortal plane, it can foreshadow an expe-rience that can happen on the mortal, conscious plane sometime in the future. He alludes to this idea in a remark published in *C. G. Jung Speak-ing*, a remark made in 1960. This material is a section from Esther Harding's *Journals*, which I edited, so I know what it actually says. I edited out Victor White's name in this material, but it refers to Victor White. Jung spoke of the clergy's reaching out for his ideas. He says:

> Only the clergy and we are concerned with the education of the soul. People may have to go back to the church when they reach a certain stage of analysis. Individuation is only for the few. . . .

... X. [a mutual acquaintance, a cleric] had never really faced his problem, nor taken up his cross, that is, the opposition that forms the cross (crossing his fingers as he spoke). He need not have been afraid; the church would not have rejected him. A Jesuit said to X. once, "You make a fist in your pocket and go on with the ritual!" But he could not face the fact of evil—just as he denied that Jesus had a shadow, though that is clearly portrayed in the records we have. Not only did he fail on Palm Sunday, allowing himself to be venerated as an imperial savior, and then cursed the fig tree because it did not fall into line, but also he was actually unable to carry his cross, someone else had to carry it for him, a most significant point. And so he had to be *fixed* on the cross. If we do not carry our own cross, we will surely be crucified. So X., who had not enough backbone to carry his cross, had an illness and must die of cancer. (Jung 1977, 440)

Shadow of Jesus – unable to carry own cross

White had intestinal cancer, and died about the age of 58. As Jung puts it:

> [T]he union of Christ with the symbol of the tree . . . would be symbolic of an entirely new psychological status. (1975a, 167)

This new psychological status is what man is moving toward—away from competing collectivities, each one of which is identified with its particular version of the God-image. These collectivities are all expressions of the God-image as an *unconscious* phenomenon. The most basic point is that it is an individual matter. *It is one individual at a time who can transform the unconscious God-image, who otherwise manifests Himself in fragmentation, each fragment being a little piece of the Deity at war with every other piece of the Deity.*

> The later development from the Christian aeon to the one of the S. spiritus [Holy Spirit] has been called the *evangelium aeternum* by Gioacchino da Fiori in a time when the great tearing apart had just begun. Such vision seems to be granted by divine grace as a sort of *consolamentum*, so that man is not left in a completely hopeless state during the time of darkness. (1975a, 136)

> Thus I am approaching the end of the Christian aeon and I am to take up Gioacchino's [[that's Joachim of Flora]] anticipation and Christ's prediction of the coming of the Paraclete. This archetypal drama is at the same time exquisitely psychological and historical.

We are actually living in the time of the splitting of the world and of the invalidation of Christ.

But an anticipation of a faraway future is no way out of the actual situation. It is a mere consolamentum for those despairing at the atrocious possibilities of the present time. (1975a, 138)

The modern world is in a state of desperate darkness. It is visible to us. We do not have to be very perceptive to look about us to see that warring opposites are tearing the world apart. They are exposing the world to an onslaught of darkness. What Jung is saying here is that, for a few anyway, there is a vision of the future, a vision of what the next aeon will bring. It will be the age of the Holy Spirit, when the warring opposites will be reconciled in the coniunctio. It is this vision of the future that Jung calls a *consolamentum*.

Consolamentum is a very significant term, considering its source and context. It is a term that derives from the heresy of the Cathars of the eleventh and twelfth centuries. The central rite of the Cathars was a rite called the *consolamentum* (Jung 1975a, 136n.). It was performed at the time when a believer was being promoted to the group called the *perfecti*. The Cathars were divided into two groups: the believers, the ordinary ones, and the *perfecti*, the elect, the ones who were totally purified. Cathars means "the purified ones." The ritual was performed when a believer was ready to be transferred from the ordinary group of believers to the special group of *perfecti*, a solemn ritual that evoked the imagery of the baptism by the Holy Spirit (or Paraclete or Comforter). After a rigid fast extending over three days, the ritual was performed, and then the applicant retired for a period of forty days more, into complete solitude. I think what happened probably, in many cases, was something like what happens to the American Indian on a vision quest; the rigors of the whole procedure would have the effect of activating the unconscious and generating a special experience. This experience was thought of as a baptism by the Paraclete. It established the individual as a member of the *perfecti*. The whole ritual was called the *consolamentum*. The word itself means a substance, an entity that conveys comfort or consolation.

The Cathar's basic theology is a derivative of the pseudo-Clementine literature (Jung 1975a, 136n.). The pseudo-Clementine literature describes the paradoxical God-image in which the right hand of the deity was Christ and the left hand of the deity was Satan. The

Cathars split the Clementine God-image into two. Their basic theological point was that there are two gods. The same god, which occupied one image for the Clementine literature, has been split. One of the gods is the omnipotent good God, the other is the malignant God. They quoted the saying of Jesus that a good tree cannot bear evil fruit to demonstrate the fact that a world which has so much evil in it, could not be the product of a good God (Matt. 7:18). Therefore, at least according to some sects of the Cathars, the world itself was created by Satan. They were involved in this conflict between the opposites—the good God and the evil God. To be one of the *perfecti* meant one could have no significant relations to the evil world, and, primarily, there could be no sexual experience and no reproductive experience. Thus if the *perfecti* occupied the entire world, the human race would soon die out. Obviously the Cathars were grappling with the same imagery of the paradoxical God that Jung is dealing with in a later, more differentiated form. Their ritual is the source of the idea of the *consolamentum*, which Jung says is granted to a few individuals who have a vision of how things are going to be in the next aeon. That vision will be something of a consolation in helping to endure the darkness of the present.

The outer difficulties now are even greater. It is my conviction that, in the area of depth psychology, example is the only real teacher. Words can point the way, but only example has the effective power to get people's attention at a depth level. It is available to everyone of us: to function out of the maximum consciousness we possess and to live our lives as exemplary of that level of consciousness, which we have reason to believe will influence a certain circle around us. That is what I think Jung is referring to. Jung himself is the outstanding example. His life is exemplary to a superlative degree.

SIX

THE LETTER TO ERICH NEUMANN WAS WRITTEN MARCH 10, 1959, IN response to a letter of Neumann's to Jung. Aniela Jaffé, in her book *The Myth of Meaning*, speaks about this letter Neumann had written to Jung. She says that after Jung had sent Neumann a draft of the last chapter of his memoirs, containing his "late thoughts" on meaning, in 1958:

> [Neumann] wrote him [Jung] a letter expressing his general agreement, while demurring on certain points. The crucial passages [[from Neumann's letter]] are as follows: "Precisely because the psyche and the archetypes with their meaning evolved in the course of natural evolution, their meaning is not something alien to nature but pertains to it from the very outset—so it seems to me. . . . This is the only thing that remains questionable: What is creation for? The answer that, what shines only in itself when unreflected may shine in infinite variety, is age-old but satisfies me." (Jaffé, 142)

Then Jaffé goes on to comment:

> Jung saw meaning in the reciprocal relationship between man's deepening self-awareness and an unfolding of the God-image (metaphorically formulated as "God's consciousness of himself"); for Neumann, there was no such retroaction on God nor did there need to be one. (142f.)

They [Neumann and Jung] had a significant difference of opinion on a central issue, which is what this letter is about. Jung writes:

> The question: *an creator sibi consciens est?* [[Is the creator conscious of himself]] is not a "pet idea" but an exceedingly painful experience with well-nigh incalculable consequences, which it is not easy to argue about. (1975a, 493)

Evidently Neumann, in his letter to Jung, called Jung's idea about the unconsciousness of God a "pet idea." It must have been very disappointing to Jung that one of his most gifted pupils did not understand and made such a shallow response, not usually characteristic of Neumann. Neumann is not characteristically shallow. It must have been particularly painful to Jung.

It brings up the crucial question: Is the creator conscious of himself? The question can be broken down into two separate questions to simplify it. The first question: Is there a creator? Not everybody acknowledges that. The second question: If there is a creator, does it know what it is doing? This issue is just one little example of how the opposites are starting to tear society apart, as concretized in the struggle between the creationists and the evolutionists. Currently, in our state school system, this controversy is operant in determining what biology textbooks are going to be used. There is a very serious political conflict on the issue of whether the creationists are going to get a full voice in biology textbooks or not. There are two opposing factions. According to the creationists, God created the world and everything in it, just the way the Bible says He did. And of course He knew exactly what He was doing, without question. The evolutionists, on the other hand, operate out of the conviction that there is no discernable purpose or intention in the universe beyond the human ego. Life emerged by chance from a random gathering of molecules that fortuitously built up some very primitive viruses, which then gradually evolved through more complex syntheses into higher forms through the process of natural selection and the survival of the fittest.

Depth psychology takes a third view, not as a matter of belief, but as a matter of reasonable supposition, based on the empirical data of depth psychology. We have data which give us reason to think there is a transpersonal center of purpose and latent intentionality—what we call the Self, which is the creator of the ego as well. It takes something of a leap, I grant, from that bit of data to establish a Creator of the world; however, we also have data indicating that manifestations of the psyche transcend time and space, and engage inorganic, material processes in the phenomena of synchronicity. On that basis it is logical to infer, at least, that the God-image that lies behind the creation of the ego may also lie behind the creation of the world. At any event, what you see being circumambulated is a third position which would transcend and reconcile the concretistic simplicities of both the creationists and the evolutionists.

Now to the other question: Is the Creator conscious of himself? Jung says:

> The question: *an creator sibi consciens est?* [[Is the Creator conscious of himself?]] is not a "pet idea" but an exceedingly painful experience with well-nigh incalculable consequences, which it is not easy to argue about. For instance, if somebody projects the self this is an unconscious act, for we know from experience that projection results only from unconsciousness.
>
> *Incarnatio* means first and foremost God's birth in Christ, hence psychologically the realization of the self as something new, not present before. (1975a, 493–94)

To repeat, we know that "if somebody projects the self, this is an unconscious act, for we know from experience that projection results only from unconsciousness."

What immediately follows from the question: "Is the Creator conscious of himself"? He is comparing God's creation of man to an individual's projection of the Self. The idea would be that God's relation to man involves a projection of the Self on the part of God. Remember we are talking in anthropomorphisms, because that is the only way we can talk about these matters. When God creates man, He creates him in God's image. It means He himself, God, the Self, projects his image into man, the ego. According to the mythological imagery, when God creates man, He creates a son or daughter as a replica image of himself, which carries his image. Our Scriptures state that explicitly. It corresponds to the human situation. When parents create a biological child, they create a new creature who carries their genetic image. They project into their child, biologically, a genetic image of themselves. At the same time, something happens psychologically. Characteristically, parents also psychologically project the image of the Self on the child; so, the child becomes concretely for the parents the supreme value, carrying the eternal qualities with the idea that the child will continue the essence of the parent beyond the parent's temporal existence. The parent's projection of the Self, the child archetype, onto the concrete child, is a fact by which nature has so cunningly assured the preservation of the race. It is this fact, when you are dealing with mature parents anyway, that leads a parent to sacrifice himself, even his own life, for the survival of the child. It is due to the fact that the child is carrying the projection of the Self. It also explains why the archetypal image of the divine child is a symbol of the Self, which we know it is. What Jung is telling us is that God functions in the same way; He generates a creature, man, by projecting his own Self-image onto man. Then, like human parents, He unconsciously expects humanity to carry the future and the supreme value for Him, just as we parents expect our children to carry the future and the supreme value for us—at least until we get sufficiently conscious to get out of that role. If God were fully conscious there would be no need for such creatures. As Jung says, unconsciousness is a prerequisite for projection.

Jung had a dream on this subject (1963b, 323). It is a dream in which he saw a UFO projecting his existence, and he realized in the dream that God is not a projection of ours. We are a projection of God. The next part of the statement follows:

> [[Incarnation]] means first and foremost God's birth in Christ, hence psychologically the realization of the self as something new, not present before. The man who was created before that is a "creature," albeit "made in the likeness" of God, and this implies the idea of the [[Sonship]] *filiatio* and [[the divine sacrifice]] *sacrificium divinum*. Incarnation is, as you say, a "new experience." (1975a, 494)

It is a very condensed statement on Jung's part. He is saying that both these events—the original creation of humanity, the original creation of Adam and Eve, and the later, purposeful incarnation of God in Christ—both events would be pointless if God were completely conscious of himself. He would not need either of these events. He would not need these human mirrors to see himself, if He could see without them. Thus God needs man and He incarnates in man in order to bring Himself to full consciousness. This humanizing process has the effect of transforming the Deity. The first creation of Adam and Eve was the first level of incarnation. He incarnates his image of himself. It says that He created man and woman in his own image. The second version, the incarnation in the Christ, was a more explicit statement of the same phenomenon.

In the Bernet letter, Jung says, "there is no consciousness without an object" (1975a, 262). Also in a later letter, the Kotschnig letter, he says:

Moreover it is impossible for us to assume that a Creator producing a universe out of nothingness can be conscious of anything, because each act of cognition is based upon a discrimination—for instance, I cannot be conscious of somebody else when I am identical with him. If there is nothing outside of God everything is God and in such a state there is simply no possibility of self-cognition. (1975a, 312)

All these things indicate that the creature, man, is essential to the Deity in order for the Deity to become conscious of himself: Jung's answer to Neumann's remark that he is just riding a hobby horse of a "pet idea."

Although the Deity is unconscious, it does not mean that chance rules. Jung writes:

Since the laws of probability give no ground for assuming that higher syntheses such as the psyche could arise by chance alone, there is nothing for it but to postulate a latent meaning in order to explain not only the synchronistic phenomena but also the higher syntheses. (1975a, 495)

It is an argument which applies to all levels of organic life. The whole evolutionary history of life gives us a picture of higher and higher syntheses of biological existence being created out of the evolutionary process. That is an impossible consequence of random events. It violates the second law of thermodynamics, which applies to all mechanical, random systems: energy systems tend to reach a neutral level of entropy. It would be an impossible miracle for one particular area to start building up higher and higher levels of energy unless some agency were pouring that energy into it. For that reason we have to assume some kind of latent, creative intentionality to account for the phenomenon of the historical evolution of life as we see it, not to speak of the higher and higher syntheses on the psychological level, which is what Jung is thinking of here primarily.[1]

Since a creation without the reflecting consciousness of man has no discernible meaning, the hypothesis of a latent meaning endows

---

[1]See also Teilhard de Chardin 1965, *The Phenomenon of Man*, described by Jung as a great book in Miguel Serrano 1966, 100f., *C. G. Jung and Hermann Hesse: A Record of Two Friendships*.

man with a cosmogonic significance, a true *raison d'être*. If on the other hand the latent meaning is attributed to the Creator as part of a conscious plan of creation, the question arises: Why should the Creator stage-manage this whole phenomenal world since he already knows what he can reflect himself in, and why should he reflect himself at all since he is already conscious of himself? Why should he create alongside his own omniscience a second, inferior consciousness—millions of dreary little mirrors—when he knows in advance just what the image they reflect will look like? (1975a, 495)

The theme is the cosmogonic significance of consciousness. This is the basis for Jung's new myth. The same theme is reflected from a different angle in the letter to Frau N., written June 28, 1956. A footnote tells that Frau N. is the mother of an imbecile child, which is all we need to know to understand what this letter is about. It contains a beautiful description of what Jung has to offer a person who has been struck with a terrible misfortune.

I think, as analysts, it is a good letter to keep in mind. I have two or three letters of Jung's that I have bookmarks in, as I use them so often. One of them is his letter to a woman who wanted to commit suicide, telling her why he would not recommend that (1975a, 25–26, 278–79). Another is this one, because it gives us his reaction, his advice, about how to deal with a terrible blow of fate such as giving birth to a mentally defective child. What a terrible blow the parents are subjected to when that happens. Of course what he has to say applies to all such misfortunes. He says:

> It is hard to accept the fate you have described. Quite apart from the moral achievement required, complete acceptance depends very much on the conception you have of fate. An exclusively causal view is permissible only in the realm of physical or inorganic processes. The teleological view is more important in the biological sphere and also in psychology, where the answer makes sense only if it explains the "why" of it. So it is pointless to cling on to the causes, since they cannot be altered anyway. It is more rewarding to know what is to be done with the consequences, and the kind of attitude one has—or should have—to them. Then the question at once arises: Does the event have a *meaning?* Did a hidden purpose of fate, or God's will, have a hand in it, or was it nothing but "chance," a "mishap." (1975a, 310–11)

How well one endures such a misfortune will depend on the conception one has of fate, as opposed to mechanical causation. For instance, we can be quite sure that this woman who gave birth to the mentally defective child surely must have tortured herself with causal questions. What did I do during the pregnancy? Did I take some drugs? Did I drink too much alcohol? Did I smoke? What did I do? What caused it? That is the eternal round of the ego, because these are the only terms the ego can think in, the terms of causality, mechanical causality. It is what Aristotle called the efficient cause, as opposed to the final cause. As Jung says, what is required is that one have a conception of fate. What would that be?

We have several words for fate in English: destiny, providence. The ancients had two quite explicit words for it, each with different implications: *heimarmene* and *moira*. *Heimarmene* has the meaning of predetermined fate, but in the sense of the compulsion of the stars. Jung talks about this whole idea of *heimarmene* in *Mysterium Coniunctionis*, where he says, in interpreting some of the alchemical material, "unity is not subject to *heimarmene*" (1955, par. 308). In other words, *heimarmene* is a fate that can be altered with sufficient consciousness. It is not irrevocable fate. It is like being caught up in parental complexes which do not undergo resolution. *Heimarmene* can be modified with consciousness.

The other term, *moira*, is generally interpreted as destiny. Its basic meaning is one's portion, one's allotment. It would correspond to our idea of the deal we are given by the divine card dealer. He gives us a certain hand and we have got to play that hand. We cannot turn that hand in for a new one; we are stuck with the one we have got. It is our portion. According to ancient mythology, even the gods, and Zeus himself, were subject to *moira*. *Moira* was beyond the gods themselves; it is a personification of destiny, of what is ordained above both gods and men: unalterable destiny. Of course, we never know in a given situation whether we are dealing with *heimarmene* or *moira*, so we have to go on the assumption that it is the former. We have to go on the assumption that it can be modified by consciousness. Whenever we are confronted with a *fait accompli*, a misfortune that has already happened, then the difference disappears, and we are dealing with *moira*. It is our established destiny. If one gives birth to a mentally defective child, it is *moira*.

If one takes Jung's advice about misfortune and says, "Well, this is my destiny," then the task is to accept the destiny. Recognizing that it is destiny is the first step, because one recognizes one did not cause it. One recognizes that a transpersonal agency is responsible for it. That is Job's question; he was hit by profound misfortune and he would not accept the advice of his comforters to take the blame himself. He persevered until he found the meaning that was satisfying to him. What is required in all such misfortunes is to find the meaning.

If one is dealing with an unconscious God, then an event of misfortune, which is attributable to transpersonal destiny, cannot be assumed to have a predetermined, conscious meaning. The most one can assume is that it has a latent meaning. Then, if one realizes it is an event of destiny, then it is the task of the ego, perhaps in cooperation with the unconscious—the unconscious usually does give some very good hints at that point—to discover the meaning. If the meaning is discovered, then the individual can accept it, and until the meaning is discovered, he cannot accept it. He fights against it. He is at war with life, with God, and with his whole fate. If the meaning and purpose can be located, then it can be accepted. What Jung elaborates regarding the Book of Job is that such "Job experiences" have as their basic meaning the realization that God does not know his total condition and that by getting a glimpse of that total condition, man is helping God become more conscious. That is the meaning that Jung extracts from the Book of Job, which is, potentially, the meaning that any individual can extract from a misfortune that befalls one. Of course, it cannot be imposed just arbitrarily; such realization has to grow organically from within. If it does, then the misfortune can be accepted and assimilated.

Job fulfilled the human task of mirroring the nature of God to himself. As a consequence of being shown what the Job mirror showed Him, Yahweh was obliged to undergo a process of Self-transformation, which is at the same time an incarnation and a humanization. He has to become; He has to participate more concretely in that mirroring phenomenon which has brought Him this consciousness, the mirroring phenomenon that is man. Emptying Himself of his divinity and entering the body of the slave (the slave that is the dependent human ego, the human being) is a Self-sacrifice of the unconscious Deity, who participates in the human consciousness that has mirrored His real being for Him and who as a process of that participation must experience, then, the suffering that characterizes human existence. He does so as a Self-sacrifice for the purpose of the transformation of His nature.

'Job experiences'

70

Buddhist Wheel of Life

Jung goes on to introduce the notion of the Nidhana-chain:

With no human consciousness to reflect themselves in, good and evil simply happen, or rather, there is no good and evil, but only a sequence of neutral events, or what the Buddhists call the Nidhana-chain, the uninterrupted causal concatenation leading to suffering, old age, sickness, and death. Buddha's insight and the Incarnation in Christ break the chain through the intervention of the enlightened human consciousness, which thereby acquires a metaphysical and cosmic significance. (1975a, 311)

The last sentence is one of the finest diamond jewels of Jungian wisdom and something really to ponder.

Buddha's insight and the Incarnation in Christ break the chain through the intervention of the enlightened human consciousness, which thereby acquires a metaphysical and cosmic significance.

What is meant by the Nidhana-chain? (see below). It is called the Nidhana-chain of suffering, or the Chain of Dependent Origination. It

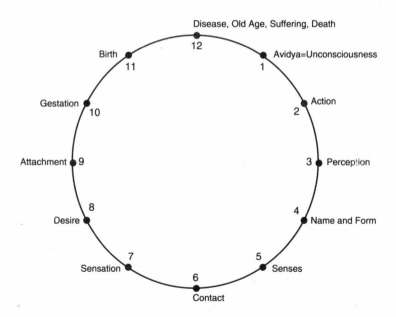

The Nidhana-Chain

71

is a process the Buddha discovered by contemplating the evils of old age, disease, suffering, and death. He asked, "where do they come from?" He traced each answer he got back through a whole series of so-called causes.

The word *Nidhana* means cause or origination. Working forward rather than backward (Buddha discovered the chain working backwards), the chain begins prior to one's existence, according to Buddhist conception, with *avidya*, ignorance. We could also translate it unconsciousness. All these terms are not relevant to modern thinking, rather it is the total sequence that is significant.

Ignorance leads to action or motivation, of some kind. Action leads to perception, some kind of dim awareness. Perception leads to conceptualizations, what are called name and form. Name and form lead to the senses, which brings about contact with objects. The senses lead to sensation itself. Sensation generates desire or craving. Desire generates attachment. Attachment leads to becoming or existence, sometimes also translated gestation. Becoming leads to birth. Once you are born, you are then exposed to disease, suffering, old age, and death. Once you are born, your unconsciousness causes you to initiate the whole process all over again, so you bring to birth another generation. So it goes on—endlessly. That is the Nidhana-chain of suffering.

One powerful illustration of the Nidhana-chain appears in Joseph Campbell's *The Mythic Image*; it is entitled "The Wheel of Becoming" (Campbell 1974, 400–401). It is a wheel, a mandala. The chain of suffering is the outermost circle. The innermost circle has at its center the three basic motivations of human existence, represented by the pig, the cock, and the serpent—ignorance, desire, and power. These are the three basic motivations of natural existence. You will notice it is a triadic mandala. It is based on the number three. There are three animals at the center, and there are six divisions of the larger circle. It is an expression of the wholeness of life as perceived from the standpoint of the ego rather than from the standpoint of the Self. (See chapter 8, in which the Trinity archetype is discussed in more detail, including one of the important symbolisms of the number three—egohood.) This picture represents that the cycle of natural ego, of spatio-temporal existence is a vicious circle, a torture wheel that is fueled by ignorance, lust, and power. It is also a mandala, an image of the unconscious Self, an image of the unconscious Deity as experienced by the ego. It is a picture of the state of affairs that exists as long as the ego is identified with this unconscious condition. Only consciousness brings release. As Jung says:

Buddha's insight and the Incarnation in Christ break the chain [of suffering] through the intervention of the enlightened human consciousness.

The beginning of the chain is unconsciousness. It is at this point that the chain is broken by consciousness. Buddha saw the chain. He found the Archimedean point outside of this circle which enabled him to see the whole circle. In the process of seeing the whole circle, he broke it. He is no longer contained in it. He is no longer a fish swimming in the pond. This chain of suffering repeats itself endlessly as long as objective consciousness is lacking. It is like the fiery torture wheel of Ixion in the Greek myth. He is forever bound to revolve on that wheel by virtue of his unconscious identification with the Self. With Buddha's insight, mankind is rescued or redeemed from identification with that unconscious Deity. A similar redemption occurs with the incarnation in Christ, because the incarnation in Christ comes as a consequence of Job's insight. Just like Buddha, Job saw the unconscious Deity in His entirety. He saw the backside of Yahweh. He saw the whole picture. He found the Archimedean point outside of the Deity. He also saw Behemoth and Leviathan, just as Buddha saw the snake, the cock, and the pig, as the center of natural existence. The result of Job's insight was then that Yahweh was obliged to incarnate and involve Himself in a Self-sacrifice in order to become man and to undergo humanization. Therefore Buddha's insight and Job's insight, which are identical, and the incarnation in Christ are all aspects of the same psychological phenomenon. It is a remarkable insight not easy to achieve.

This type of seeing, of course, is the miracle of how one discovers the Archimedean point. Buddha found it. He experienced enlightenment, but his followers, although studying the teachings and imitating him, did not. I have been told by someone knowledgeable about schools of Buddhism that the whole idea of where to break the chain led to different schools, that is, one school ignorance, another school desire (the ascetic school, the denial of desire). Buddha tried asceticism and realized it was not the way. Nevertheless, one school attacks the chain at the link of desire. You don't get outside the circle that way. As long as you fight some link, you are still in it.

Can one see one's own life within the framework of destiny? Many years ago—October 29, 1956—to be exact, I had a dream that I call a destiny dream. It pictures in an interesting way how the determinism that destiny assumes and the freedom of the will interact. It is part of a longer dream; some of the details are omitted for the sake of brevity.

I was in a strange and alien world involving conflict and intrigue. Two levels of action seemed to be going on at once. On the one level, I felt a prisoner to the situation and to the people in it. On the other hand, I felt I had been made to play the principal role in an important drama. During the dream I felt that I had read the whole plot and story at one time in a science fiction book but couldn't quite remember it. I made up my dialogue as I went along, since I didn't know the lines and seemed to be doing very well. I was quite natural and spontaneous. I believe I was helped by the fact that I had once read the story, and when each situation came up, it struck some chord of memory which came to my assistance. At a crucial moment I have a realization. I have told the people surrounding me that I have a slight cold. Those around me show they are deathly afraid of being infected by my germs if I speak in their direction. They cower away from me in fear. With this I joyfully realize I am free and no longer their prisoner. I dance a little jig and I say, "Jumping Jehosaphat."

Even during this exciting discovery, which I was absolutely certain meant real freedom, I realized also this was part of the preordained play. I was meant to be confused and uncertain at first and then to have the light suddenly dawn on me. I was playing the role perfectly just because I was reliving it at the same time. Thus my experiences were completely real, completely natural and spontaneous and nevertheless part of a play or story I was acting, which I had once read but forgotten.

The basic theme of my dream is the theme of determinism versus free will. If destiny controls us totally, free will does not exist; it is just an illusion. That would correspond to the feeling, on the one hand, that I was a prisoner. But on the other hand, my captors were deathly afraid of my words. My word had power. That conveyed the experience of freedom. I was convinced I was free; I had the joyful experience of being free, and not subject to being a prisoner of determinism. Nevertheless I could not escape the sense that I was also living out a story that had already been laid down. The opposites are really reconciled in the dream about as well as they can be in human consciousness. I think it is an interesting example of how the unconscious engages the issue of destiny versus freedom.

PART THREE

CONTINUING INCARNATION

The ego participates in God's suffering. We have become participants in the divine nature. We are the vessel . . . of the Deity suffering in the body of the "slave" (Phil. 2:6). Buddha's insight and the incarnation in Christ break the chain through the intervention of the enlightened human consciousness which thereby acquires a metaphysical and cosmic significance. Individuation and individual existence are indispensable for the transformation of God. Human consciousness is the only seeing eye of the Deity.

C. G. Jung, Nietzsche's Zarathustra,
336, 409; Letters II, 314ff.

SEVEN

THE KOTSCHNIG LETTER OF JUNE 30, 1956, IS PERHAPS THE SINGLE MOST explicit description of Jung's vision of the evolving God-image and of the human ego's relation to it. Jung says:

> When we consider the data of palaeontology with the view that a conscious creator has perhaps spent more than a thousand million years, and has made, as it seems to us, no end of detours to produce consciousness, we inevitably come to the conclusion that—if we want to explain His doings at all—His behavior is strikingly similar to a being with an at least very limited consciousness. Although aware of the things that are and the next steps to take, He has apparently neither foresight of an ulterior goal nor any knowledge of a direct way to reach it. Thus it would not be an absolute unconsciousness but a rather dim consciousness. Such a consciousness would necessarily produce any amount of errors and impasses with the most cruel consequences, disease, mutilation, and horrible fights, i.e., just the thing that has happened and is still happening throughout all realms of life. (1975a, 312)

It is an explicit description of the image of the dimly conscious God. This particular God-image reconciles the conflict between the evolutionists and the creationists, for example. Jung is saying here that the world and biological and human life have all been created by an innate purposefulness, not by chance, but the purposeful agent is almost blind. It is only dimly conscious of what it is doing, which accounts for all the errors, the impasses, the "cruel consequences, disease, mutilation, horrible fights," et cetera, which constitute the history of biological evolution and the history of humanity. (In another letter, Jung speaks of human history as a great morass: "the morass of human history.") Jung describes a *totally new* God-image. It is the picture of an entity who may very well have absolute knowledge and boundless power, *but does not know it or forgets it,* or as Jung describes in *Answer to Job,* forgets to consult its omniscience at crucial moments" (1969a, par. 634). Such a God-image requires an interaction with human consciousness in order to achieve progressive self-realization.

It is most certainly not a creed, not something for religious belief; rather, it is a scientific hypothesis which best fits the accumulated facts of depth psychology as we currently possess them. At this time, troublingly few people are aware of the facts of depth psychology. For those who are, the God-image that Jung expounds is the best hypothesis that we have to encompass the scientific data of depth psychology.

There is a similar example of Jung's point of view mentioned by Margaret Ostrowski-Sachs:

> It looks as if God was unconscious. Anyone who knew the goal would not have taken such a roundabout way with creation. It took a long time for the brain to appear on the earth. Dinosaurs give the impression of having completely empty heads. Then bumps appeared, then much later horns grew from the head. Much later still the brain was formed. It seems as if there was an urge to create something. The least differentiated animals developed the most. Only that which is incomplete can perfect itself. Only an unconscious creative power could have worked so hesitantly, which is why I think the creator God was unconscious. This assumption also accounts for the many prehistoric catastrophes. It does not imply that creation was accidental but that it seems as if its intention was limited in scope. . . . If the creator knew everything in advance, history would seem like a badly running machine, misfiring now and then. God would be responsible for each catastrophe because it must have arisen from his mistakes. The assumption of divine prescience or of a personal God makes nonsense of the world. . . . If God were almighty, how could it have taken 400 million years to reach this point from a time when only fish existed, if creation was not an unconscious search and a groping in the dark. How could we account for the enormous quantities of fish before new beings could come into existence. This is my myth about God and his creation. (Ostrowski-Sachs, 40–41)

The Kotschnig letter continues:

> The clear recognition of the fatal unreliability of the deity led Jewish prophecy to look for a sort of mediator or advocate, representing the claims of humanity before God. As you know, this figure is already announced in Ezekiel's vision of the Man and Son of Man. The idea was carried on by Daniel and then in the Apocryphal writings, particularly in the figure of the female Demiurge, viz., Sophia, and in the male form of an administrator of justice, the Son of Man, in the Book of Enoch, written about 100 B.C. and very popular at the time of Christ. It must have been so well-known, indeed, that Christ called himself "Son of Man" with the evident presupposition of everybody knowing what he was talking about. (Jung 1975a, 313)

Jung is reviewing the same sequence previously mentioned in *Answer to Job*. It is the evolving sequence of the image and concept of the Son of Man. It starts with Ezekiel's vision, in which God revealed himself in human form to Ezekiel, called the Son of Man. The image continues in Daniel [chapter] 7. Daniel had a vision where he saw someone like the Son of Man coming in the clouds of heaven. It is connected with the emerging image of Sophia, the divine wisdom, who was spoken of in Proverbs and other places as the playmate of the Deity, and who functioned as a mediator between God and man. It follows in more explicit form in the Book of Enoch, where a series of visions of heaven is described involving the Son of Man. Jung thought that Christ was so familiar with the Book of Enoch and the image of the Son of Man in it that he deliberately identified himself with it. There are several visions in the Book of Enoch which speak of the Son of Man. Here is one example:

> And there I saw One who had a head of days,
> And His head was white like wool,
> And with Him was another being whose countenance had the appearance of a man,
> And his face was full of graciousness, like one of the holy angels.
> And I asked the angel who went with me and showed me all the hidden things, concerning that Son of Man,
> Who he was, and whence he was, (and) why he went with the Head of Days?

And he answered and said unto me: This is the Son of Man who hath
righteousness,
With whom dwelleth righteousness.

(Charles 1913, 2:214)

Jung also refers specifically to Enoch's vision of the Son of Man in
Answer to Job; he says:

> Enoch is so much under the influence of the divine drama, so
> gripped by it, that one could almost suppose that he had a quite spe-
> cial understanding of the coming Incarnation. "The Son of Man" who
> is with the "Head [or Ancient] of Days" looks like an angel (i.e., like
> one of the sons of God). He "hath righteousness"; "with him dwelleth
> righteousness.". . . It is probably no accident that so much stress is
> laid on righteousness, for it is the one quality Yahweh lacks. (1969a,
> par. 678)

According to Jung's thinking, Job's encounter with Yahweh and his
view of Yahweh had the effect of generating a mediating figure called
the Son of Man, who makes an approach to Yahweh and starts to build
a bridge between the ego and the Self. The basic idea is that Job's consciousness concerning the nature of the Deity initiated a process in the
archetypal realm. It set into motion what Jung calls a *divine drama,* in
which the ego and the Self make overtures to each other, the end result of which is the transformation of God through a double process of
the humanizing of the Self and the deifying of the ego. It is a double
process of overtures. From the human side a figure of the Son of Man
makes his appearance, who starts to bridge the gap from the human
side; and with the incarnation of Christ there is an overture from the
opposite direction: the Son of God descends from the divine realm and
incarnates in man. Interestingly, the figure of Christ is given both those
names: He is called the Son of Man *and* the Son of God. He is a kind
of double personification of these twofold, reciprocal overtures that are
taking place between the ego and the Self, between the personal and
the divine realm. Jung further expounds in the Kotschnig letter:

> [Christ] was up against an unpredictable and lawless God who would
> need a most drastic sacrifice to appease His wrath, viz. the slaughter
> of His own son. Curiously enough, as on the one hand his self-sacri-
> fice means admission of the Father's amoral nature, he taught on the

other hand a new image of God, namely that of a Loving Father in whom there is no darkness. This enormous antinomy needs some explanation. It needed the assertion that he was the Son of the Father, i.e., the incarnation of the Deity in man. As a consequence the sacrifice was a self-destruction of the amoral God, incarnated in a mortal body. Thus the sacrifice takes on the aspect of a highly moral deed, of a self-punishment, as it were. (1975a, 313)

This idea goes so deep and is in such concentrated form that one must read it many times to begin to assimilate what is being said. The consequence of the self-sacrifice of the amoral God is its transformation to a good God, as preached by Christ. However, that transformation is not total because as Jung informs us:

Inasmuch as God proves His goodness through self-sacrifice He is incarnated, but in view of His infinity and the presumably different stages of cosmic development we don't know of, how much of God—if this is not too human an argument—has been transformed? (1975a, 314)

To simplify, one does not know how much of God has been transformed. He has been transformed by the self-sacrifice, but one cannot be sure it is a total transformation. If it is not a total transformation, then:

In this case it can be expected that we are going to contact spheres of a not yet transformed God when our consciousness begins to extend into the sphere of the unconscious. (1975a, 314)

He is describing in these archetypal images, of course, the data of depth psychology. When one subjects himself and his patients to a depth analysis, he encounters regions of a "not yet transformed Deity." No student of Jungian psychology has any doubt about that. That is what this material means psychologically. When one examines the unconscious, what one comes across is the unconscious Self, the unconscious, primordial God-image, which is amoral. In some respects it corresponds to the Freudian *id*. One of the ways one can see its characteristics is by observing the behavior of those people who are unconsciously identified with the Self: infants, psychotics, criminals, religious fanatics, and indeed everyone, when caught in a state of possession by a passionate affect. What we see on most immediate observation

81

is that the goals of this unconscious, amoral God-image are power, pleasure, and fulfillment in all senses of the word. One can also observe this amoral Self by observing our own unconscious affective reactions. Looking at them in personalistic terms, one can describe them as infantile, because one of the characteristics of infantile psychology is that the latent, emerging ego is identified with the Self and therefore has many of the characteristics of the unconscious Deity. Some other examples may assist in recognizing this phenomenon.

Suppose, for example, hurrying to get to class one evening, one carelessly cuts off a car on the freeway. Depending on who was driving that car one might be in trouble. He might drive alongside and shoot. It does happen now and then. More often, and who has not had this experience, he will run alongside, give a vulgar gesture accompanied by a stream of epithets. If he had the power of omniscience, one would be damned to hell. In that sequence one is witnessing the phenomenology of the behavior of the amoral Deity who has been offended. It does not matter that the offense was unintentional. It is an example of "vengeance is mine sayeth the Lord."

Another example, a literary example, is particularly illustrative of what everyone experiences to some degree. It comes from Herman Melville's novel *White Jacket*. It is about a sailor who shipped aboard an American man-of-war, a warship of the early nineteenth century. This protagonist, who is an upright, decent young man, has been wrongly accused of ignoring a specific order by the Captain. He protests; he says that he never heard of being assigned to that post, that he was not ignoring his duty.

> "It's impossible, sir," said that officer, striving to hide his vexation, "but this man must have known his station."
> "I have never known it before this moment, Captain Claret," said I.
> "Do you contradict my officer?" he returned. "I shall flog you."
> I had now been on board the frigate upward of a year, and remained unscourged.

There used to be flogging in the American navy.

> [T]he ship was homeward-bound, and in a few weeks, at most, I would be a free man. And now, after making a hermit of myself in some things, in order to avoid the possibility of the scourge, here it was hanging over me for a thing utterly unforeseen, for a crime of

which I was utterly innocent. But all that was as naught. I saw that my case was hopeless; my solemn disclaimer was thrown in my teeth, and the boatswain's mate stood curling his fingers through the cat [[i.e., the cat-o-nine tails they used for flogging]].

There are times when wild thoughts enter a man's heart, when he seems almost irresponsible for his act and his deed. The Captain stood on the weather-side of the deck. Sideways, on an unobstructed line with him, was the opening of the lee-gangway, where the side-ladders are suspended in port. Nothing but a slight bit of sinnate-stuff served to rail in this opening, which was cut right down to the level of the Captain's feet, showing the far sea beyond. I stood a little to windward of him, and, though he was a large, powerful man, it was certain that a sudden rush against him, along the slanting deck, would infallibly pitch him headforemost into the ocean, though he who so rushed must needs go over with him. My blood seemed clotting in my veins; I felt icy cold at the tips of my fingers, and a dimness was before my eyes. But through that dimness the boatswain's mate, scourge in hand, loomed like a giant, and Captain Claret, and the blue sea seen through the opening at the gangway, showed with an awful vividness. I cannot analyze my heart, though it then stood still within me. But the thing that swayed me to my purpose was not altogether the thought that Captain Claret was about to degrade me, and that I had taken an oath with my soul that he should not. No, I felt my man's manhood so bottomless within me, that no word, no blow, no scourge of Captain Claret could cut me deep enough for that. I but swung to an instinct in me—the instinct diffused through all animated nature, the same that prompts even a worm to turn under the heel. Locking souls with him, I meant to drag Captain Claret from this earthly tribunal of his to that of Jehovah, and let Him decide between us. No other way could I escape the scourge.

Nature has not implanted any power in man that was not meant to be exercised at times, though too often our powers have been abused. The privilege, inborn and inalienable, that every man has, of dying himself, and inflicting death upon another, was not given to us without a purpose. These are the last resources of an insulted and un-endurable existence.

"To the gratings, sir!" said Captain Claret; "do you hear?"

My eye was measuring the distance between him and the sea. (Melville 279–80)

He was spared at the last moment. Someone came to bear witness for him. White Jacket was intending to behave in approximately the same way as the man cut off on the freeway. It is the same basic dynamic. The Self, the amoral unconscious Self, will not stand to be offended. It will, if necessary, murder its offender and take the ego down with it. It does not know what it is doing. White Jacket was in the grips of this Deity who in the name of justice was going to commit a double murder. You could hardly call that moral, even though it was in the name of justice. Melville describes so well what he calls the *innate instinct*: It is the God-image within us, an expression of the unconscious Self.

The same phenomena lay behind the duels of honor in the eighteenth century. "You offend me, my honor requires that you give me satisfaction. You give me the chance to kill you." That is the amoral Deity speaking. Whenever one falls into an unconscious power reaction, one is living out a small version of the same thing. Job did not make the mistake of having a similar lapse of consciousness as White Jacket. He maintained his integrity even while seeing the nature of the Deity. His wife told him to "curse God and die." His wife would have him behave the way White Jacket was planning to behave.

There is a requirement not only for consciousness but also for a discriminating consciousness which can make ethical decisions. Jung says,

> Although the divine incarnation is a cosmic and absolute event, it only manifests empirically in those relatively few individuals capable of enough consciousness to make ethical decisions, i.e., to decide for the Good. Therefore God can be called good only inasmuch as He is able to manifest His goodness in individuals. . . .
>
> The knowledge of what is good is not given *a priori*; it needs discriminating consciousness. . . . There is no such thing as the "Good" in general, because something that is definitely good can be as definitely evil in another case. . . . For instance generosity is certainly a virtue, but it instantly becomes a vice when applied to an individual that misunderstands it. (1975a, 314)

At issue is what is called psychological ethics. From the standpoint of depth psychology, it is not so easy to answer the question: What is good? As Jung says, "There is no such thing as the 'Good' in general." Psychological ethics does not mean the ethics of the penal code, of just staying within the law of a particular country, of minimal standards. Psychological ethics also does not mean staying within the conventional social code of one's collective group, which is not necessarily the same as the penal code at all. Also, it is not even true that psychological ethics is following one's conscience. Jung speaks of choosing the soul over the conscience. Conscience is a complicated psychological dynamism. It is a combination of superego introjects and directions from the Self, sometimes also contaminated by various complexes. The unanalyzed conscience does not constitute the basis for psychological ethics.

There is an anecdote that Viktor Frankl (1962), the father of logotherapy, told that illustrates a point on this subject. A well known Freudian psychoanalyst had come to give a lecture to Viktor Frankl's logotherapy group, probably in Vienna. After the lecture, Frankl had taken the analyst to dinner, where they talked about their theoretical differences in psychology. Logotherapy is a kind of spiritual therapy, which does not involve the unconscious. Frankl said to the analyst that there really is such a thing as a conscience and that the analyst had demonstrated the fact of conscience by the excellent lecture he gave. The Freudian analyst replied with some irritation that it was not conscience; it was narcissism.

The virtue of such a reply is that it shows the awareness of the shadow. The psychoanalyst did not fall victim to the shallow notion of virtue because he was aware of the shadow dimension of one's behavior. The crucial feature of psychological ethics is that *one's actions are based on a thorough awareness of the shadow* in oneself and in others. One is not a naïve innocent, either in relation to the motivations of others or in relation to the motivations of oneself. An awareness of the shadow also goes along with an awareness of the opposites. It is a version of that process too. With a good awareness of the opposites, one can never be too sure where the "Good" actually resides. It does not necessarily reside where it appears best. In fact, when one has a good sense of the dynamism of the opposites, whenever one gets too much on one side or the other, one must start looking for its contrary, as it will be lurking around somewhere. A favorite passage of Jung's in this regard is a non-canonical saying of Jesus that Jung quotes a number of times in his works. Certain manuscripts of Luke at Luke 6:4 have an addition which reads:

On the same day seeing one working on the Sabbath, He [[namely, Christ]] said unto him, "Man if indeed thou knowest what thou doest, thou art blest; but if thou knowest not thou art cursed and a transgressor of the law."

Jung quotes that passage to illustrate the fact that, so far as psychological ethics are concerned, the accompanying consciousness, to a large extent, determines the nature of what one is doing. He also makes clear in various places that being aware that an act is evil does not eliminate the fact that it is evil. It just means that one carries the guilt of doing it consciously.

The ability to carry the opposites consciously ushers in the possibility of the *continuing incarnation*.

We ought to remember that the Fathers of the Church have insisted upon the fact that God has given Himself to man's death on the Cross so that we may become gods. The Deity has taken its abode in man with the obvious intention of realizing its Good in man. Thus we are the vessel or the children and the heirs of the Deity suffering in the body of the "slave." (1975a, 315)

This statement announces what Jung calls the *continuing incarnation*. He says, we are "the children and the heirs of the Deity suffering in the body of the 'slave.'" This statement is a reference to a passage in Paul's Letter to the Philippians 2:5–9 (Jerusalem Bible), where we read:

In your minds you must be the same as Christ Jesus:

His state was divine,
yet he did not cling
to his equality with God
but emptied himself
to assume the condition of a slave,
and became as men are;
and being as all men are,
he was humbler yet,
even to accepting death,
death on a cross.
But God raised him high
and gave him the name
which is above all other names.

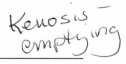

This passage is the basis of what is called the doctrine of *kenosis*, of emptying. The idea, very relevant to our understanding of the relation between the ego and the Self, is that the Deity, the Self, desiring to come into conscious realization, must flow into an ego. In order to do that it must divest itself of divinity and become a slave: namely, the weak, feeble, limited human ego. The result then is that the Self is emptied and the ego is filled. The Self is humanized by its connection to the limited human ego, and the ego is deified by its connection to the transpersonal aspects of the Self. A similar meaning is found in Christ's statement, "You are Gods," a phrase from Psalms 82:6, which Christ quoted, and which Jung quotes a number of times in these letters and elsewhere in his later writings. He elaborates this point further:

> The significance of man is enhanced by the incarnation. We have become participants of the divine life and we have to assume a new responsibility, viz. the continuation of the divine self-realization, which expresses itself in the task of our individuation. Individuation does not only mean that man has become truly human as distinct from animal, but that he is to become partially divine as well. This means practically that he becomes adult, responsible for his existence, knowing that he does not only depend on God but that God also depends on man. Man's relation to God probably has to undergo a certain important change: Instead of the propitiating praise to an unpredictable king or the child's prayer to a loving father, the responsible living and fulfilling of the divine will in us will be our form of worship of and commerce with God. His goodness means grace and light and His dark side the terrible temptation of power. (1975a, 316; see also Jung 1963b, 209; 1975a, 265, 322–24)

Here the operative statement is another one of those diamond gems. He tells us what *psychological maturity* means from the standpoint of Jungian psychology. He says it means "the responsible living and fulfilling of the divine will in us." What is that? How can we do that? How can we even know the divine will? All sorts of questions arise from this simple statement. One might very well say, "I don't know anything about divine will; all I know is what I want; how could I know what God wants? I would not presume as much." It is the problem of distinguishing between the ego and the Self. In the first half of life that distinction is not going to be made. The first half of life, barring exceptions, is characterized by a degree of identification between the ego and the Self which does not allow their distinction. In the second half of life, ideally at least, the ego and Self have started to undergo some degree of separation. It becomes possible in a few cases for the ego to become aware that a transpersonal center is calling the shots in his life. If that level of awareness takes place, then the ego begins to get some idea of what is meant by "the divine will in us." That event, however, does not take place without substantial psychological development.

A woman once wrote me a letter asking me about this issue. She was a stranger; I did not know her personally. I get these letters every now and then from people who have read some of my books. She said to me, "I desperately want to do the will of God. Please tell me what it is or at least tell me how do I find out what God wants of me?" That is the question. If we are not members of a particular creed that tells us what God wants—which is the function of a religious creed, it tells you and then you obey those religious rules, the laws of God according to that creed and you are justified—but if you are not that fortunate, then one must discover it for oneself. That is where the analytic process, that is where the process of the serious attention to the unconscious, comes in. I think there is reason to believe, which is implied by what Jung is saying, that even God does not know what his will is until the individual makes the discovery. It may be that consciousness happens simultaneously to both the ego and the Self. If one is not able to accept a conventional, collective answer to the question of "what is God's will?", then one is obliged to look for an individual, experiential answer. One must then seek the divine will for oneself. It is a search of discovery, and it becomes a depth psychological adventure for each individual who undertakes it.

There is a similar reference in the Kelsey letter, [in which Jung addresses the question:] whence evil?

> [T]his age-old question is not answered unless you assume the existence of a [supreme] being *who is in the main unconscious*. Such a model would explain why God has created a man gifted with consciousness and why He seeks His goal in him. In this the Old Testament, the New Testament, and Buddhism agree. Meister Eckhart said it: "God is not blessed in His Godhead, He must be born in man forever." This is what happens in Job: *The creator sees himself through the eyes of man's consciousness* and this is the reason why God had to become man, and why man is progressively gifted with the dangerous prerogative of the divine "mind." You have it in the saying: "Ye are gods," and man

has not even begun yet to know himself. He would need it to be prepared to meet the dangers of the *incarnatio continua*, which began with Christ and the distribution of the "Holy Ghost" to poor, almost unconscious beings. We are still looking back to the pentecostal events in a dazed way instead of looking forward to the goal the Spirit is leading us to. Therefore mankind is wholly unprepared for the things to come. Man is compelled by divine forces to go forward to increasing consciousness and cognition, developing further and further away from his religious background because he does not understand it any more. His religious teachers and leaders are still hypnotized by the beginnings of a then new aeon of consciousness instead of understanding them and their implications. What one once called the "Holy Ghost" is an impelling force, creating wider consciousness and responsibility and thus enriched cognition. The real history of the world seems to be the progressive incarnation of the deity. (1975a, 435–36; see also Jung 1971, par. 418)

That is a marvelous summation: "The real history of the world seems to be the progressive incarnation of the deity."

We have a whole new world-view laid open in this paragraph. The key sentence is the one Jung italicizes: *The creator sees himself through the eyes of man's consciousness.* This idea of the divine nature of consciousness appeared in the Tanner letter also:

> Nobody seems to have noticed that without a reflecting psyche the world might as well not exist, and that, in consequence, consciousness is a second world-creator, and also that the cosmogonic myths do not describe the absolute beginning of the world but rather the dawning of consciousness as the second Creation. (1975a, 487)

It appears, too, in the Neumann letter:

> After thinking all this over I have come to the conclusion that being "made in the likeness" applies not only to man but also to the Creator: he resembles man or is his likeness, which is to say that he is just as unconscious as man or even more unconscious, since according to the myth of the incarnatio he actually felt obliged to become man and offer himself to man as a sacrifice. (1975a, 495–96)

These two statements sum up and, I believe, constitute the basic principles that establish Jung's new myth. The two statements are these. *The creator sees himself through the eyes of man's consciousness, and consciousness is a second world-creator.* This is Jung's new myth, which I talk about in *The Creation of Consciousness* (Edinger 1984). He had the full revelation of it in Africa, in Kenya.

Jung describes this revelation also in *Memories, Dreams, Reflections*. It is Jung's discovery of the new myth as he experienced it subjectively:

> From Nairobi we used a small Ford to visit the Athi Plains, a great game preserve. From a low hill in this broad savanna a magnificent prospect opened out to us. To the very brink of the horizon we saw gigantic herds of animals: gazelle, antelope, gnu, zebra, warthog, and so on. Grazing, heads nodding, the herds moved forward like slow rivers. There was scarcely any sound save the melancholy cry of a bird of prey. This was the stillness of the eternal beginning, the world as it had always been, in the state of non-being; for until then no one had been present to know that it was this world. I walked away from my companions until I had put them out of sight, and savored the feeling of being entirely alone. There I was now, the first human being to recognize that this was the world, but who did not know that in this moment he had first really created it.
>
> There the cosmic meaning of consciousness became overwhelmingly clear to me. "What nature leaves imperfect, the art perfects," say the alchemists. Man, I, in an invisible act of creation put the stamp of perfection on the world by giving it objective existence. This act we usually ascribe to the Creator alone, without considering that in so doing we view life as a machine calculated down to the last detail, which, along with the human psyche, runs on senselessly, obeying foreknown and predetermined rules. In such a cheerless clockwork fantasy there is no drama of man, world, and God; there is no "new day" leading to "new shores," but only the dreariness of calculated processes. My old Pueblo friend came to my mind. He thought that the *raison d'être* of his pueblo had been to help their father, the sun, to cross the sky each day. I had envied him for the fullness of meaning in that belief, and had been looking about without hope for a myth of our own. Now I knew what it was, and knew even more: that man is indispensable for the completion of creation; that, in fact, he himself is the second creator of the world, who alone has given to the world its objective existence—without which, unheard, unseen, silently eating, giving birth, dying, heads nodding through hundreds of millions of years, it would have gone on in the profoundest night of non-being down to its unknown end. Human consciousness created objective existence and meaning, and man found his indispensable place in the great process of being. (1963b, 255–56)

EIGHT

THE LETTER TO PASTOR LACHAT WAS WRITTEN MARCH 27, 1954, IN response to Jung's receiving his book on the Holy Spirit. The title of the book was *The Reception and Action of the Holy Spirit in Personal Life and in the Community*. This subject obviously caused a vigorous reaction in Jung, who leaves us quite a spirited essay on the psychology of the Holy Spirit. It is as though the dynamism of that symbol itself is constellated and brought into living action just by being talked about. It happens not infrequently. The very process of talking about archetypal contents constellates them, and suddenly they are in our midst. It is an unusually spirited letter on Jung's part.

Jung assumes one is familiar with the mythological theology of the Trinity. The Holy Spirit or Holy Ghost is one of the three persons of the Trinity, the basic God-image of the Christian aeon. It is the myth we are just now starting to emerge from. The basic image is the Trinity:

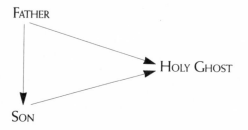

FATHER

HOLY GHOST

SON

The image is stated in the Nicene creed. There are a number of different versions of the creed. The version Jung quotes in his "Trinity" essay is the creed each Christian would confess:

> We firmly believe and wholeheartedly confess that there is only one true God, eternal, infinite, and unchanging; incomprehensible,

almighty, and ineffable; Father and Son and Holy Ghost; three Persons, but one essence; entirely simple in substance and nature. The Father is of none, the Son is of the Father alone, and the Holy Ghost is of both equally; for ever without beginning and without end; the Father begetting, the Son being born, and the Holy Ghost proceeding; consubstantial and coequal and coalmighty and coeternal. (Jung 1969a, par. 219)

The creed above comes from the Lateran Council of 1215. This creed derives from a conflict of considerable heat in the early church. It states that the Holy Spirit proceeds from both the Father and the Son. The Son derives from the Father, and the Holy Spirit comes from both of them. Obviously the basic Christian Trinity is based on the symbolism of the number *three*.[1]

In his "Trinity" essay, Jung makes two chief points. The first point is that the Trinity image is an incomplete quaternity and, therefore, needs to be completed. The feminine, the devil and matter have been left out. From the second standpoint, the Trinity image is quite complete inasmuch as it refers to three stages of a developmental process. Jung makes the very interesting observation that the Father, the Son and the Holy Spirit can be representative of three different stages of psychological development. Concerning the Father, he says:

The world of the father typifies an age, which is characterized by a pristine oneness with the whole of nature. (1969a, par. 201)

A feeling of oneness far removed from critical judgement and moral conflict . . . (1969a, par. 199)

It is . . . man in his childhood state. (1969, par. 201)

It describes the state of the original containment in nature. Then the world of the Son is described next:

It is . . . a world filled with longing for redemption and for that state of perfection in which man was still one with the Father. Longingly he looked back to the world of the Father, but it was lost forever, because an irreversible increase in man's consciousness

---

1. For a more detailed exposition, see Jung 1969a, "A Psychological Approach to the Dogma of the Trinity"; see also Edinger 1987b, chap. 7.

had taken place in the meantime and made it independent. (1969a, par. 203)

The stage of the "Son" is a conflict situation *par excellence*. . . . "Freedom from the law" brings a sharpening of opposites. (1969a, par. 272)

Then follows the third stage, which is the stage of the Holy Spirit or the Holy Ghost. Jung says:

[T]he advance to the third stage (the Holy Ghost) means something like a recognition of the unconscious if not actual subordination to it. . . . Just as the transition from the first stage to the second demands the sacrifice of childish dependence, so at the transition to the third stage an exclusive independence has to be relinquished. (1969a, par. 273)

This third stage means articulating one's ego-consciousness with a supraordinate totality, of which one cannot say that it is "I," but which is best visualized as a more comprehensive being. (1969a, par. 276)

These extractions from Jung's "Trinity" essay can also be found in *Ego and Archetype* (Edinger 1987b, 181). It is a totally different approach to Trinitarian symbolism, and it corresponds to the fact that the Christian aeon has been very much preoccupied with historical factors: linear, developmental, temporal, historical factors. The speculations of Joachim of Flora, whom Jung speaks of in several places, illustrate a consciousness of the historical nature of the process even before Jung. Joachim, who died in 1202, elaborated the idea of the Trinity as a historical process. His idea was that the first millenium before Christ—the millenium following the establishment of Mosaic law on Sinai—was the age of the Father. The millenium after Christ, from A.D. 1 to A.D. 1000, he called the age of the Son. The third millenium was to be the age of the Holy Ghost. Joachim predicted that the church would die in that millenium, and that the new "spiritual church" would be born to take its place. He had a strictly historical symbolism attached to the Trinity. Jung sees it in much the same way, except Joachim was a little ahead of himself. Jung sees the age of the Holy Spirit beginning with the new aeon, now (von Franz 1975).

One must keep in mind, while reading this letter, that Jung is talking to a Protestant pastor who has a largely conventional religious
viewpoint. Jung's letter will therefore be somewhat compensatory, because Jung always talks very specifically to the individual person. It
means he will emphasize the negative and dangerous aspects of the
Holy Spirit to correct. Lachat's one-sided, innocent, positive view
about the theological Holy Spirit.

The symbolism of the Holy Spirit runs throughout the Bible. The
traditional view has always been that it revealed itself initially at the
creation in Genesis. The Holy Spirit was the creative entity. In the
course of the Old Testament it inspired deeds of valor and, later, the
utterance of the prophets. In the New Testament, through the over-
shadowing of the Holy Spirit, Mary conceived Christ. The Holy Spirit
descended on Christ at the time of his baptism as a dove. It was
thought, conventionally, to have operated throughout Christ's min-
istry. After His death it descended again at Pentecost upon his
disciples, and according to the Church, the Church was born at that
time. The Church became the container and guardian of the Holy Spirit,
or as Jung puts it, the Church keeps it well chained up. This letter examines some specific items pertaining to the Holy Spirit. Jung says:

> [T]he Holy Spirit would not be easy to apprehend; it would even be
> highly dangerous to attract the divine attention by specially pious
> behavior (as in the case of Job and some others). . . . It is very com-
> forting to be assured by the Catholic Church that it "possesses" the
> Spirit, who assists regularly at its rites. Then one knows that he is
> well chained up. Protestantism is no less reassuring in that it repre-
> sents the Spirit to us as something to be sought for, to be easily
> "drunk," even to be possessed. We get the impression that he is some-
> thing passive which cannot budge without us. He has lost his dan-
> gerous qualities, his fire, his autonomy, his power. He is represented
> as an innocuous, passive, and purely beneficent element, so that to be
> afraid of him would seem just stupid. . . .
> . . . [[This account has]] failed to explain to us clearly what it
> has done with the *Deus absconditus*. (Jung 1975b, par. 1534–35)

Absconditus means hidden. It is a favorite expression of Jung's—*Deus
absconditus*, the hidden God. In English, that stem shows up in the verb
to abscond. A robber can abscond with the money he has stolen; he
steals it and hides it away. The *Deus absconditus* has that quality: the

[handwritten margin notes: "Deus absconditus = dark, dangerous, hidden God (uc) contained by religious institut."]

dark, dangerous, hidden God. Jung is contradicting the Pastor's naïve notion of the nature of the Holy Spirit. Jung is talking about the living, psychological reality, not theological abstraction. There is a world of difference between those two. Since it is truly dangerous, its containment in a religious institution is indeed desirable as long as that containment works. It also may be contained in political institutions. It can be contained in authority of any kind, to which one gives one's allegiance. If one gives devoted allegiance to an institution of any kind, then the religious dimension of the Holy Spirit has been chained up. One takes his orders from the establishment, rather than from the autonomous psychic content, a situation that is safer. In dreams, the Holy Ghost is signified chiefly by three images: wind, fire, and birds—especially big birds.

[handwritten margin notes: "H.G. in dreams: wind, fire, birds"]

Jung continues on the theme of the danger of the Holy Spirit:

> But the action of the Holy Spirit does not meet us in the atmosphere of a normal, bourgeois (or proletarian!), sheltered, regular life, but only in the insecurity outside the human economy, in the infinite spaces where one is alone with the *providentia Dei* [[the providence of God]]. We must never forget that Christ was an innovator and revolutionary, *executed with criminals*. The reformers and great religious geniuses were *heretics*. It is there that you find the footprints of the Holy Spirit, and no one asks for him or receives him *without having to pay a high price*. The price is so high that no one today would dare to suggest that he possesses or is possessed by the Holy Spirit, or he would be too close to a psychiatric clinic. The danger of making oneself ridiculous is too real, not to mention the risk of offending our real god: *respectability*. (1975b, par. 1539)

The implication for analytic practice is that opening up the unconscious is dangerous. I do not think that fact is always appreciated (Jung 1966, pars. 225ff.). In doing depth analysis, assuming one is open to the depth level of the psyche, one may constellate in the patient a connection with that same depth, which can be dangerous. Very definitely. Jung once said, "Whoever comes to see me takes his life in his hands." It is a good thing to remember, so one does not get caught in the innocent notion that one can be only a purveyor of nurturing acceptance and healing. That notion can be a dangerous illusion, because good ego intentions cannot banish what Jung calls the *Deus absconditus*. If the unconscious opens up, it may manifest.

One must always remember that the unconscious contains the opposites and thus appears to the ego as an antinomy.

The idea that the unconscious is the abyss of all the horrors is a bit out of date. The collective unconscious is neutral; it is only nature, both spiritual and chthonic. To impute to my psychology the idea that the Holy Spirit is "only a projection of the human soul" is false. He is a transcendental fact which presents itself to us under the guise of an archetypal image. (Jung 1975b, par. 1536)

Like God, then, the unconscious has two aspects: one good, favorable, beneficent, the other evil, malevolent, disastrous. The unconscious is the immediate source of our religious experiences. This psychic nature of all experience does not mean that the transcendental realities are also psychic. (Jung 1975b, par. 1538)

The image of the Holy Spirit, which is a psychic image because it is all we can experience, reflects or indicates a transcendental fact. However, as Jung says, "This psychic nature of all experience does not mean that the transcendental realities are also psychic." This statement is a reference to Kantian epistemology as discussed in chapter 1. Even though our experience is limited to psychic realities, that does not mean that psychic reality is all that exists. We have good reason to believe that the external world exists, and we have equally good reason to believe that a transcendental, metaphysical world exists. It is just that we cannot know either of these worlds. Jung is clearly refuting here what is so often laid against him, so-called *psychologism*—that way of thinking which reduces everything to psychology, which is not the case. It is just that our experience is *psychology* only. But what the psychological images derive from is of an unknown realm.

The ambivalent nature of the unconscious was presaged in Clement of Rome's notion of the two hands of God:

In these circumstances it becomes very difficult to know what to make of prayer. Can we address our prayer to the good God to the exclusion of the demon, as Schweitzer recommends? Have we the power of dissociating God like the country woman who said to the child Jesus, when he interrupted her prayer to the Virgin: "Shhh, child, I'm talking to your mother"? Can we really put on one side the God who is dangerous to us? Do we believe that God is so powerless that we can say to him: "Get out, I'm talking to your better half"? . . . [W]e're going to have our bathe in the river, and never mind the crocodiles. (Jung 1975b, par. 1537)

Jung is vigorous in his reaction to the idea of a simple, childlike faith. The question comes up: what about prayer from a psychological standpoint? I think prayer, psychologically understood, is active imagination. It is not a request for anything specific. It is a request that the unconscious reveal itself with an image of some kind, which can then lead to a dialogue. That is prayer. Also I consider it legitimate to ask for help in time of need if one does not specify what it is. I think consulting the *I Ching* in times of uncertainty is a kind of prayer, for instance.

[margin handwritten notes: prayer as active imagination]

There is another letter of Jung's on the same subject. It was written to an anonymous person who had asked him about the question of prayer. Jung replied:

> This was and still is a problem for me. Some years ago I felt that all demands which go beyond what *is* are unjustified and infantile, so that we shouldn't ask for anything that is not granted. We can't remind God of anything or prescribe anything for him, except when he tries to force something on us that our human limitation cannot endure. The question is, of course, whether such things happen. I think the answer is yes, for if God needs us as regulators of his incarnation and his coming to consciousness, it is because in his boundlessness he exceeds all the bounds that are necessary for becoming conscious. Becoming conscious means continual renunciation because it is an ever deepening concentration.
>
> If this is right, then it may be that God has to be "reminded." The innermost self of every man and animal, of plants and crystals, is God, but infinitely diminished and approximated to his ultimate, individual form. In approximating to man he is also "personal," like an antique god, and hence in the "likeness of a man" (as Yahweh appeared to Ezekiel).
>
> An old alchemist formulated the relation to God thus: "Help me, that I may help you!" (1975a, 120)

In Jung's view one is not entitled to pray for anything at all, except one thing: remind the Self to go easy on the ego, that it is expecting too much. One must remind the Self how things are up here in the material world, and thus not break the fragile bonds of the ego by demanding too much. Take it easy, let up a bit. That is what Jung thinks is legitimate prayer.

He refers to the three stages or persons of the Trinity:

1. The Father. The opposites not yet differentiated; Satan is still numbered among the "sons of God." Christ then is only hinted at.

2. God is incarnated as the "Son of Man." Satan has fallen from heaven. He is the other "son." The opposites are differentiated. [[It is the age of the Son.]]

3. [[The age of the Holy Spirit:]] The Holy Spirit is One, his prototype is the Ruach Elohim, an emanation, an active principle, which proceeds (as quintessence) [[from the Father and the Son]] a *Patre Filioque*. Inasmuch as he proceeds also from the Son he is different from the Ruach Elohim, who represents the active principle of Yahweh. (1975b, par. 1549)

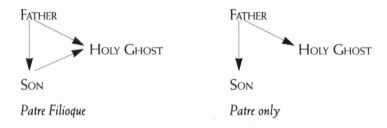

FATHER   HOLY GHOST   FATHER   HOLY GHOST

SON   SON

Patre Filioque   *Patre only*

The Holy Spirit was the agency of the father God in the Old Testament. In the new dispensation, as it is worked out in the Christian Trinity, the Holy Spirit derives not only from the Father-God, but also from the Son. There was a great dispute in the early Christian centuries about this question. The question was: does the Holy Spirit proceed from the Father only, or does it proceed from the Father and the Son? Does it proceed from a *Patre* period—or does it proceed from a *Patre Filioque*? *Filioque* means "and the Son." This is the *Filioque* controversy (Jung 1969a, pars. 217ff, 289). The *Filioque* controversy is the controversy between two different God-images.

Modern people have a great deal of trouble understanding how the early Christian Fathers could get worked up over such matters, just as we have trouble understanding how the medievalists could be so interested in how many angels can stand on the head of a pin. If we understand it psychologically, it is a very important question. The pin question asks psychologically: what is the connecting link between the transpersonal archetypal world and the material ego world? It is a legitimate question once you understand it in psychological terms. The same thing applies to the *Filioque* controversy. It is one of the bases of the split between the Eastern and Western Church. The Western Roman Church adopted the *Filioque* formula and established a God-image in which the Holy Spirit proceeds from both the Father and the Son. The Eastern Orthodox Church rejected that formula and created a different God-image, still a Trinitarian one, but one in which the Holy Spirit proceeds only from the Father.

Psychologically, we can understand that by allowing the Son, the *import of ego* Christ-Son, who has human aspects, to be the one who generates the Holy Spirit, the ego is given a special function. The whole Western *in Western* tradition then has built into it, in its mythology, an importance to the *Christian* ego that the Eastern tradition does not grant. This difference could *tradition* very well account for the fact that the Eastern Orthodox Church has never had a Protestant reformation, which would represent psychologically an ego development of major proportions. Jung goes on to say, as a result of all these considerations:

> *Thus the ordinary man became a source of the Holy Spirit. . . .* This fact signifies the continued and progressive divine incarnation. Thus man is received and integrated into the divine drama. He seems destined to play a decisive part in it; that is why he must receive the Holy Spirit. I look upon the receiving of the Holy Spirit as a highly revolutionary fact which cannot take place until the ambivalent nature of the Father is recognized. (1975b, par. 1551)

Similar to "the responsible living and fulfilling of the divine will in us," is another such cryptic statement: *"the receiving of the Holy Spirit."* It is an elaboration of what Jung means by the *continuing incarnation.* He says further:

> A conscientious clarification of the idea of God would have consequences as upsetting as they are necessary. They would be indispensable for an interior development of the trinitarian drama and of the role of the Holy Spirit. The Spirit is destined to be incarnate in man or to choose him as a transitory dwelling-place. . . . he must not be identified with Christ. We cannot receive the Holy Spirit unless

we have accepted our own individual life as Christ accepted his. Thus we become the "sons of god" fated to experience the conflict of the divine opposites, represented by the crucifixion. (1975b, par. 1551)

It seems to me to be the Holy Spirit's task and charge to reconcile and reunite the opposites in the human individual through a special development of the human soul. (1975b, par. 1553)

He is elaborating about the images of receiving the Holy Spirit, which is part of the process of continuing incarnation, those two images: *receiving the Holy Spirit* and *continuing incarnation*. One of the basic symbolic images that lies at the root of these ideas is the conception of Christ in Mary's womb through the agency of the Holy Spirit. That is a traditional symbolic example of what it means to receive the Holy Spirit: to be fertilized by it, to gestate and bring to birth the new organism that has been conceived by the connection of receiving the Holy Spirit. The basic image then, certainly in terms of Western symbolism, is the image of the Annunciation, which comes from Luke, chapter 1, verses 26–38:

> And in the sixth month the angel Gabriel was sent from God unto a city of Galilee, named Nazareth,
> To a virgin espoused to a man whose name was Joseph, of the House of David; and the virgin's name was Mary.
> And the angel came in unto her, and said, Hail, thou that art highly favoured, the Lord is with thee: blessed art thou among women.
> And when she saw him, she was troubled at his saying, and cast in her mind what manner of salutation this should be.
> And the angel said unto her, Fear not, Mary: for thou hast found favour with God.
> And, behold, thou shalt conceive in thy womb, and bring forth a son, and shalt call his name Jesus.
> He shall be great, and shall be called the Son of the Highest: and the Lord God shall give unto him the throne of his father David:
> And he shall reign over the house of Jacob forever; and of his kingdom there shall be no end.
> Then said Mary unto the angel, How shall this be, seeing I know not a man?

And the angel answered and said unto her, The Holy Ghost shall
come upon thee, and the power of the Highest shall overshadow
thee: therefore also that holy thing which shall be born of thee shall
be called the Son of God. . . .
For with God nothing shall be impossible.
And Mary said, Behold the handmaiden of the Lord; be it unto me
according to thy word. And the angel departed from her.

In the traditional paintings of this phenomenon, one might see the
angel Gabriel making the announcement, while simultaneously a dove is
descending from heaven: the Holy Ghost coming in to fertilize Mary's
womb. We have similar images in Greek mythology; for example,
Perseus is conceived by Zeus through a golden shower. In that case the
golden shower is the Holy Spirit. It is a general archetypal image, but
it has been elaborated most fully in Christian symbolism. It is the basic
image of the incarnation, and of what it means to be a recipient of the
Holy Spirit.

The dream of a patient is also an example of that image. A woman
had malignant melanoma, had surgery and did not know whether she
was cured or not: an apparent cure. She had this dream:

*I am standing on a flat, grassy mound. A small woodland creature runs through
my legs. I think it is a squirrel. Suddenly I am lifted up by a great, black cloud—
off the ground. I am held there, cradled by the cloud underneath the branches of a
great tree. I am terrified and screaming for help. No one comes. Eventually I come
down to earth again. I am shaken and reach out and touch my cat and say, "So
this is God."*

A few months later she had this dream:

*A great black cloud has come again. It is terrible; I can't handle it. Then a voice
comes and says, "You can handle it." I say, "No, I can't." The voice says, "Yes,
you can."*

The next day following this dream, the dreamer learned that her most
beloved brother had been killed in a plane crash the night before. This
event initiated a deep depression that lasted for several months—the
black cloud. But out of this agonizing experience a whole new level of
development took place. She became a Jungian analyst. This drama
took place twenty years ago, but she was cured of cancer.

This dream is an annunciation dream. She was under the cloud of the Highest, you see; it is the very image used in the Annunciation passage: "The power of the Highest shall overshadow thee." That word *overshadow* in Greek is an ominous word, like being under the shadow of something ominous. It is the way a chicken might feel under the shadow of a chicken hawk. It is what the Annunciation looks like close up, so to speak, from the point of view of psychological realities.

Jung goes on to speak of the image of *wholeness*:

> This is true inasmuch as the Father by descending from the cosmic immensity became the least by incarnating himself within the narrow bounds of the human soul. . . . Doubtless the presence of the Holy Spirit enlarges human nature by divine attributes. Human nature is the divine vessel and as such the union of the Three. This results in a kind of quaternity which always signifies *totality*, while the triad is rather a process, but never the natural division of the *circle*, the natural symbol of wholeness. The quaternity as union of the Three seems to be aimed at by the *Assumption of Mary*. This dogma adds the feminine element to the masculine Trinity, the terrestrial element (*virgo terra!*) to the spiritual, and thus sinful man to the Godhead. (1975b, par. 1552)

He is referring to the dogma of the Assumption of Mary into heaven, which he talks about also in other places and which he thinks is such a major event for our collective psychology (1969a, pars. 748ff.). The result is that the Trinity has had a fourth personage added to it—namely, Mary. Symbolically she brings the attributes of matter, flesh, and humanity—sinful humanity. It is one of Jung's basic ideas, therefore, that depth psychology is transforming the Trinitarian God-image of the Christian aeon into a quaternity God-image of the coming aeon. It is another expression for the idea of the *continuing incarnation*, because with Mary being added to the Godhead, all humanity is dragged with her. It means all humanity becomes available for the incarnating process of the quaternity God-image.

Symbols of the Holy Spirit appear in modern dreams. In *Memories, Dreams, Reflections*, Jung reports a dream:

> Then, around Christmas of 1912, I had a dream. In the dream I found myself in a magnificent Italian loggia with pillars, a marble floor, and a marble balustrade. . . .

Suddenly a white bird descended, a small sea gull or a dove. . . . Immediately, the dove was transformed into a little girl, about eight years of age, with golden blond hair. . . .

The little girl returned and tenderly placed her arms around my neck. Then she suddenly vanished; the dove was back. (1963b, 171–72)

This dream is an encounter with the Holy Spirit. I see it as analogous to the baptismal image of Christ involving the descent of the Holy Spirit. This dream foreshadowed Jung's whole confrontation with the unconscious.

Another example I have published in *Anatomy of the Psyche*. A young research scientist made a brilliant formulation in a scientific paper based on an important discovery. The professor who held authority over him had belittled his conclusions without reading the paper. At this point the young scientist, who was usually very mild-mannered, replied with great intensity: "Professor—, if you are going to criticize my paper you must read it and give it careful thought." This was done with great intensity, and he was alarmed by the intensity of his response. After a flare of anger the professor acknowledged his mistake, read the paper, and recognized its value. The night before this crucial encounter, which had important consequences for the young scientist's career, he had this dream:

> *I am sitting at a dinner table with guests. Suddenly something spills and catches fire. Then the whole table is covered with little flames shifting around from one side to the other. It is a beautiful sight. On awakening I think of the miracle at Pentecost.* (Edinger 1985, 37)

Another one I have published in *The Creation of Consciousness*. It is the dream of a woman, a painter, who was in the process of committing herself seriously to her artistic vocation:

> *I am with a few people and we are suddenly startled to see a gigantic bird overhead. His wingspread is enormous—twenty to thirty feet. As he swoops down low we are in his awesome shadow. This bird has numbers on his wing, and I know that he belongs to a man who will be very distressed that he has flown away. We must capture him and return him to the man. The bird lands on the ground, not afraid of us. One man picks up his hind hoof and begins tapping the dirt out of it (the way one does to a horse). This hoof is no ordinary hoof, it is inlaid with jewels; that is why*

it is being cleaned. Later a freight train comes by and we are able to load the huge bird aboard the train for his trip home. We have sedated him to make the trip easier, and he is carefully secured. (Edinger 1984, 112)

In this modern image the Holy Ghost is in distress, somewhat like an endangered species that needs the help of the human ego to be rescued. It is another version of the same imagery.

There is another related image that comes from antiquity. It is an ancient legend told about one of the early kings of Rome. This account comes from the Roman historian Livy in *The Early History of Rome*. The story concerns a man by the name of Lucumo Tarquin, later called Lucius Tarquin Priscius, who decided to emigrate from Tarquinii to Rome. He thought his prospects would be better in Rome. Tarquin and his wife [Tanaquil] are on their way to Rome:

> The pair had reached Janiculum and were sitting together in their carriage, when an eagle dropped gently down and snatched off the cap which Lucumo was wearing. Up went the bird with great clangour of wings until, a minute later, it swooped down again and, as if it had been sent by heaven for that very purpose, neatly replaced the cap on Lucumo's head, and then vanished into the blue. Tanaquil like most Etruscans was well skilled in celestial prodigies, and joyfully accepted the omen.

Remember we have talked before about the auguries. Here was a real augury, unplanned:

> Flinging her arms around her husband's neck, she told him that no fortune was too high to hope for. "Only consider," she cried, "from what quarter of the sky the eagle came, what god sent it as his messenger! Did it not declare its message by coming to your *head*—the highest part of you? Did it not take the crown, as it were, from a human head, only to restore it by heaven's approval, where it belongs?" Thus dreaming of future greatness, Lucumo and Tanaquil drove on into Rome. (Livy 1960, 57)

Indeed, later, he [Tarquin] became King of Rome. It is another example corresponding to Christ's baptism. It is an image of encountering the Holy Spirit and of being baptized with one's vocation, with one's calling. One finds, not too infrequently in people who achieve a certain level of greatness, that they have had experiences of that sort, in which they have met destiny and they know they have been singled out. They have had the experience. It is another aspect of what it is like to have a living encounter with the Holy Spirit.

On several occasions I have been asked if the Christian Trinity has any parallel in Jewish symbolism. The answer is "yes." Jung addresses this issue in a letter to James Kirsch, written on November 18, 1952. Kirsch had written to Jung, asking him the role that Christ, and the Christian mystery, play in the Jewish psyche. Jung responded:

> I can call your attention to the extraordinary development in the Kabbalah. I am rather certain that the *sefiroth* tree contains the whole symbolism of Jewish development parallel to the Christian idea. The characteristic difference is that God's incarnation is understood to be a historical fact in the Christian belief, while in the Jewish Gnosis it is an entirely pleromatic process symbolized by the concentration of the supreme triad of Kether, Hokhmah, and Binah in the figure of Tifereth. Being the equivalent of the Son and the Holy Ghost, he is the *sponsus* [[bridegroom]] bringing about the great solution through his union with Malkhuth. This union is equivalent to the *assumptio beatae virginis* [[assumption of the blessed virgin]], but definitely more comprehensive than the latter as it seems to include even the extraneous world of the Kelipoth [[the shards—the dark, abysmal world of shards]]. (1975a, 92)

The Kabbalah elaborates a complex God-image, which it pictures as a series of interrelated emanations from the original, primordial source. The top three entities—Kether, Hokhmah, and Binah—are equivalent to the Christian Trinity, as Jung alludes to in *Mysterium Coniunctionis*. According to the *Zohar*, the first three sefiroth are three lights. The second light is said to proceed from the first light, and the third light proceeds from both the first and the second (Jung 1955, pars. 18f., 619n., 643n.).

It is an exact parallel to the formula for how the Holy Spirit proceeds from the Father and the Son. Furthermore, the major image of the Kabbalah, the ultimate goal of the whole historical and mystical process, is the wedding of Tifereth, a personification of the upper trinity, the bridegroom, with Malkhuth (Malchuth), the bride. Malkhuth is thought of as having split off from the rest of the Deity and as having gone into exile, in the same way that Israel had gone into exile. They were thought to represent parallel phenomena. Malkhuth corresponds to the Shekinah, the feminine divine presence which got split off from the Deity to wander around in the world. When she is reunited with the Deity, the Messiah comes, the event that would be represented by the wedding of Malkhuth with Tifereth. The image corresponds to the Christian image of the assumption of the Virgin. In each case the result would be that a spiritual entity would be enlarged upon and completed by a corporeal or material entity pertaining to the world. The wedding of Malkhuth and Tifereth is the event that Jung experienced in his great *coniunctio* vision (1963b, 294). As Jung says in *Mysterium Coniunctionis*:

> In this wicked world ruled by evil Tifereth is *not* united with Malchuth. But the coming Messiah will reunite the King with the Queen, and this mating will restore to God his original unity. (1955, par. 18)

What Jung illustrates is a good example that psychological facts will manifest themselves in different symbolic contexts.

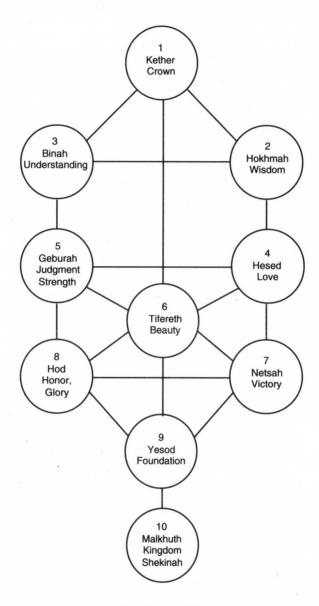

The Sefirothic Tree

Concentrating on the "central pillar": Kether combined with his emanations of Hokhmah and Binah undergoes personification in Tifereth which will be wedded to the split off Malkhuth "when the Messiah comes."

NINE

THE COX LETTERS WERE WRITTEN SEPTEMBER 25, 1957, AND NOVEMBER 12, 1957. In the first letter to David Cox, Jung gives a description of the historical evolution of the God-image from two different standpoints. The first standpoint is what he calls the euhemeristic standpoint, which refers to the ancient figure Euhemerus, who lived about 300 B.C. He developed a personalistic, rational interpretation of mythology. His idea was that mythology was, of course, "all the bunk"; that it does not refer to anything transcendent. There are no such things as gods. *euhemer-ism* Rather, mythology derives from certain prominent human beings who made an impression on their contemporaries. These larger-than-life human heroes then got translated into myth. Such a rational, personalistic attitude is called *euhemerism* today. Jung says it is one way of looking at the evolution of the God-image. From that standpoint, Jung says, we can see that development:

as a development of man's understanding of the supreme powers be- *modern rational personalistic viewpoint* yond his control. [The process consists of the following stages:] (1) Gods. (2) A supreme Deity ruling the gods and demons. (3) God shares our human fate, is betrayed, killed, or dies, and is resurrected again. There is a feminine counterpart dramatically involved in God's fate. (4) God becomes man in the flesh and thus historical. He is identified with the abstract idea of the *summum bonum* and loses the feminine counterpart. The female deity is degraded to an ancillary position (Church). Consciousness begins to prevail against the unconscious. This is an enormously important step forward in the emancipation of consciousness and in the liberation of thought from its involvement in things. Thus the foundation of science is laid, but on the other hand, that of atheism and materialism. Both are inevitable consequences of the basic split between spirit and matter in Christian philosophy, which proclaimed the redemption of the spirit from the body and its fetters. (5) The whole metaphysical world is understood as a psychic structure projected into the sphere of the unknown. (1975b, par. 1658)

The metaphysical world is understood as the projection of human psychology, so that the whole transpersonal dimension that used to be experienced as part of the realm of the gods is explained away euhemeristically. It is the common modern viewpoint. According to this description then, the ego outgrows the gods. The result is that it is left in a dissociated state, because it is cut off from the transpersonal dimension out of which it came.

Since a dissociated state is not satisfactory, Jung goes on to speak of the other way of looking at it: from the standpoint of the archetype. From that standpoint the evolution of the God-image is thought of as a dynamic process of development in the archetype itself. It does not just reflect the development of human consciousness but is an image of its own inner evolution. The result is that, following the incarnation, something has been left out:

> [T]he indispensable dark side has been left behind or stripped off, and the feminine aspect is missing. Thus a further act of incarnation becomes necessary. Through atheism, materialism, and agnosticism, the powerful yet one-sided aspect of the *summum bonum* is weakened, so that it cannot keep out the dark side, and incidentally the feminine factor, any more. "Antichrist" and "Devil" gain the ascendancy: God asserts his power through the revelation of his darkness and destructiveness. (1975b, par. 1660)

This process, then, according to Jung, is how the *continuing incarnation* first announces itself. It announces itself by intruding via the negative and destructive side into the human psyche, expressing itself negatively, because that specifically is the aspect of the Deity that had been left out of account before. Following the rule of the return of the repressed, the missing side of the God-image must show up first. There is a very profound dynamic being expressed here. Then Jung finishes this paragraph by saying:

> As God lives in everybody in the form of the *scintilla* of the self, man could see his "daemonic," i.e., ambivalent, nature in himself and thus

he could understand how he is penetrated by God or how God incarnates in man. (1975b, 1660)

An exposition of the *continuing incarnation* follows:

> Through his further incarnation God becomes a fearful task for man, who must now find ways and means to unite the divine opposites in himself. He is summoned and can no longer leave his sorrows to somebody else, not even to Christ, because it was Christ that has left him the almost impossible task of his cross. Christ has shown how everybody will be crucified upon his destiny, i.e., upon his self, as he was . . . . We are in the soup that is going to be cooked for us, whether we claim to have invented it or not. Christ said to his disciples "Ye are gods." This word becomes painfully true. If God incarnates in the empirical man, man is confronted with the divine problem. Being and remaining man he has to find an answer. It is the question of the opposites, raised at the moment when God was declared to be good only. Where then is his dark side? Christ is the model for the human answers and his symbol is the *cross*, the union of the opposites. This will be the fate of man, and this he must understand if he is to survive at all. We are threatened with universal genocide if we cannot work out the way of salvation by a symbolic death. (1975b, par. 1661)

As he says in another place, "Modern man is a vessel filled with divine conflict," because he is wide open to experiencing the divine opposites that constitute the paradoxical God (1969a, par. 740). It is that state of affairs that threatens "universal genocide if the way of salvation cannot be worked out by a symbolic death." One of the ways to describe the paradoxical God is to speak of it as an unconscious *coniunctio*. It is an unconscious union of opposites, which is the phenomenology of the Self in the unconscious state. As soon as the conscious ego gets a glimpse of this unconscious God, the opposites immediately split. When they are touched by consciousness, they split. It is part of the incarnation process. The result is that the individual ego that has gotten that glimpse is then filled with that divine conflict. The split opposites, then, pour into the ego. It is not one's personal conflict, but one is not very likely aware of that fact, because when these things happen, when the content pours into the ego, the ego, generally, is not able to hold onto its objective standpoint. It immediately identifies with what pours into it, and so it experiences itself as the conflict; but the conflict does not belong to the ego. It is the conflict of the archetypal God-image.

One sees this phenomenology everywhere: externally and internally. Externally the opposites that derive from the paradoxical God-image are pouring into the body-social. They manifest in the polarities and conflicts that develop in the collective psyche. When Jung was writing, he, of course, was particularly impressed with the polarization that existed between the East and the West, which at the moment appears to have been resolved. Only, do not be too sure. What is clear is that the constellation of the divine conflict between the opposites, if it does not settle in one place, will shift over to another place. Although divisions between the United States and the Soviet Union have been mitigated, the splits have gone elsewhere. Now one sees them emerging in localized, ethnic splits of various kinds. The split between Islam and the West is becoming much more prominent. We have quite intense, emerging factional splits between traditional religionists and secularists everywhere. The economic, ethnic, and sexual interest factions—all of these—are contributing to the phenomenology of the divine conflict between the opposites. What is happening in all these cases is that the paradoxical God-image, which is destined to appear in our age, is incarnating in the human psyche. First of all, it is showing up in the collective psyche. What it is doing is obliging humanity to live out collectively on the social plane the divine conflict contained within the paradoxical God. Jung makes a telling remark in *Answer to Job*, where he says, "The image of God pervades the whole human sphere and makes mankind its involuntary exponent," which is how the paradoxical God manifests itself externally in the collective psyche (1969a, par. 660).

It also manifests itself internally, in the individual. When that happens the individual ego encounters conflicts having an archetypal charge behind them: they are not little conflicts; they are big conflicts. Everything that activates serious, paralyzing ambivalence will fall into this category. The individual, then, takes that inner state of conflict as his own inner division and he becomes neurotic. Neurosis is, by definition, to be split, which of course is where the analytic procedure comes in. Jung says in this paragraph that we can be rescued from this danger, only if we "work out the way of salvation by a symbolic death." The idea seems to be that a death is in the cards: if it is not one kind, it will

be the other. I would understand this symbolic death to refer to the individual's task of individuation, in which each individual ego experiences the symbolic death that occurs when the ego has the experience
of being relativized. You remember Jung's remark in *Mysterium*, he says:
"the experience of the self is always a defeat for the ego" (1955, par. 778). A death.
The idea would be that if enough individuals engage the problem of
the divine conflict within their own psyches, if enough individuals experience symbolic death, which accompanies a conscious reconciliation of the opposites, namely a conscious *coniunctio*, that then has the
effect of transforming the paradoxical God. If enough individuals have
had that transformative experience within themselves, then they become seeds sown in the collective psyche which can promote the uni-
fication of the collective psyche as a whole.

Society is no more than the sum total of all the individuals that
make it up. It is not anything else. Therefore, the collective psyche of
the human race is the sum total of all the individual psyches. If a certain number of individual psyches have had the experience whereby
the God-image, by reaching consciousness, has achieved the transformation, then those few individuals will function something like yeast
in the dough. The interesting question, of course, is how many will it
take? The Old Testament went into this question. You remember,
Abraham disputed with Yahweh about how many righteous men there
would have to be in a city before he would decline to destroy it. He
[Abraham] got Him down to ten. I think we have to take that symbolically rather than literally. There is no way of knowing. I think each individual ought to live his life out of the hypothesis that, maybe, one
would do (Jung 1975a, 510f.)

Jung makes it clear that the task is a dangerous one:

> In order to accomplish this task [[this is the task of the union of
> the opposites, the incarnation task]], man is inspired by the Holy
> Ghost in such a way that he is apt to identify him with his own mind.
> He even runs the grave risk of believing he has a Messianic mission,
> and forces tyrannous doctrines upon his fellow-beings. He would do
> better to dis-identify his mind from the small voice within, from
> dreams and fantasies through which the divine spirit manifests itself.
> One should listen to the inner voice attentively, intelligently and
> critically (*Probate spiritus!*) [[test the spirits]], because the voice one
> hears is the *influxus divinus* consisting, as the Acts of John aptly state,

[margin notes: critical mass whereby God-image transformed in collective; must listen to inner voice critically]

Middle way)

of "right" and "left" streams, i.e., of opposites. They have to be clearly separated so that their positive and negative aspects become visible. Only thus can we take up a middle position and discover a middle way. That is the task left to man, and that is the reason why man is so important to God that he decided to become a man himself. (1975b, par. 1662)[1]

Again, as the Self comes into consciousness, it splits into opposites, into a right and a left stream, as the referred text indicates. It means one must be very careful listening to this inner voice, because it does not come with a label around its neck saying, "I'm the left stream." One has to be aware that these things are mixed up. This Latin phrase *Probate spiritus* is a favorite expression of Jung's. You will find it scattered around in his *Collected Works*. *Test the spirits*. It comes from First John 4:1, where John says, "Do not believe every spirit, but test the spirits whether they are of God." It means every stream of libido, every inclination, every fantasy stream that comes up, has to be critically examined. It has to be related to by a conscious, critical, judging, moral ego.

I was very struck by an event that happened some years ago that I read about in the newspaper. A sixteen-year-old boy lay in wait in the bushes for his parents to come home and shot them both dead. When he was questioned about it, he said, "God told me to do it." That boy did not test the spirit that was talking to him. If he had gone back to that spirit at a later time, it is quite possible that that same voice, after the murder, might have said, "You fool, you took a symbolic statement literally. It's your own fault." It is evident without knowing anything more about this boy's psychology. He is a sixteen-year-old who kills his parents. With that kind of story, it is evident that his unconscious is telling him that it is time the parent-figures be killed in his psyche, and that he achieve a greater level of independence. The unconscious, however, speaks in direct, primitive images. Not uncommonly one gets dreams in adolescence of the sort, that the parents have died or need to die some way or another. This story is an extreme example of the sort of thing one encounters all the time in dealing with the unconscious. We must always *test the spirits*, not just do what they recommend, innocently.

---

[1] In Jung 1975b, par. 1662, footnote 23 should read the "Acts of John," not the "Acts of Peter."

From the standpoint of the ego, the nature of the unconscious is profoundly ambiguous. Thus Jung writes about Yahweh:

> God in the Old Testament is a guardian of law and morality, yet is himself unjust. He is a moral paradox, unreflecting in an ethical sense. . . . The divine paradox is the source of unending suffering to man. Job cannot avoid seeing it and thus he sees more than God himself. This explains why the God-image has to come down "into the flesh." The paradox . . . is clearly discernible in the fact that the "Suffering Righteous man" is, historically speaking, an erroneous conception, not identical with the suffering God, because he is Jesus Christ, worshipped as a separate God (he is a mere prefiguration, painfully included in a trinity) and not an ordinary man who is forced to accept the suffering of intolerable opposites he has not invented. They were preordained. He is the victim, because he is capable of three-dimensional consciousness and ethical decision. (1975b, par. 1680)

According to the myth, Christ was God and therefore not ordinary, suffering man. Sinful, ordinary man is the agent of *continuing incarnation* in the present. Jung goes on to say:

> Man's suffering does not derive from his sins but from the maker of his imperfections, the paradoxical God. The righteous man is the instrument into which God enters in order to attain self-reflection and thus consciousness and rebirth as a divine child trusted to the care of adult man. (1975b, par. 1681)

This striking statement lays down a whole new basic assumption for the new aeon. The basic idea is that the ego did not make itself. It is not responsible for its imperfections, its weaknesses, its lapses. Now, that is a very radical statement. It goes against the collective wisdom of the centuries. It contradicts the collective standpoint of our current functioning. The fact is that much of our inner suffering is due to identification with our subjectivity, based on the erroneous assumption that the "I," the ego, is responsible for what happens within the psyche.

The ego does have to take responsibility for its behavior, but it is not responsible for what goes on within the psyche. It is not its own creator, although it has been operating out of that assumption for quite a while. Therefore, the task of the suffering ego becomes the objectification of its subjectivity. As Jung says in the Lang letter:

must dis-identify
@/ subjectivity
(You/ego) does not create images of psyche

Though I am sure of my subjective experience, I must impose on myself every conceivable restriction in interpreting it. I must guard
against identifying with my subjective experience. (1975a, 376)

If one identifies with one's subjective experience, then one assumes
he is the creator of it. Whereas, if you know you did not create the
thoughts and images that come into your head, then you are dis-
identifying from your subjective experience, a major aspect of the analytic process. We examine dreams, we do active imagination, we make
sand-trays, we paint pictures and what-not, all for the same purpose of
trying to promote dis-identification from our subjectivity. In other
words, to render our subjectivity objective. The constant danger that
we have to be alert for is the unconscious assumption that is always
stalking us: I created that (when I did not).

To conclude, I want to summarize the seminar by offering this series of
quotations from Jung's letters:

[G]ive due regard to the epistemological premises. (1975a, 262)

[H]ere that threshold which separates two epochs plays the principal role. I mean by that threshold the theory of knowledge whose
starting point is Kant. On that threshold minds go their separate
ways: those that have understood Kant, and the others that cannot
follow him. (1975a, 375)

I cannot but regard all assertions about God as relative because subjectively conditioned—and this out of respect for my brothers,
whose other conceptions and beliefs have as much to justify them as
mine. . . . Though I am sure of my subjective experience, I must impose on myself every conceivable restriction in interpreting it. I must
guard against identifying with my subjective experience. (1975a,
376)

I am sorry to say that everything men assert about God is twaddle.
(1975a, 377)

When you ask me if I am a believer I must answer "no." I am loyal
to my inner experience and have *pistis* in the Pauline sense, but I do
not presume to believe in my subjective interpretation. (1975a, 378)

[T]he charisma of faith was denied me. I was thrown on experience
alone. Always Paul's experience on the road to Damascus hovered be-

fore me. . . . I drew the conclusion that you must obviously fulfill
your destiny in order to get to the point where a *donum gratiae* [[gift of
grace]] might happen along. . . .

. . . only by going my own way, integrating my capacities headlong (like Paul), and thus creating a foundation for myself, could
something be vouchsafed to me or built upon it. . . .

The only way open to me was the experience of religious realities.
(1975a, 257f.)

The whole course of individuation is dialectical, and the so-called
"end" is the confrontation of the ego with the "emptiness" of the centre. . . . But if the ego usurps the centre it loses its object (inflation!)

. . . In the individuation process the ego is brought face to face
with an unknown superior power which is likely to cut the ground
from under its feet and blow consciousness to bits. (1975a, 259f.)

All statements about and beyond the "ultimate" are anthropomorphisms. (1975a, 260f.)

[[God]] is an apt name given to all overpowering emotions in my own
psychic system, subduing my conscious will and usurping control
over myself. This is the name by which I designate all things which
cross my wilful path violently and recklessly, all things which upset
my subjective views, plans, and intentions and change the course of
my life for better or worse. (1975a, 525)

By "religion," then, I mean a kind of attitude which takes careful
and conscientious account of certain numinous feelings, ideas, and
events and reflects upon them; . . . [[and by the]] exercise of the "religious function." . . . I mean the allegiance, surrender, or submission
to a supraordinate factor or to a "convincing" [=overpowering!] principle. (1975a, 483f.)

Myth is pre-eminently a social phenomenon: it is told by the many
and heard by the many. It gives the ultimately unimaginable religious
experience an image, a form in which to express itself, and thus
makes community life possible. (1975a, 486)

myth is a social phenomenon

Nobody seems to have noticed that without a reflecting psyche the
world might as well not exist, and that, in consequence, consciousness is a second world-creator, and also that the cosmogonic myths
do not describe the absolute beginning of the world but rather the
dawning of consciousness as the second Creation. (1975a, 487)

We are actually living in the time of the splitting of the world and of the invalidation of Christ.

But an anticipation of a faraway future is no way out of the actual situation. It is a mere *consolamentum* for those despairing at the atrocious possibilities of the present time. (1975a, 138)

I think that the great split in those days was by no means a mistake but a very important collective fact of synchronistic correspondence with the then new aeon of Pisces. (1975a, 165)

When Christ withstood Satan's temptation, that was the fatal moment when the shadow was cast off. Yet it had to be cast off in order to enable man to become morally conscious. (1975a, 166)

The question: *an creator sibi consciens est?* [[is the Creator conscious of himself?]] is not a "pet idea" but an exceedingly painful experience with well-nigh incalculable consequences. (1975a, 493)

Since a creation without the reflecting consciousness of man has no discernible meaning, the hypothesis of a latent meaning endows man with a cosmogonic significance, a true *raison d'être*. If on the other hand the latent meaning is attributed to the Creator as part of a conscious plan of creation, the question arises: Why should the Creator stage-manage this whole phenomenal world since he already knows what he can reflect himself in, and why should he reflect himself at all since he is already conscious of himself? Why should he create alongside his own omniscience a second, inferior consciousness—millions of dreary little mirrors when he knows in advance just what the image they reflect will look like? (1975a, 495)

With no human consciousness to reflect themselves in, good and evil simply happen, or rather, there is no good and evil, but only a sequence of neutral events, or what the Buddhists call the Nidhana-chain, the uninterrupted causal concatenation leading to suffering, old age, sickness, and death. Buddha's insight and the Incarnation in Christ break the chain [of suffering] through the intervention of the enlightened human consciousness, which thereby acquires a metaphysical and cosmic significance. (1975a, 311)

When we consider the data of palaeontology with the view that a conscious creator has perhaps spent more than a thousand million years, and has made, as it seems to us, no end of detours to produce consciousness, we inevitably come to the conclusion that . . . His behavior is strikingly similar to a being with an at least very limited consciousness. . . . not . . . an absolute unconsciousness but a rather dim consciousness. (1975a, 312)

[[Christ]] was up against an unpredictable and lawless God who would need a most drastic sacrifice to appease His wrath, namely the slaughter of His own son. Curiously enough, as on the one hand his self-sacrifice means admission of his Father's amoral nature, he taught on the other hand a new image of God, namely that of a Loving Father in whom there is no darkness. This enormous antinomy needs some explanation. It needed the assertion that he was the Son of the Father, that is, the incarnation of the Deity in man. As a consequence the sacrifice was a self-destruction of the amoral God, incarnated in a mortal body. Thus the sacrifice takes on the aspect of a highly moral deed, of a self-punishment, as it were. (1975a, 313)

Although the divine incarnation is a cosmic and absolute event, it only manifests empirically in those relatively few individuals capable of enough consciousness to make ethical decisions, that is, to decide for the Good. Therefore God can be called good only inasmuch as He is able to manifest His goodness in individuals. His moral quality depends upon individuals. That is why He incarnates. Individuation and individual existence are indispensable for the transformation of God the Creator. (1975a, 314)

[[Man]] does not only depend on God but . . . God also depends on man. Man's relation to God probably has to undergo a certain important change: Instead of the propitiating praise to an unpredictable king or the child's prayer to a loving father, the responsible living and fulfilling of the divine will in us will be our form of worship of and commerce with God. His goodness means grace and light and His dark side the terrible temptation of power. (1975a, 316)

[T]his age old question [[whence evil?]] is not answered unless you assume the existence of a [supreme] being *who is in the main unconscious.* Such a model would explain why God has created a man gifted with consciousness and why He seeks His goal in him. . . . *The creator sees himself through the eyes of man's consciousness* and this is the reason why God had to become man, and why man is progressively gifted with the dangerous prerogative of divine "mind.". . . The real history of the world seems to be the progressive incarnation of the deity. (1975a, 435)

[T]he action of the Holy Spirit does not meet us in the atmosphere of a normal, bourgeois (or proletarian!), sheltered, regular life, but only in the insecurity outside the human economy, in the infinite spaces where one is alone with the *providentia Dei* [[divine providence]]. We must never forget that Christ was an innovator and revolutionary, *executed with criminals*. The reformers and great religious geniuses were *heretics*. It is there that you find the footprints of the Holy Spirit, and no one asks for him or receives him *without having to pay a high price*. (1975b, par. 1539)

Thus the ordinary man became a source of the Holy Spirit, though certainly not the only one. . . . This fact signifies the continued and progressive divine incarnation. Thus man is received and integrated into the divine drama. He seems destined to play a decisive part in it; that is why he must receive the Holy Spirit. I look upon the receiving of the Holy Spirit as a highly revolutionary fact which cannot take place until the ambivalent nature of the Father is recognized. (1975b, par. 1551)

Man's suffering does not derive from his sins but from the maker of his imperfections, the paradoxical God. The righteous man is the instrument into which God enters in order to attain self-reflection and thus consciousness and rebirth as a divine child trusted to the care of adult man. (1975b, par. 1681)

APPENDIX

SELECTIONS FROM JUNG'S LETTERS

To Bernhard Lang

Dear Colleague,   June 1957

Many thanks for your friendly letter, which shows that the Buber-Jung controversy is a serious matter for you.[1] And so indeed it is, for here that threshold which separates two epochs plays the principal role. I mean by that threshold the theory of knowledge whose starting-point is Kant. On that threshold minds go their separate ways: those that have understood Kant, and the others that cannot follow him. I will not enter here into the *Critique of Pure Reason*, but will try to make things clear to you from a different, more human standpoint.

Let us take as an example the believing person who has Buber's attitude to belief. He lives in the same world as me and appears to be a human being like me. But when I express doubts about the absolute validity of his statements, he expostulates that he is the happy possessor of a "receiver," an organ by means of which he can know or tune in the Transcendent. This information obliges me to reflect on myself and ask myself whether I also possess a like receiver which can make the Transcendent, i.e., something that transcends consciousness and is by definition unknowable, knowable. But I find in myself nothing of the sort. I find I am incapable of knowing the infinite and eternal or paradoxical; it is beyond my powers. I may *say* that I know what is infinite and eternal; I may even assert that I have experienced it; but that one could actually *know* it is impossible because man is neither an infinite nor an eternal being. He can know only the part but not the whole, not the infinite and eternal. So when the believer assures me that I do not possess the organ he possesses, he makes me aware of my humanity, of my limitation which he allegedly does not have. He is the superior one, who regretfully points out my deformity or mutilation. Therefore I speak of the *beati possidentes* of belief, and this is what I reproach them with: that they exalt themselves above our human stature and our human limitation and won't admit to pluming themselves on a possession which distinguishes them from the ordinary mortal. I start with the confession of not knowing and not being able to know; believers start with the assertion of knowing and being able to know. There is now only one truth, and when we ask the believers what this truth is they give us a number of very different answers with regard to which the one sure thing is that each believer announces his own particular truth. Instead of saying: To me personally it seems so, he says: It is so, thus putting everybody else automatically in the wrong.

Now in my estimation it would be more human, more decent, and altogether more appropriate if we carefully inquired beforehand what other people think and if we expressed ourselves less categorically. It would be more becoming to do this than to believe subjective opinions and to damn the opinions of others as fallacies. If we do not do this, the inevitable consequence is that only my subjective opinion is valid, I alone possess the true receiver, and everyone else is deformed who lacks such an important organ as belief is considered to be. Buber is unconscious of the fact that when he says "God" he is expressing his subjective belief and imagining by "God" something other people could not sanction. What, for instance, would a Buddhist say about Buber's conception of God? My human limitation does not permit me to assert that I know God, hence I cannot but regard all assertions about God as relative because subjectively conditioned—and this out of respect for my brothers, whose other conceptions and beliefs have as much to justify them as mine. If I am a psychologist I shall try to take these differences seriously and to understand them. But under no circumstances shall I assume that if the other person doesn't share my opinion it is due to a deformity or lack of an organ. How could I have any communication at all with a person if I approached him with the absolutist claims of the believer? Though I am sure of my subjective experience, I must impose on myself every conceivable restriction in interpreting it. I must guard against identifying with my subjective experience. I consider all such identifications as serious psychological mistakes indicative of total lack of criticism. For what purpose am I endowed with a modicum of intelligence if I do not apply it in these decisive matters? Instead of being delighted with the fact of my inner experience, I am then using it merely to exalt myself, through my subjective belief, above all those who do not accept my interpretation of the experience. The experience itself is not in question, only the absolutizing interpretation of it. If I have a vision of Christ, this is far from proving that it was Christ, as we know only too well from our psychiatric practice. I therefore treat all confessions of faith with extreme reserve. I am ready at any time to confess to the inner experience but not to my metaphysical interpretation, otherwise I am implicitly laying claim to universal recognition. On the contrary, I must confess that I cannot interpret the inner experience in its metaphysical reality, since its essential core is of a transcendental nature and beyond my human grasp. Naturally I am free to believe something about it, but that is my subjective prejudice which I don't want to thrust on other people, nor can I ever prove that it is universally valid. As a matter of fact we have every reason to suppose that it is not.

I am sorry to say that everything men assert about God is twaddle, for no man can know God. Knowing means seeing a thing in such a way that all can know it, and for me it means absolutely nothing if I profess a knowledge which I alone possess. Such people are found in the lunatic asylum. I therefore regard the proposition that belief is knowledge as absolutely misleading. What has really happened to these people is that they have been overpowered by an inner experience. They then make an interpretation which is as subjective as possible and believe it, instead of remaining true to the original experience. Take as an example our national saint Nicholas von der Flüe: he sees an overwhelmingly terrifying face which he involuntarily interprets as God and then twiddles it around until it turns into the image of the Trinity, which still hangs today in the church at Sachseln.[2] This image has nothing to do with the original experience, but represents the Summum Bonum and divine love, which are miles away from God's Yahwistic terrors or the "wrath fire" of Boehme. Actually after this vision Nicholas should have preached: "God is terrible." But he believed his own interpretation instead of the immediate experience.

This is a typical phenomenon of belief and one sees from it how such confessions of faith come about. Because this so-called knowledge is illegitimate, inner uncertainty makes it fanatical and generates missionary zeal, so that through the concurrence of the multitude the subjective interpretation, precarious enough as it is, may not be shaken still further. But the certitude of inner experience generates greater certainty than the interpretation we have imposed upon it. Buber fails to see that when he says "My experience is God" he is interpreting it in such a way as to force everyone into believing his opinion—because he himself is uncertain; for confronted with the great mystery no mortal man can aver that he has given a reliable interpretation, otherwise it would no longer be a mystery. It is only too plain to see that such people have no mysteries any more, like those Oxfordites who think they can call up God on the telephone.

When you ask me if I am a believer I must answer "No." I am loyal to my inner experience and have *pistis* in the Pauline sense,[3] but I do not presume to believe in my subjective interpretation, which would seem to me highly obnoxious when I consider my human brothers. I "abhor" the belief that I or anybody else could be in possession of an absolute truth. As I have said, I regard this unseemliness as a psychological mistake, a hidden inflation. If you have inner experiences you are always in danger of identifying with them and imagining that you are specially favoured, or are a special species of man who possesses one organ more than others. I know only too well how difficult it is for people to stand off from their own experience far enough to see the difference between the authentic experience and what they have made of it. For if they stood by it, they would reach very weighty conclusions which could severely shake their interpretation. Obviously they want to avoid these consequences, and my critical psychology is therefore a thorn in their flesh. I can also confirm that I regard all declarations of faith, which Buber for instance has in mind, as an object of psychological research, since they are subjective human statements about actual experiences whose real nature cannot be fathomed by man in any case. These experiences contain a real mystery, but the statements made about them don't. Thus it remained a real mystery to Brother Klaus what that terrifying countenance of God actually meant.

Incidentally, I would like to remark that the concept "transcendent" is relative. Transcendence is simply that which is unconscious to us, and it cannot be established whether this is permanently inaccessible or only at present. In the past many things were transcendent that are now the subject-matter of science. This should make one cautious—especially when dealing with ultimate things man cannot know about. We cannot, after all, assert that belief enables us to attain godlike knowledge. We merely believe we can become godlike, but we must modestly accept the fact that we cannot thrust this belief on anybody else. We could never prove that this would not be an unbelievable presumption. I for one am convinced that it is.

All that I have written you is Kantian epistemology expressed in everyday psychological language. I hope by this means to have gained your ear.

In case my idea of interpretation should seem unintelligible to you, I would like to add a few words more. Interpretation by faith seeks to represent the experienced content of a vision, for instance, as the visible manifestation of a transcendental Being, and it invariably does so in terms of a traditional system and then asserts that this representation is the absolute truth. Opposed to this is my view, which also interprets, in a sense. It interprets by comparing *all* traditional assumptions and does not assert that Transcendence itself has been perceived; it insists only on the reality of the fact that an experience has taken place, and that this is exactly the form it took. I compare this experience with all other experiences of the kind and conclude that a process is going on in the unconscious which expresses itself in various forms. I am aware that this process is actually going on, but I do not know what its nature is, whether it is psychic, whether it comes from an angel or from God himself. We must leave these questions open, and no belief will help us over the hurdle, for we do not know and can never know. With collegial regards,

Yours sincerely, C. G. JUNG

Notes

(*Letters* II, 375–79)
1. Lang asked: "Do you regard yourself as a believing person and is your statement 'modern consciousness abhors belief' simply the legitimate, descriptive statement of a scientist about the present state of consciousness, or do you identify yourself personally with this attitude?"

2. Nicholas von der Flüe was baptized and buried in the church of Sachseln, Cant. Unterwalden. Cf. Jung, "Brother Klaus," and Jung's letter to Fritz Blanke, 2 May 1945, n. 12, in *Letters* I, 365.

3. Cf. "Psychology and Religion," par. 9: "pistis, that is to say, trust or loyalty, faith and confidence in a certain experience of a numinous nature. . . . The conversion of Paul is a striking example of this." Also I Cor. 12:9: "To another faith by the same Spirit . . ."

To Pastor Walter Bernet

Dear Pastor Bernet,   13 June 1955

At last I have got down to reading and studying your book[1] which you so kindly sent me. Please put the slowness of this procedure down to my old age! It was certainly not lack of interest that kept me reading so long, but rather a curiosity or—more accurately—a need to familiarize myself with and learn to understand the theological mode of thinking, which is so alien to me. I have been able to assimilate this thinking only very fragmentarily, if at all, in spite or perhaps because of the fact that I come from a theological milieu on my mother's side, and my father was himself a clergyman. It was the tragedy of my youth to see my father cracking up before my eyes on the problem of his faith and dying an early death.[2] This was the objective outer event that opened my eyes to the importance of religion. Subjective inner experiences prevented me from drawing negative conclusions about religion from my father's fate, much as I was tempted to do so. I grew up in the heyday of scientific materialism, studied natural science and medicine, and became a psychiatrist. My education offered me nothing but arguments against religion on the one hand, and on the other the charisma of faith was denied me. I was thrown back on experience alone. Always Paul's experience on the road to Damascus hovered before me, and I asked myself how his fate would have fallen out but for his vision. Yet this experience came upon him while he was blindly pursuing his own way. As a young man I drew the conclusion that you must obviously fulfill your destiny in order to get to the point where a *donum gratiae* might happen along. But I was far from certain, and always kept the possibility in mind that on this road I might end up in a black hole. I have remained true to this attitude all my life.

From this you can easily see the origin of my psychology: only by going my own way, integrating my capacities headlong (like Paul), and thus creating a foundation for myself, could something be vouchsafed to me or built upon it, no matter where it came from, and of which I could be reasonably sure that it was not merely one of my own neglected capacities.

The only way open to me was the experience of religious realities which I had to accept without regard to their truth. In this matter I have no criterion except the fact that they seem meaningful to me and harmonize with man's best utterances. I don't know whether the archetype is "true" or not. I only know that it lives and that I have not made it.

Since the number of possibilities is limited, one soon comes to a frontier, or rather to frontiers which recede behind one another presumably up to the point of death. The experience of these frontiers gradually brings the conviction that what is experienced is an endless approximation. The goal of this approximation seems to be anticipated by archetypal symbols which represent something like the circumambulation of a centre. With increasing approximation to the centre there is a corresponding depotentiation of the ego in favour of the influence of the "empty" centre, which is certainly not identical with the archetype but is the thing the archetype points to. As the Chinese would say, the archetype is only the *name* of Tao, not Tao itself. Just as the Jesuits translated Tao as "God," so we can describe the "emptiness"[3] of the centre as "God." Emptiness in this sense doesn't mean "absence" or "vacancy," but something unknowable which is endowed with the highest intensity. If I call this unknowable the "self," all that has happened is that the effects of the unknowable have been given an aggregate name, but its contents are not affected in any way. An indeterminably large part of my own being is included in it, but because this part is the unconscious I cannot indicate its limits or its extent. The self is therefore a *borderline concept*, not by any means filled out with the known psychic processes. On the one hand it includes the phenomena of synchronicity, on the other its archetype is embedded in the brain structure and is physiologically verifiable: through electrical stimulation of a certain area of the brain-stem of an epileptic it is possible to produce mandala visions (*quadratura circuli*). From synchronistic phenomena we learn that a peculiar feature of the psychoid[4] background is transgressivity[5] in space and time. This brings us directly to the frontier of transcendence, beyond which human statements can only be mythological.

The whole course of individuation is dialectical, and the so-called "end" is the confrontation of the ego with the "emptiness" of the centre. Here the limit of possible experience is reached: the ego dissolves as the reference-point of cognition. It cannot coincide with the centre, otherwise we would be insensible; that is to say, the extinction of the ego is at best an endless approximation. But if the ego usurps the centre it loses its object (inflation!).[6]

Even though you add to my "ultimate" an "absolute ultimate," you will hardly maintain that my "ultimate" is not as good an "ultimate" as yours. In any case all possibility of cognition and predication ceases for me at this frontier because of the extinction of the ego. The ego can merely affirm that something vitally important is happening to it. It may conjecture that it has come up against something greater, that it feels powerless against this greater power; that it can cognize nothing further; that in the course of the integration process it has become convinced of its finiteness, just as before it was compelled to take practical account of the existence of an ineluctable archetype.

The ego has to acknowledge many gods before it attains the centre where no god helps it any longer against another god.

It now occurs to me—and I hope I am not deceiving myself—that from the point where you introduce the "absolute ultimate" which is meant to replace my descriptive concept of the self by an empty abstraction, the archetype is increasingly detached from its dynamic background and gradually turned into a purely intellectual formula. In this way it is neutralized, and you can then say "one can live with it quite well." But you overlook the fact that the self-constellating archetypes and the resultant situations steadily gain in numinosity, indeed are sometimes imbued with a positively eerie daemonism and bring the danger of psychosis threateningly close. The upsurging archetypal material is the stuff of which mental illnesses are made. In the individuation process the ego is brought face to face with an unknown superior power which is likely to cut the ground from under its feet and blow consciousness to bits. The archetype is not just the formal condition for mythological statements but an overwhelming force comparable to nothing I know. In view of the terrors of this confrontation I would never dream of addressing this menacing and fascinating opponent familiarly as "Thou," though paradoxically it also has this aspect. All talk of this opponent is mythology. All statements about and beyond the "ultimate" are anthropomorphisms and, if anyone should think that when he says "God" he has also predicated God, he is endowing his words with *magical power*. Like a primitive, he is incapable of distinguishing the verbal image from reality. In one breath he will endorse the statement *Deus est ineffabilis* without a thought, but in the next he will be speaking of God as though he could express him.

It seems to me—and I beg your pardon in advance if I am doing you an injustice—that something of the sort has happened to you. You write, apparently without any misgivings, that I equate God with the self. You seem not to have noticed that I speak of the *God-image and not of God* because it is quite beyond me to say anything about God at all. It is more than astonishing that you have failed to perceive this fundamental distinction, it is shattering. I don't know what you must take me for if you can impute such stupidities to me after you yourself have correctly presented my epistemological standpoint at the beginning of your book. I have in all conscience never supposed that in discussing the psychic structure of the God-image I have taken God himself in hand. I am not a word-magician or word-fetishist who thinks he can posit or call up a metaphysical reality with his incantations. Don't Protestant critics accuse the Catholic Mass of magic when it asserts that by pronouncing the words *Hoc est corpus meum* Christ is actually present?

In *Job* and elsewhere I am always explicitly speaking of the *God-image*. If my theologian critics choose to overlook this, the fault lies with them and not with me. They obviously think that the little word "God" conjures him up in reality, just as the Mass forces Christ to appear through the words of the Consecration. (Naturally I am aware of the dissident Catholic explanation of this.) I do not share your overvaluation of words, and have never regarded the equation Christ = Logos as anything else than an interesting symbol conditioned by its time.

This credulity and entrapment in words is becoming more and more striking nowadays. Proof of this is the rise of such a comical philosophy as existentialism, which labours to help being become being through the magical power of the word. People still believe that they can posit or replace reality by words, or that something has happened when a thing is given a different name. If I call the "ultimate" the self and you call it the "absolute ultimate," its ultimateness is not changed one whit. The name means far less to me than the view associated with it. You seem to think that I enjoy romping about in a circus of archetypal figures and that I take them for ultimate realities which block my view of the Ineffable. They guide but they also mislead; how much I reserve my criticism for them you can see in *Answer to Job*, where I subject archetypal statements to what you call "blasphemous" criticism. The very fact that you consider this critique of anthropomorphisms worthy of condemnation proves how strongly you are bound to these psychic products by word-magic. If theologians think that whenever they say "God" then God is, they are deifying anthropomorphisms, psychic structures and myths. This is exactly what I don't do, for, I must repeat, I speak exclusively of the *God-image* in *Job*. Who talks of divine knowledge and divine revelation? Certainly not me. "Ultimately" I have really reached the ultimate with my presumptuous anthropomorphisms which feign knowledge and revelation! I see many God-images of various kinds; I find myself compelled to make mythological statements, but I know that none of them expresses or captures the immeasurable Other, even if I were to assert it did.

However interesting or enthralling metaphysical statements may be, I must still criticize them as anthropomorphisms. But here the theologian buttonholes me, asseverating that *his* anthropomorphism is God and damning anyone who criticizes any anthropomorphic weaknesses, defects, and contradictions in it as a blasphemer. It is not God who is insulted by the worm but the theologian, who can't or won't admit that his concept is anthropomorphic. With this he puts an end to the much needed discussion and understanding of religious statements. Just as Bultmann's demythologizing procedure stops at the point where the demagicking of words no longer seems advisable to him, so the theologian treats exactly the same concept as mythological, i.e., anthropomorphic at one moment and as an inviolable taboo at the next.

I have begged four distinguished (academic) theologians to tell me what exactly is the attitude of modern Protestantism to the question of the identity of the God of the Old Testament with the God of the New, between whom the layman thinks he can spot quite a number of differences. The question is so harmless that it is like asking what the difference is between Freud's view of the unconscious and mine. Two didn't answer at all despite repeated requests. The third told me that there was no longer any talk of God in the theological literature of the last twenty years anyway. The fourth said the question was very easy to answer: Yahweh was simply a somewhat archaic God-concept in comparison with that of the New Testament. Whereupon I replied: "Look, my dear Professor, this is just the kind of psychologism the theologians accuse me of. Suddenly the divine revelation in the OT is nothing but an archaic *concept* and the revelation in the NT is simply a modern one. But the next moment this same revelation is God himself and no concept at all."

So you ride the hobby-horse of your choice. In order to do away with such tricks, I stick to my proposal that we take all talk of God as mythological and discuss these mythologems honestly. As soon as we open our mouths we speak in traditional verbal images, and even when we merely think we think in age-old psychic structures. If God were to reveal himself to us we have nothing except our psychic organs to register his revelation and could not express it except in the images of our everyday speech.

Let the Protestant theologian therefore abandon his hieratic word-magic and his alleged knowledge of God through faith and admit to the layman that he is mythologizing and is just as incapable as he is of expressing God himself. Let him not vilify and condemn and twist the arguments of others who are struggling just as earnestly to understand the mysteries of religion, even if he finds these arguments personally disagreeable or wrong in themselves. (I cannot exempt you, for one, from the obligation to give due regard to the epistemological premises of *Answer to Job* if you want to criticize it.)

So long as we are conscious of ourselves, we are supported by the psyche and its structures and at the same time imprisoned in them with no possibility of getting outside ourselves. We would not feel and be aware of ourselves at all were we not always confronted with the unknown power. Without this we would not be conscious of our separateness, just as there is no consciousness without an object.

We are not delivered from the "sin" of mythologizing by saying that we are "saved" or "redeemed" through the revelation of God in Christ, for this is simply another mythologem which does, however, contain a psychological truth. Consequently we can understand the "feeling of redemption" which is bound up with this mythologem; but the statement "revelation in Christ" merely affirms that a myth of this kind exists which evidently belongs to the symbolism of the self.

What impresses me most profoundly in discussions with theologians of both camps is that metaphysical statements are made apparently without the slightest awareness that they are talking in mythic images which pass directly as the "word of God." For this reason it is so often thoughtlessly assumed that I do the same thing, whereas quite to the contrary I am trained by my daily professional work to distinguish scrupulously between idea and reality. The recognition of projections is indeed one of the most important tasks of psychotherapy.

I have read your erudite book with great interest and profit and find it all the more regrettable that in spite of your admirably objective presentation of my standpoint at the beginning you nevertheless go off the rails at the end. You think *I* have deviated from my epistemological position in *Job*. Had you read the introduction you could never have pronounced this false judgment.

I can understand very well that you are shocked by the book; I was too, and by the original Job into the bargain. I feel that you have in general too poor an opinion of me when you charge me with the arrogance of wanting to write an *exegesis* of Job. I don't know a word of Hebrew. As a layman, I have only tried to read the translated text with psychological common sense, on the assumption, certainly, that I am dealing with anthropomorphisms and not with magical words that conjure up God himself. If in the Jewish commentaries the high priest takes the liberty of admonishing Adonai to remember his good rather than his bad qualities,[7] it is no longer so shocking if I avail myself of a similar criticism, especially as I am not even addressing Adonai, as the high priest did, but merely the anthropomorphic God-image, and expressly refrain from all metaphysical utterances, which the high priest did not. You will scarcely suppose that, despite my assurance to the contrary, the mere pronouncing of God's name conjures up God himself. At all events Adonai took the high priest's criticism and a number of other equally drastic observations without a murmur, thereby showing himself to be more tolerant than certain theologians. The reason why mythic statements invariably lead to word-magic is that the archetype possesses a numinous autonomy and has a psychic life of its own. I have dealt with this particular difficulty at some length in *Job*. Perhaps I may remark in conclusion that the theory of archetypes is more difficult, and I am not quite so stupid as you apparently think.

I cannot omit to thank you, all the same, for the great trouble you have taken in going into my proposition so thoroughly. It is obvious that this cannot be done without difficulties and misunderstandings, especially in view of the fact that our age is still for the most part trapped in its belief in words. Ancient Greece was on an even lower level, as the term *phrenes* with its psychic connotation shows.[8] The Pueblo Indians of New Mexico still think in the "heart" and not in the head.[9] Tantra Yoga gives the classic localizations of thought: *anahata*, thinking (or localization of consciousness) in the chest region (*phrenes*); *visuddha* (localized in the larynx), verbal thinking; and *ajna*,[10] vision, symbolized by an eye in the forehead, which is attained only when verbal image and object are no longer identical, i.e., when their *participation mystique*[11] is abolished.

I have this advance of human consciousness particularly at heart. It is a difficult task to which I have devoted all my life's work. This is the reason why I venture to plague you with such a long letter.[12]

Yours sincerely, C. G. JUNG

Notes

(*Letters* II, 257–65)
Letter was addressed to Bern, Switzerland.

1. *Inhalt und Grenze der religiösen Erfahrung* (1952). [The Scope and Limit of Religious Experience.]
2. Cf. *Memories, Dreams, Reflections*, 91ff./ 96ff.
3. For the Buddhist concept of *sunyata*, emptiness, cf. Jung's letter to W. Y. Evans-Wentz, 8 December 1938, n. 3, in *Letters* I, 249. Also "Psychology and Religion," *CW* 11, par. 136.
4. Cf. Jung's letter to Dr. H., 30 August 1951, in *Letters* II, 22, n. 5.
5. "Synchronicity," *CW* 8, par. 964.
6. *Aion*, *CW* 9ii, pars. 44f., 79.
7. *Aion*, par. 110.
8. The midriff or diaphragm; among the pre-Socratics, the seat of consciousness. In Homer, however, *phrenes* meant the lungs.
9. *Memories, Dreams, Reflections*, 248/233.
10. *Anahata, visuddha,* and *ajna* are three of the seven *chakras* in Kundalini Yoga. Cf. Jung's letter to Elined Kotschnig, 23 July 1934, n. 2, in *Letters* I, 170; and Jung, "The Realities of Practical Psychotherapy," *CW* 16 (2d ed.), Appendix, par. 560.
11. A term coined by Lévy-Bruhl for the "prelogical" mentality of primitives, but later abandoned by him. Jung made frequent use of it to denote the state of projection in which internal and external events are inextricably mixed up, resulting in an irrational and unconscious identity of inside and outside.
12. A decade later, Bernet published extracts from Jung's letter with comments in an essay on Jung in *Tendenzen der Theologie im 20. Jahrhundert. Eine Geschichte in Porträts*, ed. H. J. Schulz (1966). He concluded: ". . . this outsider of theology has, with the relentless determination with which he demands experience of man, with his uncomfortable criticism of ecclesiastical talk of God, with his bold vision in particular of the Protestant Church, urged upon contemporary theological thought questions which in the interest of theology are absolutely necessary and which in their rigour show the way."

To Valentine Brooke

[ORIGINAL IN ENGLISH]

Dear Sir,   16 November 1959

As you have learned from Mr. Richardson's account,[1] I am an irritating person. I am dealing with doubts and views which puzzle the modern mind consciously as well as unconsciously. I am treading on corns right and left. As a consequence I have to spend a great amount of my time in handing out apologies and explanations for saying things which allude to facts and ideas unknown to the reader. Moreover the reader is handicapped by his positivistic premise that the truth is simple and can be expressed by one short sentence. Yet "nothing is quite true and even this is not quite true," as Multatuli says. A psychologist concerned with the treatment of mental disturbances is constantly reminded of the fallacies in our verbal formulations. In spite of all the difficulties besetting my way, I will try to explain my standpoint.

Whatever I perceive from without or within is a representation or image, a psychic entity caused, as I rightly or wrongly assume, by a corresponding "real" object. But I have to admit that my subjective image is only *grosso modo* identical with the object. Any portrait painter will agree with this statement and the physicist will add that what we call "colours" are really wave-lengths. The difference between image and real object shows that the psyche, apperceiving an object, alters it by adding or excluding certain details. The image therefore is not entirely caused by the object; it is also influenced by certain pre-existent psychic conditions which we can correct only partially. (We cannot remove colour perception, f.i.) Moreover we know from experience that all acts of apperception are influenced by pre-existent patterns of perceiving objects (f.i., the premise of causality), particularly obvious in pathological cases (being exaggerations or distortions of so called "normal" behaviour). They are presuppositions pertaining to the whole of humanity. The history of the human mind offers no end of examples (f.i., folklore, fairy tales, religious symbolism, etc.). To explain the spontaneous origin of such parallelisms, the theory of migration[2] is insufficient. I call them archetypes, i.e., instinctual forms of mental functioning. *They are not inherited ideas, but mentally expressed instincts, forms and not contents.*

They influence our image-formation. As experience shows, archetypes are equipped with a specific energy without which they could not have causal effects. Thus when we try to form an image of the fact one calls "God" we depend largely upon innate, pre-existent ways of perceiving, all the more so as it is a perception from within, unaided by the observation of physical facts which might lend their visible forms to our God-image (though there are plenty cases of the sort).

"God" therefore is *in the first place* a mental image equipped with instinctual "numinosity," i.e., an emotional value bestowing the characteristic autonomy of the affect on the image.

This is my chief statement. Now people unaccustomed to proper thinking assume that it is a final statement. No scientific statement is final: it is a likely formulation of observation and analysis. It goes as far as a scientific statement can go. But it does not and cannot say what "God" is; it only can define what He is in our mind. The mind is neither the world in itself nor does it reproduce its accurate image. The fact that we have an image of the world does not mean that there is only an image and no world. But this is exactly the argument of those who assume that when I speak of the God-image I mean that God does not exist, *as He is only an image.*

Our images are, as a rule, *of something,* and even delusions are "images" of something, as modern psychology has amply shown. If f.i. I imagine an animal which does not exist in reality as we know it, I form the picture of a mythological entity, following the age-old activity of our ancestors in imagining fairy beasts and "doctor animals." I am functioning within the frame of an archetype. I am in this case strongly influenced by it. (The archetype has efficacy.) But although we can be fairly certain that no such animal exists in physical reality, there is nevertheless a real cause which has suggested the creation of the dragon. The dragon-image is its expression.

The God-image is the expression of an underlying *experience of something* which I cannot attain to by intellectual means, i.e., by scientific cognition, unless I commit an unwarrantable transgression.

When I say that I don't need to believe in God because I "know," I mean I know of the existence of God-images in general and in particular. I know it is matter of a universal experience and, in so far as I am no exception, I know that I have such experience also, which I call God. It is the experience of my will over against another and very often stronger will, crossing my path often with seemingly disastrous results, putting strange ideas into my head and maneuvering my fate sometimes into most undesirable corners or giving it unexpected favourable twists, outside my knowledge and my intention. The strange force against or for my conscious tendencies is well known to me. So I say: "I know Him." But why should you call this something "God"? I would ask: "Why not?" It has always been called "God." An excellent and very suitable name indeed. Who could say in earnest that his fate and life have been the result of his conscious planning alone? Have we a complete picture of the world? Millions of conditions are in reality beyond our control. On innumerable occasions our lives could have taken an entirely different turn. Individuals who believe they are masters of their fate are as a rule the slaves of destiny. A Hitler or Mussolini could believe they were such masterminds. *Respice finem!* I know what I want, but I am doubtful and hesitant whether the Something is of the same opinion or not.[3]

Hoping I have succeeded in elucidating the puzzle,

Sincerely yours, C. G. JUNG

Notes

(*Letters* II, 520–23)

Letter was addressed to Worthing, Sussex.

1. On 22 October 1959, the British Broadcasting Corporation broadcast a television interview with Jung conducted by John Freeman in the series "Face to Face." In the course of the interview Freeman asked: "Do you believe in God?" to which Jung answered after a long pause: "I don't need to believe, I know." These words gave rise to considerable argument, and Brooke sent Jung a rather derogatory review of the broadcast by Maurice Richardson in the *London Observer*, 25 Oct. 1959, as well as some of the correspondence published in the same paper about Jung's words. Brooke asked for their exact meaning. The interview with Freeman is published in *C. G. Jung Speaking.*

2. Cf. Jung's letter to Henri Flournoy, 29 March 1949, n. 3, in *Letters* I, 525.

3. Most of this paragraph is reproduced in Jaffé, *The Myth of Meaning* (1971), 53.

To Robert C. Smith

[ORIGINAL IN ENGLISH]
Dear Mr. Smith,   29 June 1960

Buber and I[1] start from an entirely different basis: I make no transcendental statements. I am essentially empirical, as I have stated more than once.
I am dealing with psychic phenomena and not with metaphysical assertions.
Within the frame of psychic events I find the fact of the belief in God. It *says:*
"God is." This is the fact I am concerned with. I am not concerned with the
truth or untruth of God's existence. *I am concerned with the statement only,* and I am
interested in its structure and behaviour. It is an emotionally "toned" complex
like the father- or mother-complex or the Oedipus complex. It is obvious that
if man does not exist, no such statement can exist either, nor can anybody
prove that the statement "God" exists in a non-human sphere.

What Buber misunderstands as Gnosticism is *psychiatric observation,* of
which he obviously knows nothing. It is certainly not my invention. Buber has
been led astray by a poem in Gnostic style I made 44 years ago for a friend's
birthday celebration[2] (a private print!), a poetic paraphrase of the psychology
of the unconscious.

"Every pioneer is a monologist" until other people have tried out his
method and confirmed his results. Would you call all the great minds which
were not popular among their contemporaries, monologists, even that "voice
of one crying in the wilderness"?

Buber, having no practical experience in depth psychology, does not know
of the *autonomy of complexes,* a most easily observable fact however. Thus God, as
an autonomous complex,[3] is a *subject* confronting me. One must be really blind
if one cannot get that from my books. Likewise the *self* is a redoubtable reality,
as everybody learns who has tried or was compelled to do something about it.
Yet I define the Self as a *borderline concept.* This must be a puzzler for people like
Buber, who are unacquainted with the empiricist's epistemology.

Why cannot Buber get into his head that I deal with psychic facts and not
with metaphysical assertions? Buber is a theologian and has far more information about God's true existence and other of His qualities than I could ever
dream of acquiring. My ambitions are not soaring to theological heights. I am
merely concerned with the practical and theoretical problem of how-do-
complexes-behave? F.i. how does a mother-complex behave in a child and in
an adult? How does the God-complex behave in different individuals and

societies? How does the self-complex compare with the *Lapis Philosophorum* in Hermetic philosophy and with the Christ-figure in patristic allegories, with Al Chadir in Islamic tradition, with Tifereth in the Kabbalah, with Mithras, Attis, Odin, Krishna, and so on?

As you see, I am concerned with *images*, human phenomena, of which only the ignorant can assume that they are within our control or that they can be reduced to mere "objects." Every psychiatrist and psychotherapist can tell you to what an enormous degree man is delivered over to the terrific power of a complex which has assumed superiority over his mind. (*Vide* compulsion neurosis, schizophrenia, drugs, political and private nonsense, etc.) Mental possessions are just as good as ghosts, demons, and gods.

It is the task of the psychologist to investigate these matters. The theologian certainly has not done it yet. I am afraid it is sheer prejudice against science which hinders theologians from understanding my empirical standpoint. Seen from this standpoint the "experience of God" is *nolens volens* the psychic fact that I find myself confronted with, a factor in myself (more or less represented also by external circumstances) which proves to me to be of insurmountable power. F.i. a most rational professor of philosophy is entirely possessed by the fear of cancer which he knows does not exist. Try to liberate such an unfortunate fellow from his predicament and you will get an idea of "psychic autonomy."

I am sorry if X. bothers about the question of the basis upon which "religion rests." This is a metaphysical question the solution of which I do not know. I am concerned with *phenomenal religion*, with its observable facts, to which I try to add a few psychological observations about basic events in the collective unconscious, the existence of which I can prove. Beyond this I know nothing and I have never made any assertions about it.

How does Buber know of something he cannot "experience psychologically"? How is such a thing possible at all? If not in the psyche, then where else? You see, it is always the same matter: *the complete misunderstanding of the psychological argument:* "God" within the frame of psychology is an *autonomous complex, a dynamic image, and that is all psychology is ever able to state.* It cannot know more about God. It cannot prove or disprove God's actual existence, but it does know how fallible images in the human mind are.

If Niels Bohr compares the model of atomic structure with a planetary system, he knows it is merely a model of a transcendent and unknown reality, and if I talk of the God-image I do not deny a transcendental reality. I merely insist on the psychic reality of the God-complex or the God-image, as Niels Bohr proposes the analogy of a planetary system. He would not be as dumb as to believe that his model is an exact and true replica of the atom. No empiricist in his senses would believe his models to be the eternal truth itself. He knows too well how many changes any kind of reality undergoes in becoming a conscious representation.

All my ideas are names, models, and hypotheses for a better understanding of observable facts. I never dreamt that intelligent people could misunderstand them as theological statements, i.e., hypotheses. I was obviously too naïve in this regard and that is the reason why I was sometimes not careful enough to repeat time and again: "But what I mean is only the psychic image of a *noumenon*"[4] (Kant's thing-in-itself, which is not a negation as you know).

My empirical standpoint is so disappointingly simple that it needs only an average intelligence and a bit of common sense to understand it, but it needs an uncommon amount of prejudice or even ill-will to misunderstand it, as it seems to me. I am sorry if I bore you with my commonplaces. But you asked for it. You can find them in most of my books, beginning with the year 1912,[5] almost half a century ago and not yet noticed by authorities like Buber. I have spent a lifetime of work on psychological and psychopathological investigations. Buber criticizes me in a field in which he is incompetent and which he does not even understand.

Sincerely yours, C. G. JUNG

Notes

(*Letters* II, 570–73)
Letter was addressed to Mr. Smith, then in Villanova, Pennsylvania. Now assistant professor of philosophy and religion, Trenton State College (New Jersey). At the time of writing Smith was preparing as a thesis "A Critical Analysis of Religious and Philosophical Issues Between Buber and Jung." Cf. Jung's letter to Erich Neumann, 28 February 1952, n. 9, in *Letters* II, 243.

1. In his letter Smith had reported a conversation with Buber in which the latter had accused Jung of being a "monologist," having reduced God to an object, and maintaining that Jung's statement that without man no God would be possible was an ontological denial of God.

2. *Septem Sermones ad Mortuos.* Cf. Jung's letter to Alphonse Maeder, 19 January 1917, n. 1, in *Letters* I, 34.

3. Cf. Jung's letter to Father Victor White, 5 October 1945, n. 2, in *Letters* I, 384.

4. "An object of purely intellectual intuition, devoid of all phenomenal attributes" (*Shorter Oxford Dict.*). The term was introduced by Kant to distinguish between "noumenon" and "phenomenon" as "an immediate object of perception."

5. Date of publication of *Wandlungen und Symbole der Libido* (orig. version of *Symbols of Transformation*).

To Pastor Tanner

Dear Pastor Tanner, 12 February 1959

Before going into the question[1] you have asked me I would like to thank you for the sympathetic interest you have taken in my opinions.

As you rightly remark, it is difficult to discuss the question of "faith without religion" because we must first establish what exactly we mean by "religion." Naturally I can define this concept only in psychological terms, and this definition is fundamental to everything I say about religion. I distinguish between "religion" and "creed"; the one is generic, the other specific. The ancients derived *religio* from *relegere* or *religere*, to ponder, to take account of, to observe (e.g., in prayer). Cicero: *religiosus ex relegendo;*[2] *religens* = god-fearing. A *conscientias scrupulus*[3] has *religio*. *Religio is iustitia erga deos*[4] (Cicero). *Divum religio i.e. religio erga deos*[5] (Lucretius). *Conficere sacra Cereris summa religione*[6] (Cicero). The Church Fathers, among them St. Augustine, derive it from *religare*, to bind, to reconnect: *Religio ex eo dicta est, quod nos religat Deo,*[7] and: *Religio vera ea est, qua se uni Deo anima, unde se peccato velut abruperat, reconcilatione religat.*[8]

The latter interpretation derives on the one hand from the Jewish idea of marriage with God,[9] to which man can be unfaithful, and on the other hand from the character of Yahweh, i.e., from his injustice, which in Hellenistic times led to the conception of an *advocate*, foreshadowed in the Book of Job, who represents man at the heavenly court, as in Daniel and especially in the Book of Enoch (1st cent.). The distance between God and man is so great that Yahweh sees himself obliged to set up an embassy among men—the ambassador is his own son—and to deliver a missive to them (the gospel). At the same time Christ is the mediator with the title of *filius hominis*, Son of Man, as in Daniel and Enoch, and, as such, also an advocate.

The Jewish conception of the religious relationship with God as a legal contract (covenant!) gives way in the Christian conception to a love relationship, which is equally an aspect of the marriage with God. The bond of love can also be severed by estrangement and adultery.

As a contrast to this Judaeo-Christian conception we have the totally alien views current in pagan antiquity: the gods are exalted men and embodiments of ever-present powers whose will and whose moods must be complied with. Their *numina*[10] must be carefully studied, they must be propitiated by sacrifices just as the favour of archaic princes is won by gifts. Here religion means a watchful, wary, thoughtful, careful, prudent, expedient, and calculating attitude towards the powers-that-be, with not a trace of that legal and emotional contract which can be broken like a marriage.

Obviously the idea of marriage with God is a later and special development, whereas the original form of *religio* is, without question, aptly characterized by the implications of *relegere*. I prefer this interpretation of *religio* because it is in better accord with the general psychological findings.

By "religion," then, I mean a kind of attitude which takes careful and conscientious account of certain numinous feelings, ideas, and events and reflects upon them; and by "belief" or "creed" I mean an organized community which collectively professes a specific belief or a specific ethos and mode of behaviour. "Faith without religion" could therefore be translated as "(non-denominational) religion without creed," manifestly an unorganized, non-collective, entirely individual exercise of the "religious function." (By the latter I mean the allegiance, surrender, or submission to a supraordinate factor or to a "convincing" [= overpowering!] principle: *religio erga principium*.[11]) This trend is characteristic of present-day humanity, especially the young. The reason for this singular phenomenon, as I see it, is that people have grown rather *tired of believing* and are worn out by the effort of having to cling on to ideas which seem incomprehensible to them and are therefore quite literally *unbelievable*. This doubt is only reinforced by contemporary events. Things are going on in the world which make the public ask: Is it possible that a world in which such things happen is ruled by a good God, by a Summum Bonum? Our world is actually riven in two by an Iron Curtain, and in one half all religious activity is discouraged or suppressed, and the "Prince of Lies," the devil, who in our half has lost all substance by evaporating into a mere *privatio boni*, has for reasons of state been elevated into the supreme principle of political action. These facts have a highly suggestive effect on Christians who profess the collective belief. Whenever *belief is* stressed, demanded or expected, *doubt* infallibly increases and so does the vulnerability of belief in particular tenets.

In consequence, the tenets of belief have to be purified, or made easier, by being relieved of their principal encumbrances, which for the rationalist are their particularly obnoxious "mythological" components. Bultmann's endeavours are obviously intended to serve this purpose. Where they should or could stop is highly questionable. Christ as "Redeemer," for instance, is a mythologem of the first order, and so too is the "Son of God," the "Son of Man," the "Son of the Virgin," etc. "Faith without religion" or "religion without creed" is simply a logical consequence which has got out of Bultmann's control.

But if the believer without religion now thinks that he has got rid of mythology he is deceiving himself: he cannot get by without "myth." *Religio is* by its very nature always an *erga*, a "towards," no matter whether the following accusative be "God," "Redeemer," a philosophical idea or an ethical principle;

it is always a "mythic" or transcendental statement. This is naturally also the case when the ultimate principle is called "matter." Only the totally naïve think this is the opposite of "myth." *Materia* is in the end simply a chthonic mother goddess, and the late Pope seems to have had an inkling of this. (Cf. the second Encyclical[12] to the dogma of the Assumption!)

Clearly the anti-mythological trend is due to the difficulties we have in clinging on to our previous mythological tenets of belief. Nowadays they demand too much of the effort to believe. This was not so in earlier centuries, with their very limited knowledge of nature. It needed no *sacrificium intellectus* to believe in miracles, and the report of the birth, life, death, and resurrection of the Redeemer could still pass as biography. All this has radically changed in recent times under the compelling influence of scientific rationalism, and the aversion of the younger generation for mythology seems the natural outcome of the premise: we are tired of the excessive effort of having to believe, because the object of belief is no longer inherently convincing. The dogma of the Trinity, the divine nature of the Redeemer, the Incarnation through the Holy Ghost, Christ's miraculous deeds and resurrection, are more conducive to doubt than to belief. One dogma after another falls. The "message of the Crucified and Risen Christ" is just not understood any more, but is, at most, felt as a well-meant object lesson in ethics that is conceded to have some practical utility. From here it is but a short step to the view that certain ethical principles can be acquired without the mythological trimmings.

But for people with religious sensibilities this rationalism is not enough; they have a dim suspicion that ethics needs a different foundation from the one which Janus-faced reason grants it. "Reason" is, notoriously, not necessarily ethical any more than intelligence is. These people sense in religion an indispensable I-Thou relationship which is not at hand in any rational decisions based on ego-conditioned judgments. They therefore reserve for themselves a personal relationship to Christ, as can plainly be seen in the Christocentric trend of recent developments in Protestantism. This conception of belief presupposes only *one* mythologem: the continuing, living presence of the Risen Christ. For many religious people today even this concession to myth is dropped and they content themselves with a bashfully veiled theism[13] which has a minimum of the traditional mythic encumbrances. Beyond that there are only surrogates like exotic theosophical ideas or other regressive -isms, all of which culminate in materialism, where one succumbs to the illusion of having finally escaped each and every mythological bugbear.

With this radical "demythologization" *religious communication* comes to a dead end too. Myth is pre-eminently a social phenomenon: it is told by the many and heard by the many. It gives the ultimately unimaginable religious experience an image, a form in which to express itself, and thus makes community life possible, whereas a merely subjective religious experience lacking the traditional mythic imagery remains inarticulate and asocial, and, if it does anything at all, it fosters a spiritually *anchoritic life*.

Although the anchorite does not represent a model for living, the solitude of religious experience can be, and will be, an unavoidable and necessary transitional phase for everyone who seeks the essential experience, that is to say the *primordial* religious experience. This alone forms the true and unshakable foundation of his inner life of belief. But once he has attained this certitude, he will in the normal course of things be unable to remain alone with it. His fulfillment spills over in communication, and communication requires language. But what language shall he choose? Obviously one that is generally understood. So for practical reasons he will not invent a new idiom, which would merely do him a bad service by branding him as an unintelligible eccentric, but will be bound to make use of the immemorial myth, in this case the Christian myth, even at the risk of being accused of pouring new wine into old bottles. If his individual experience is a living thing, it will share the quality of all life, which does not stagnate but, being in continual flux, brings ever new aspects to light. The old myth, which always holds within it something yet older and more aboriginal, remains the same, this being an essential quality of all forms of religion; it only undergoes a new interpretation. Thus the Reformation was no more a repristination of the early Church than the Renaissance was a mere revival of antiquity, but a new exposition which could not throw off its own historical evolution.

The imageless and unbiased experience modern man strives for will—unless he aspires to the role of the prophet—lead to the modest conclusion that notwithstanding its numinosity it was after all only his own subjective experience. If he has the necessary knowledge at his disposal, he will also come to see that it was not unique in its substance but has been observed in many other cases as well. Furthermore, he will have no difficulty in understanding that experiences of this kind are inherent in the nature of the psyche at all times, no matter to what causative God they may be attributed. We can in imagination and belief go beyond the psyche, just as in fantasy we can go beyond the three-dimensional world. But we can have immediate *knowledge* only of the psychic, even though we may be *sure* that our imageless experience was an "objective" fact—a fact, however, that can never be proved.

Nowadays one very often hears people asserting that something or other is "only" psychic, as though there were anything that is *not* psychic. When we assert that something is present, we must necessarily have "representation," i.e., an image of it. If we had none, it would at the very least be unconscious to us. But then we would not be able to assert, let alone prove, anything about it either. The presence of objects is entirely dependent on our powers of representation, and "representation" is a psychic act. But these days "only psychic" simply means "nothing." Outside psychology only modern physics has had to acknowledge that no science can be carried on without the psyche.[14]

For more than a hundred years the world has been confronted with the concept of an unconscious,[15] and for more than fifty years with the empirical investigation of it, but only a very few people have drawn the necessary conclusions. Nobody seems to have noticed that without a reflecting psyche the world might as well not exist, and that, in consequence, consciousness is a second world-creator, and also that the cosmogonic myths do not describe the absolute beginning of the world but rather the dawning of consciousness as the second Creation.

Myths are descriptions of psychic processes and developments, therefore. Since these, so long and so far as they are still in the unconscious state, prove to be inaccessible to any arbitrary alteration, they exert a compelling influence on consciousness as pre-existent conditioning factors. This influence is neither abolished nor corrected by any environmental conditions. From ancient times, therefore, it has been deemed a *daemonium*.[16] No amount of reason can conjure this empirical fact out of existence.

Now whether these archetypes, as I have called these pre-existent and pre-forming psychic factors, are regarded as "mere" instincts or as daemons and gods makes no difference at all to their dynamic effect. But it often makes a mighty difference whether they are undervalued as "mere" instincts or overvalued as gods.

These new insights enable us to gain a new understanding of mythology and of its importance as an expression of intrapsychic processes. And from this in turn we gain a new understanding of the Christian myth, and more particularly of its apparently obnoxious statements that are contrary to all reason. If the Christian myth is not to become obsolete—which would be a sell-out with quite unpredictable consequences—the need for a more psychologically oriented interpretation that would salvage its meaning and guarantee its continuance forces itself upon us. The danger of its final destruction is considerable when even the theologians start to demolish the classic world of mythological ideas without putting a new medium of expression in its place.

I must apologize, my dear Pastor, for the unusual prolixity of my letter. Considering the importance of your question my exertions are small enough. At the age of 84 I am somewhat tired, but I am concerned about our culture, which would be in danger of losing its roots if the continuity of tradition were broken. For close on sixty years I have felt the pulse of modern man from all continents of the earth, and have experienced far too much of the woes of our time not to take the gravity of your question profoundly to heart.

Yours sincerely, C. G. JUNG

Notes

(*Letters* II, 482–88)

Tanner's first name was not obtained. Letter was addressed to Kronbühl, Canton St. Gallen, Switzerland.

1. Tanner asked Jung's opinion on the teachings of certain theologians, in particular the followers of Dietrich Bonhoeffer (1906–45), according to which modern man needs a "faith without religion."

2. "Those who carefully . . . retraced everything which concerned the worship of the gods were called religious from *relegere*." Cicero, *De natura deorum*, 2, 28.

3. = scruples of conscience.

4. "Religion (is) that which gives due reverence [lit. does justice] to the gods." Cicero, *De partitione oratoriae*, 78.

5. "*Divum religio* here means reverence towards the gods." Lucretius, *De rerum natura*, 6, 1276.

6. "To perform the sacred rites of Ceres with the strictest reverence." Cicero, *Pro Balbo*, 24.

7. "The word religion is derived from what binds us to God." Augustine, *Retractiones*, 1.13.9.

8. "True religion is that by which the soul binds itself to the One God by reconciliation, whence by sin in the same manner it has severed itself." Augustine, *De quantitate animae*, 36.

9. Hosea 2:19: "And I will betroth thee unto me for ever."

10. *Numen* (whence *numinosum*) means "nod" (of the head); in a narrower sense, the god showing his will by nodding his head. Cf. *Aion*, *CW* 9ii, par. 110, quoted passage.

11. = religion (due reverence) towards a principle.

12. *Ad Caeli Reginam*. Cf. Jung's letter to Upton Sinclair, 7 January 1955, n. 7, in *Letters* II, 203.

13. Belief in a god, but with denial of revelation.

14. Cf. Jung's letter to Edward Whitmont, 4 Mar. 1950, n. 1, in *Letters* I, 546–7.

15. For instance C. G. Carus, *Psyche* (1846). The book opens with the sentence: "The key to knowledge of the nature of conscious psychic life lies in the realm of the unconscious."

16. The intermediate realm of supernatural powers between gods and men.

To Father Victor White

[ORIGINAL IN ENGLISH]

Dear Victor, 24 November 1953

Forget for once dogmatics and listen to what psychology has to say concerning your problem: *Christ as a symbol is far from being invalid,*[1] although he is one side of the self and the devil the other. This pair of opposites is contained in the creator as his right and left hand, as Clemens Romanus says.[2] From the psychological standpoint the experience of God the creator is the perception of an overpowering impulse issuing from the sphere of the unconscious.[3] We don't know whether this influence or compulsion deserves to be called good or evil, although we cannot prevent ourselves from welcoming or cursing it, giving it a bad or a good name, according to our subjective condition. Thus Yahweh has either aspect because he is essentially the creator *(primus motor)* and because he is yet unreflected in his whole nature.

With the *incarnation* the picture changes completely, as it means that God becomes manifest in the form of Man who is conscious and therefore cannot avoid judgment. He simply has to call the one good and the other evil. It is a historical fact that the real devil only came into existence together with Christ.[4] Though Christ was God, as Man he was detached from God and he watched the devil falling out of heaven,[5] removed from God as he (Christ) was separated from God inasmuch as he was human. In his utter helplessness on the cross, he even confessed that God had forsaken him. The Deus Pater would leave him to his fate as he always "strafes" those whom he has filled before with this abundance by breaking his promise.[6] This is exactly what S. Joannes à cruce describes as the "dark night of the soul." It is the reign of darkness, which is also God, but an ordeal for Man. The Godhead has a double aspect, and as Master Eckhart says: God is not blissful in his mere Godhead, and that is the reason for his incarnation.[7]

But becoming Man, he becomes at the same time a definite being, which is this and not that. Thus the very first thing Christ must do is to sever himself from his shadow and call it the devil (sorry, but the Gnostics of Irenaeus[8] already knew it!).

When a patient in our days is about to emerge from an unconscious condition, he is instantly confronted with his *shadow* and he has to decide for the good, otherwise he goes down the drain. *Nolens volens* he "imitates" Christ and follows his example. The first step on the way to individuation consists in the discrimination between himself and the shadow.

In this stage the Good is the goal of individuation, and consequently Christ represents the self.

The next step is the *problem of the shadow:* in dealing with darkness, you have got to cling to the Good, otherwise the devil devours you. You need every bit of your goodness in dealing with Evil and just there. To keep the light alive in the darkness, that's the point, and only there your candle makes sense.

Now tell me how many people you know who can say with any verisimilitude that they have finished their dealings with the devil and consequently can chuck the Christian symbol overboard?

As a matter of fact, our society has not even begun to face its shadow or to develop those Christian virtues so badly needed in dealing with the powers of darkness. Our society cannot afford the luxury of cutting itself loose from the *imitatio Christi,* even if it should know that the *conflict with the shadow,* i.e., Christ versus Satan, is only the first step on the way to the faraway goal of the unity of the self in God.

It is true however that the *imitatio Christi* leads you into your own very real and *Christlike conflict* with darkness, and the more you are engaged in this war and in these attempts at peacemaking helped by the anima, the more you begin to look forward beyond the Christian aeon to the *Oneness of the Holy Spirit. He is the pneumatic state the creator attains to through the phase of incarnation.* He is the experience of every individual that has undergone the complete abolition of his ego through the absolute opposition expressed by the symbol Christ versus Satan.

The state of the Holy Spirit means a restitution of the original oneness of the unconscious on the level of consciousness. That is alluded to, as I see it, by Christ's logion: "Ye are gods."[9] This state is not quite understandable yet. It is a mere anticipation.

The later development from the Christian aeon to the one of the S. spiritus has been called the *evangelium aeternum* by Gioacchino da Fiori[10] in a time when the great tearing apart had just begun. Such vision seems to be granted by divine grace as a sort of *consolamentum,*[11] so that man is not left in a completely hopeless state during the time of darkness. We are actually in the state of darkness viewed from the standpoint of history. We are still within the Christian aeon and just beginning to realize the age of darkness where we shall need Christian virtues *to the utmost.*

In such a state we could not possibly dismiss Christ as an invalid symbol although we clearly foresee the approach of his opposite. Yet we don't see and feel the latter as the preliminary step toward the future union of the divine opposites, but rather as a menace against everything that is good, beautiful, and

the "phantom menace"

holy to us. The *adventus diaboli* does not invalidate the Christian symbol of the self, on the contrary: it complements it. It is a mysterious transmutation of both.

Since we are living in a society that is unconscious of this development and far from understanding the importance of the Christian symbol, we are called upon to hinder its invalidation, although some of us are granted the vision of a future development. But none of us could safely say that he has accomplished the assimilation and integration of the shadow.

Since the Christian church is the community of all those having surrendered to the principle of the *imitatio Christi*, this institution (i.e., such a mental attitude) is to be maintained until it is clearly understood what the assimilation of the shadow means. Those that foresee, must—as it were—stay behind their vision in order to help and to teach, particularly so if they belong to the church as her appointed servants.

You should not mind if some of your analysands are helped out of the church. It is their destiny and adventure. Others will stay in it anyhow. It does not matter whether the ecclesiastical powers-that-be approve of your vision or not. When the time is fulfilled a new orientation will irresistibly break through, as one has seen in the case of the Conceptio Immaculata[12] and the Assumptio which both deviate from the time-hallowed principle of apostolic authority,[13] a thing unheard of before. It would be a lack of responsibility and a rather auto-erotic attitude if we were to deprive our fellow beings of a vitally necessary symbol before they had a reasonable chance to understand it thoroughly, and all this because it is not complete if envisaged from an anticipated stage we ourselves in our individual lives have not yet made real.

Anybody going ahead is alone or thinks he is lonely at times, no matter whether he is in the church or in the world. Your practical work as *directeur de conscience* brings to you individuals having something in their character that corresponds with certain aspects of your personality (like the many men fitting themselves as stones into the edifice of the tower in the *Shepherd of Hermas*).[14]

Whatever your ultimate decision will be, you ought to realize beforehand that staying in the church makes sense as it is important to make people understand what the symbol of Christ means, and such understanding is indispensable to any further development. There is no way round it, as little as we can eliminate from our life old age, illness, and death, or Buddha's Nidana-chain of evils.[15] The vast majority of people are still in such an unconscious state that one should almost protect them from the full shock of the real *imitatio Christi*. Moreover we are still in the Christian aeon, threatened with a complete annihilation of our world.

As there are not only the many but also the few, somebody is entrusted with the task of looking ahead and talking of the things to be. That is partially my job, but I have to be very careful not to destroy the things that are. Nobody will be so foolish as to destroy the foundations when he is adding an upper storey to his house, and how can he build it really if the foundations are not yet properly laid? Thus, making the statement that Christ is not a complete symbol of the self, I cannot make it complete by abolishing it. I must keep it therefore in order to build up the symbol of the perfect contradiction in God by adding this darkness to the *lumen de lumine*.[16]

Thus I am approaching the end of the Christian aeon and I am to take up Gioacchino's anticipation and Christ's prediction of the coming of the Paraclete. This archetypal drama is at the same time exquisitely psychological and historical. We are actually living in the time of the splitting of the world and of the invalidation of Christ.

But an anticipation of a faraway future is no way out of the actual situation. It is a mere *consolamentum* for those despairing at the atrocious possibilities of the present time. Christ is still the valid symbol. Only God himself can "invalidate" him through the Paraclete.

Now that is all I can say. It is a long letter and I am tired. If it is not helpful to you, it shows at least what I think.

I have seen X. She is as right as she can be and as she usually is, and just as wrong as her nature permits, altogether as hopeful as a hysterical temperament ever can be.

You have probably heard of the little celebration we had here round the Nag-Hamadi Gnostic Codex[17] given to the Institute by a generous donor. There was even a note in the *Times*.[18] It was a disproportionate affair and neither my doing, nor liking. But I was manoeuvred into saying in the end a few words about the relation between Gnosticism and psychology.[19]

My best wishes![20]

Yours cordially, C. G.

Notes

(*Letters* II, 133–38)
1. In a letter of 8 November 1953, White said that Jung seemed to create a dilemma by maintaining that "Christ is no longer an adequate and valid symbol of the self"—a misunderstanding which Jung tries to correct here. (Most of this letter is published in German in *Ges. Werke*, XI, Anhang, 681ff.)
2. Cf. Dr. H., 17 Mar. 51, n. 10.
3. "Psychology and Religion," *CW* 11, par. 137: ". . . it is always the overwhelming psychic factor that is called 'God.'"
4. Jung was, of course, perfectly aware of the fact that the figure of Satan oc-

curs in the Old Testament. What he means is that, Christ being the incarnation of God's goodness, the devil becomes a psychological inevitability as the incarnation of evil—in other words the devil is the personification of Christ's split-off dark side. Cf. *Aion*, *CW* 9ii, par. 113.

5. Luke 10:18.
6. Rev. 3:19.
7. Cf. *Psychological Types*, *CW* 6, par. 418.
8. *Aion*, par. 75, n. 23.
9. John 10:34, referring to Psalm 82:6.
10. Joachim of Flora (*ca.* 1145–1202), Italian mystic and theologian. He taught that there are three periods of world history: the Age of the Law, or of the Father; the Age of the Gospel, or of the Son; and the Age of the Holy Spirit, or of Contemplation. His teachings were condemned by the Fourth Lateran Council, 1215. Cf. *Aion*, pars. 137ff.
11. The rite of "consoling" or "comforting," the central rite of the Cathars (cf. ibid., pars. 225ff.). It was baptism with the Spirit, considered to be the Paraclete sent by Christ (the "comforter which is the Holy Ghost," John 14:26). The *consolamentum* freed man from original sin.
12. The dogma of the Immaculate Conception pronounced as "of faith" by Pius IX in the bull *Ineffabilis Deus* (1854).
13. The principle by which all that the Apostles were supposed to have taught was regarded as infallible, and by which nothing in religious teaching or practice was considered Christian unless it was of Apostolic origin.
14. An early Christian text ascribed to Hermas, brother of Pope Pius I (*ca.* 140–55), containing lessons to be disseminated for the instruction of the Church. Cf. *Psychological Types*, *CW* 6, pars. 381ff., esp. par. 390 for the building of the tower.
15. The twelve *nidanas* of Buddhism, starting with "ignorance" and ending with "despair," form the *nidana*-chain, the conditions which keep man a prisoner in *samsara*, the endless chain of rebirth. In Jung's *Collected Works*, *Nidana* is spelled two different ways; cf. his letter (Nidhana) to the anonymous Frau N., 28 June 1956, in *Letters II*, 311.]
16. The Council of Nicaea (325) defined the everlasting Word, "the true light" (John 1:9), as *lumen de lumine*, light of the light.
17. A Gnostic Papyrus in Coptic found in 1945 near the village of Nag-Hamâdi in Upper Egypt and acquired in 1952 for the C. G. Jung Institute. It is now known as the Codex Jung; its main part consists of the so-called "Gospel of Truth" attributed to Valentinus. This has been published under the editorship of M. Malinine, H. C. Puech, and G. Quispel as *Evangelium Veritatis* (Zurich, 1956). Two further parts: *De Resurrectione* (1963) and *Epistula Jacobi Apocrypha* (1968); the fourth part, *Tractatus Tripartitus*, is still unpublished.
18. "New Light on a Coptic Codex," *The Times*, 16 November 1953.

19. Jung's address is in *CW* 18, pars. 1514ff.

20. White answered in a short note of 20 November 1953, saying how "immensely grateful" he was for the letter, adding: ". . . the points that 'ring the bell' most immediately are those about the 'autoerotic attitude' and about 'an anticipation of a faraway future is no way out.'"

To Father Victor White

Dear Victor,   Bollingen, 10 April 1954

Your letter[1] has been lying on my desk waiting for a suitable time to be answered. In the meantime I was still busy with a preface I had promised to P. Radin and K. Kerenyi. They are going to bring out a book together about the figure of the trickster.[2] He is the collective shadow. I finished my preface yesterday. I suppose you know the Greek Orthodox priest Dr. Zacharias?[3] He has finished his book representing a reception, or better—an attempt—to integrate Jungian psychology into Christianity as he sees it. Dr. Rudin S.J. from the Institute of Apologetics did not like it. Professor Gebhard Frei on the other hand was very positive about it.

I am puzzled about your conception of Christ and I try to understand it. It looks to me as if you were mixing up the idea of Christ being human and being divine. Inasmuch as he is divine he knows, of course, everything, because all things macrocosmic are supposed to be microcosmic as well and can therefore be said to be known by the self. (Things moreover behave as if they were known.) It is an astonishing fact, indeed, that the collective unconscious seems to be in contact with nearly everything. There is of course no empirical evidence for such a generalization, but plenty of it for its indefinite extension. The *sententia*, therefore: *animam Christi nihil ignoravisse*[4] etc. is not contradicted by psychological experience. *Rebus sic stantibus*, Christ as the self can be said *ab initio cognovisse omnia* etc. I should say that Christ knew his shadow—Satan—whom he cut off from himself right in the beginning of his career. The self is a unit, consisting however of two, i.e., of opposites, otherwise it would not be a totality. Christ has consciously divorced himself from his shadow. Inasmuch as he is divine, he is the self, yet only its white half. Inasmuch as he is human, he has never lost his shadow completely, but seems to have been conscious of it. How could he say otherwise "Do not call me good . . ."?[5] It is also reasonable to believe that as a human he was not wholly conscious of it, and inasmuch as he was unconscious he projected it indubitably. The split through his self made him as a human being as good as possible, although he was unable to reach the degree of perfection his white self already possessed. The Catholic doctrine cannot but declare that *Christ even as a human being knew everything*. This is the logical consequence of the perfect union of the *duae naturae*. Christ as understood by the Church is to me a spiritual, i.e., mythological being; even his humanity

153

is divine as it is generated by the celestial Father and exempt from original sin. When I speak of him as a human being, I mean its few traces we can gather from the gospels. It is not enough for the reconstruction of an empirical character. Moreover even if we could reconstruct an individual personality, it would not fulfil the role of redeemer and God-man who is identical with the "all-knowing" self. Since the individual human being is characterized by a selection of tendencies and qualities, it is a specification and not a wholeness, i.e., it cannot be individual without incompleteness and restriction, whereas the Christ of the doctrine is perfect, complete, whole and therefore not individual at all, but a collective mythologem, viz. an archetype. He is far more divine than human and far more universal than individual.

Concerning the omniscience it is important to know that *Adam* already was equipped with supernatural knowledge according to Jewish and Christian tradition,[6] all the more so Christ.

I think that the great split[7] in those days was by no means a mistake but a very important collective fact of synchronistic correspondence with the then new aeon of Pisces. Archetypes, in spite of their conservative nature, are not static but *in a continuous dramatic flux.* Thus the self as a monad or continuous unit would be dead. But it lives inasmuch as it splits and unites again. There is no energy without opposites!

All conservatives and institutionalists are Pharisees, if you apply this name without prejudice. Thus it was to be expected that just the better part of Jewry would be hurt most by the revelation of an exclusively good God and loving Father. This novelty emphasized with disagreeable clearness that the Yahweh hitherto worshipped had some additional, less decorous propensities. For obvious reasons the orthodox Pharisees could not defend their creed by insisting on the bad qualities of their God. Christ with his teaching of an exclusively good God must have been most awkward for them. They probably believed him to be hypocritical, since this was his main objection against them. One gets that way when one has to hold on to something which once has been good and had meant considerable progress or improvement at the time. It was an enormous step forward when Yahweh revealed himself as a *jealous* God, letting his chosen people feel that he was after them with blessings and with punishments, and that God's goal was man. Not knowing better, they cheated him by obeying his Law literally. But as Job discovered Yahweh's primitive amorality, God found out about the trick of observing the Law and swallowing camels.[8]

The old popes and bishops succeeded in getting so much heathendom, barbarism and real evil out of the Church that it became much better than some centuries before: there were no Alexander VI,[9] no auto-da-fés, no thumbscrews and racks any more, so that the compensatory drastic virtues (asceticism etc.) lost their meaning to a certain extent. The great split, having been a merely spiritual fact for a long time, has at last got into the world, as a rule in its coarsest and least recognizable form, viz. as the iron curtain, the completion of the second Fish.[10]

Now a new synthesis must begin. But how can absolute evil be connected and identified with absolute good? It seems to be impossible. When Christ withstood Satan's temptation, that was the fatal moment when the shadow was cut off. Yet it had to be cut off in order to enable man to become morally conscious. If the moral opposites could be united at all, they would be suspended altogether and there could be no morality at all. That is certainly not what synthesis aims at. In such a case of irreconcilability the opposites are united by a neutral or ambivalent bridge, a symbol expressing either side in such a way that they can function together.[11] This symbol is the *cross* as interpreted of old, viz. as the tree of life or simply as the tree to which Christ is inescapably affixed. This particular feature points to the compensatory significance of the tree: the tree symbolizes that entity from which Christ had been separated and with which he ought to be connected again to make his life or his being complete. In other words, the *Crucifixus* is the symbol uniting the absolute moral opposites. Christ represents the light; the tree, the darkness; he the ʻon, it the mother. Both are *androgynous* (tree = phallus).[12] Christ is so much identical with the cross that both terms have become almost interchangeable in ecclesiastical language (f.i. "redeemed through Christ or through the cross" etc.). The tree brings back all that has been lost through Christ's extreme spiritualization, namely the elements of nature. Through its branches and leaves the tree gathers the powers of light and air, and through its roots those of the earth and the water. Christ was suffering on account of his split and he recovers his perfect life at Easter, when he is buried again in the womb of the virginal mother. (Represented also in the myth of Attis by the tree, to which an image of Attis was nailed, then cut down and carried into the cave of the mother Kybele.[13] The Nativity Church of Bethlehem is erected over an Attis sanctuary!)[14] This mythical complex seems to represent a further development of the old drama, existence becoming real through reflection in consciousness, Job's tragedy.[15] But now it is the problem of dealing with the results of conscious discrimination. The first attempt is moral appreciation and decision for the Good. Although this decision is indispensable, it is not too good in the long run. You must not get stuck with it, otherwise you grow out of life and die slowly. Then the one-sided emphasis on the Good becomes doubtful, but there is apparently no possibility of reconciling Good and Evil. That is where we are now.

The symbolic history of the Christ's life shows, as the essential teleological tendency, the crucifixion, viz. the union of Christ with the symbol of the tree. It is no longer a matter of an impossible reconciliation of Good and Evil, but of man with his vegetative (= unconscious) life. In the case of the

Christian symbol the tree however is dead and man upon the Cross is going to die, i.e., the solution of the problem takes place after death. That is so as far as Christian truth goes. But it is possible that the Christian symbolism expresses man's mental condition in the aeon of Pisces, as the ram and the bull gods do for the ages of Aries and Taurus. In this case the post-mortal solution would be symbolic of an entirely new psychological status, viz. that of Aquarius, which is certainly a oneness, presumably that of the Anthropos, the realization of Christ's allusion: "*Dii estis.*"[16] This is a formidable secret and difficult to understand, because it means that man will be essentially God and God man. The signs pointing in this direction consist in the fact that the cosmic power of self-destruction is given into the hands of man and that man inherits the dual nature of the Father. He will [mis]understand it and he will be tempted to ruin the universal life of the earth by radioactivity. Materialism and atheism, the negation of God, are indirect means to attain this goal. Through the negation of God one becomes deified, i.e., god-almighty-like, and then one knows what is good for mankind. That is how destruction begins. The intellectual schoolmasters in the Kremlin are a classic example. The danger of following the same path is very great indeed. It begins with the lie, i.e., the projection of the shadow.

There is need of people knowing about their shadow, because there must be somebody who does not project. They ought to be in a visible position where they would be expected to project and unexpectedly they do not project! They can thus set a visible example which would not be seen if they were invisible.

There is certainly Pharisaism, law consciousness, power drive, sex obsession, and the wrong kind of formalism in the Church. But these things are symptoms that the old showy and easily understandable ways and methods have lost their significance and should be slowly replaced by more meaningful principles. This indeed means trouble with the Christian vices. Since you cannot overthrow a whole world because it harbours also some evil, it will be a more individual or "local" fight with what you rightly call *avidya*. As "tout passe," even theological books are not true forever, and even if they expect to be believed one has to tell them in a loving and fatherly way that they make some mistakes. A true and honest introverted thinking is a grace and possesses for at least a time divine authority, particularly if it is modest, simple and straight. The people who write such books are not the voice of God. They are only human. It is true that the right kind of thinking isolates oneself. But did you become a monk for the sake of congenial society? Or do you assume that it isolates only a theologian? It has done the same to me and will do so to everybody that is blessed with it.

That is the reason why there are compensatory functions. The introverted thinker is very much in need of a developed feeling, i.e., of a less autoerotic, sentimental, melodramatic and emotional relatedness to people and things. The compensation will be a hell of a conflict to begin with, but later on, by understanding what *nirdvandva*[17] means, they[18] become the pillars at the gate of the transcendent function, i.e., the *transitus* to the self. . . .

Cordially yours, C. G.

Notes

(*Letters* II, 163–68)

1. White wrote a long letter on 3 March 1954 in answer to Jung's of 24 November 1953, expressing agreement with most of what he said. It deals largely with Jung's views on the problem of "Christ's shadow," which contradict the Catholic doctrine that Christ knew everything (and therefore could not have a shadow).

2. Jung's commentary "On the Psychology of the Trickster Figure" (*CW* 9i) for Paul Radin, *The Trickster* (1956; orig. *Der göttliche Schelm*, 1954). Kerényi wrote the other commentary.

3. Cf. Jung's letter to Gerhard Zacharias, 24 August 1953, in *Letters* II, 120–21.

4. "Christ's soul was not ignorant of anything." This and the following *ab initio cognovisse omnia* ("from the beginning he knew everything") are two statements of the Holy Roman Office (one of the eleven departments of the Roman Curia) laid down in 1918 and quoted by White.

5. Cf. Matthew 19:17, Mark 10:18, Luke 18:19.

6. *Mysterium Coniunctionis, CW* 14, pars. 570ff.

7. The separation of Christ, the epitome of good, from his shadow, the devil.

8. Matthew 23:24: "Ye blind guides, which strain at a gnat, and swallow a camel."

9. Rodrigo Borgia (1431–1503), the most notorious of the corrupt and venal popes of the Renaissance.

10. The astrological sign of Pisces consists of two fishes which were frequently regarded as moving in opposite directions. Traditionally, the reign of Christ corresponds to the first fish and ended with the first millennium, whereas the second fish coincides with the reign of Antichrist, now nearing its end with the entry of the vernal equinox into the sign of Aquarius. Cf. *Aion, CW* 9ii, pars. 148f., and "Answer to Job," *CW* 11, par. 725.

11. The bridge is the "uniting symbol," which represents psychic totality, the self. Cf. *Psychological Types, CW* 6, par. 828.

12. The tree often symbolizes the mother and appears as such in the numerous tree-birth myths (cf. *Symbols of Transformation, CW* 5, Part II, ch. V). But

it is also a phallic symbol and thus has an androgynous character. (For Christ's androgyny cf. *Mysterium Coniunctionis*, pars. 526, 565 & n. 63.)

13. Attis was one of the young dying gods, the lover of Kybele, the Great Mother goddess of Anatolia. In her rites, taking place in March, a pine tree, symbol of Attis, was carried into her sanctuary. Cf. Jung's letter to Father Victor White, 25 November 1950, n. 5, in *Letters* I, 566.

14. A sanctuary of Adonis, another young dying god closely related to Attis, existed since ancient times in a cave at Bethlehem. It is supposed to be identical with Christ's birthplace, over which Constantine the Great (*ca.* 288–337) had a basilica built.

15. Cf. *Memories, Dreams, Reflections*, 338f./312, and Jung's letter to Erich Neumann, 10 March 1959, in *Letters* II, 493–96.

16. "Ye are gods." John 10:34.

17. *Nirdvandva* (Sanskrit), "free from the opposites" (love and hate, joy and sorrow, etc.). Cf. *Psychological Types*, *CW* 6, pars. 327ff.

18. Here "they" refers to the compensatory (or inferior) functions. Cf. ibid., Def. 30.

To Erich Neumann

Dear friend,   10 March 1959

Best thanks for your long and discursive letter of 18.II. What Frau Jaffé sent you was a first, as yet unrevised draft,[1] an attempt to pin down my volatile thoughts. Unfortunately the fatigue of old age prevents me from writing a letter as discursive as yours.

I

The question: *an creator sibi consciens est?*[2] is not a "pet idea" but an exceedingly painful experience with well-nigh incalculable consequences, which it is not easy to argue about. For instance, if somebody projects the self this is an unconscious act, for we know from experience that projection results only from unconsciousness.

Incarnatio means first and foremost God's birth in Christ, hence psychologically the realization of the self as something new, not present before. The man who was created before that is a "creature," albeit "made in the likeness" of God, and this implies the idea of the *filiatio* and the *sacrificium divinum*. Incarnation is, as you say, a "new experience."

"It has happened almost by accident and casually . . ."[3] This sentence might well characterize the whole process of creation. The archetype is no exception. The initial event was the arrangement of indistinct masses in spherical form. Hence this primordial archetype [mandala] appears as the first form of amorphous gases, for anything amorphous can manifest itself only in some specific form or order.

The concept of "order" is not identical with the concept of "meaning." Even an organic being is, in spite of the meaningful design implicit within it, not necessarily meaningful in the total nexus. For instance, if the world had come to an end at the Oligocene period, it would have had no meaning for man. Without the reflecting consciousness of man the world is a gigantic meaningless machine, for in our experience man is the only creature who is capable of ascertaining any meaning at all.

We still have no idea where the constructive factor in biological development is to be found. But we do know that warmbloodedness and a differentiated brain were necessary for the inception of consciousness, and thus also for the revelation of meaning. It staggers the mind even to begin to imagine the accidents and hazards that, over millions of years, transformed a lemur-like tree-dweller into a man. In this chaos of chance, synchronistic phenomena were probably at work, operating both with and against the known laws of nature to produce, in archetypal moments, syntheses which appear to us miraculous. Causality and teleology fail us here, because synchronistic phenomena manifest themselves as pure chance. The essential thing about these phenomena is that an objective event coincides meaningfully with a psychic process; that is to say, a physical event and an endopsychic one have a common meaning. This presupposes not only an all-pervading, latent meaning which can be recognized by consciousness, but, during that preconscious time, a psychoid process with which a physical event meaningfully coincides. Here the meaning cannot be recognized because there is as yet no consciousness. It is through the archetype that we come closest to this early, "irrepresentable," psychoid stage of conscious development; indeed, the archetype itself gives us direct intimations of it. Unconscious synchronicities are, as we know from experience, altogether possible, since in many cases we are unconscious of their happening, or have to have our attention drawn to the coincidence by an outsider.

II

Since the laws of probability give no ground for assuming that higher syntheses such as the psyche could arise by chance alone, there is nothing for it but to postulate a latent meaning in order to explain not only the synchronistic phenomena but also the higher syntheses. Meaningfulness always appears to be unconscious at first, and can therefore only be discovered *post hoc*; hence there is always the danger that meaning will be read into things where actually there is nothing of the sort. Synchronistic experiences serve our turn here. They point to a latent meaning which is independent of consciousness.

Since a creation without the reflecting consciousness of man has no discernible meaning, the hypothesis of a latent meaning endows man with a cosmogonic significance, a true *raison d'être*. If on the other hand the latent meaning is attributed to the Creator as part of a conscious plan of creation, the question arises: Why should the Creator stage-manage this whole phenomenal world since he already knows what he can reflect himself in, and why should he reflect himself at all since he is already conscious of himself? Why should he create alongside his own omniscience a second, inferior consciousness—millions of dreary little mirrors when he knows in advance just what the image they reflect will look like?

After thinking all this over I have come to the conclusion that being "made in the likeness" applies not only to man but also to the Creator: he resembles man or is his likeness, which is to say that he is just as unconscious as man or even more unconscious, since according to the myth of the *incarnatio* he actually felt obliged to become man and offer himself to man as a sacrifice.

Here I must close, aware as I am that I have only touched on the main points (so it seems to me) in your letter, which I found very difficult to understand in parts. It is not levity but my *molesta senectus*[4] that forces economy on me. With best greetings,

Sincerely yours, C. G. JUNG

Notes

(*Letters* II, 493–96)

Parts of this letter were published in Jung and Jaffé, *Erinnerungen, Träume, Gedanken*, 376ff. (not in *Memories, Dreams, Reflections*). The whole letter, together with Neumann's of 18 February 1959, is in Jaffé, *Der Mythus vom Sinn im Werk von C. G. Jung* (1967), 179ff. (not in tr., *The Myth of Meaning*).

1. The first draft of ch. XII, "Late Thoughts," in *Memories, Dreams, Reflections*.
2. = is the creator conscious of himself?
3. Paraphrase of a passage in *Memories, Dreams, Reflections* (which Neumann had read in MS form): "Natural history tells us of a haphazard and casual transformation of species over hundreds of millions of years of devouring and being devoured" (339/312). He objected to the "Darwinistic residue" in "haphazard and casual transformation" and suggested a different theory "in which your concept of the archetype and of absolute and extraneous knowledge will play a part." Concerning Neumann's concept of extraneous knowledge—a knowledge steering the life process and in which the division between inner and outer reality, psyche and world, is transcended in a "unitary reality"—cf. his "Die Psyche und die Wandlung der Wirklichkeitsebenen," *Eranos Jahrbuch 1952*.
4. = burdensome old age.

Anonymous

Dear Frau N.,   28 June 1956

It is hard to accept the fate you have described.[1] Quite apart from the moral achievement required, complete acceptance depends very much on the conception you have of fate. An exclusively causal view is permissible only in the realm of physical or inorganic processes. The teleological view is more important in the biological sphere and also in psychology, where the answer makes sense only if it explains the "why" of it. So it is pointless to cling on to the causes, since they cannot be altered anyway. It is more rewarding to know what is to be done with the consequences, and the kind of attitude one has—or should have—to them. Then the question at once arises: Does the event have a *meaning*? Did a hidden purpose of fate, or God's will, have a hand in it, or was it nothing but "chance," a "mishap"?

If it was God's purpose to try us, why then must an innocent child suffer? This question touches on a problem that is clearly answered in the Book of Job. Yahweh's amorality or notorious injustice changes only with the Incarnation into the exclusive goodness of God. This transformation is connected with his becoming man and therefore exists only if it is made real through the conscious fulfillment of God's will in man. If this realization does not occur, not only the Creator's amorality is revealed but also his unconsciousness. With no human consciousness to reflect themselves in, good and evil simply happen, or rather, there is no good and evil, but only a sequence of neutral events, or what the Buddhists call the Nidhana-chain, the uninterrupted causal concatenation leading to suffering, old age, sickness, and death. Buddha's insight and the Incarnation in Christ break the chain through the intervention of the enlightened human consciousness, which thereby acquires a metaphysical and cosmic significance.

In the light of this realization, the mishap changes into a happening which, if taken to heart, allows us to glimpse deeply into the cruel and pitiless imperfections of Creation and also into the mystery of the Incarnation. The happening then turns into that *felix culpa*[2] which Adam brought on himself by his disobedience. Suffering, Meister Eckhart says, is the "swiftest steed that bears you to perfection." The boon of increased self-awareness is the sufficient answer even to life's suffering, otherwise it would be meaningless and unendurable. Though the suffering of the Creation which God left imperfect cannot be done away with by the revelation of the good God's will to man, yet it can be mitigated and made meaningful.

Yours sincerely, C. G. JUNG

Notes

(*Letters* II, 310–11)

Frau N. was a woman in Switzerland.

1. N. was the mother of an imbecile child.
2. = happy fault. Cf. Jung's letter to Upton Sinclair, 7 January 1955, n. 2, in *Letters* II, 201–8.

To Elined Kotschnig

[ORIGINAL IN ENGLISH]

Dear Mrs. Kotschnig,   30 June 1956

It is not quite easy to answer your question[1] within the space of a letter. You know that we human beings are unable to explain anything that happens without or within ourselves otherwise than through the use of the intellectual means at our disposal. We always have to use mental elements similar to the facts we believe we have observed. Thus when we try to explain how God has created His world or how He behaves toward the world, the analogy we use is the way in which our creative spirit produces and behaves. When we consider the data of palaeontology with the view that a conscious creator has perhaps spent more than a thousand million years, and has made, as it seems to us, no end of detours to produce consciousness, we inevitably come to the conclusion that—if we want to explain His doings at all—His behaviour is strikingly similar to a being with an at least very limited consciousness. Although aware of the things that are and the next steps to take, He has apparently neither foresight of an ulterior goal nor any knowledge of a direct way to reach it. Thus it would not be an absolute unconsciousness but a rather dim consciousness. Such a consciousness would necessarily produce any amount of errors and impasses with the most cruel consequences, disease, mutilation, and horrible fights, i.e., just the thing that has happened and is still happening throughout all realms of life. Moreover it is impossible for us to assume that a Creator producing a universe out of nothingness can be conscious of anything, because each act of cognition is based upon a discrimination—for instance, I cannot be conscious of somebody else when I am identical with him. If there is nothing outside of God everything is God and in such a state there is simply no possibility of self-cognition.

Nobody can help admitting that the thought of a God creating any amount of errors and impasses is as good as a catastrophe. When the original Jewish conception of a purposeful and morally inclined God marked the end of the playful and rather purposeless existence of the polytheistic deities in the Mediterranean sphere, the result was a paradoxical conception of the supreme being, finding its expression in the idea of divine justice and injustice. The clear recognition of the fatal unreliability of the deity led Jewish prophecy to look for a sort of mediator or advocate, representing the claims of humanity before God. As you know, this figure is already announced in Ezekiel's vision of the Man and Son of Man.[2] The idea was carried on by Daniel[3] and then in the Apocryphal writings, particularly in the figure of the female Demiurge, viz. Sophia,[4] and in the male form of an administrator of justice, the Son of Man, in the Book of Enoch, written about 100 B.C. and very popular at the time of Christ. It must have been so well-known, indeed, that Christ called himself "Son of Man" with the evident presupposition of everybody knowing what he was talking about. Enoch is exactly what the Book of Job expects the advocate of man to be, over against the lawlessness and moral unreliability of Yahweh. The recently discovered scrolls of the Dead Sea mention a sort of legendary mystical figure, viz. "the Teacher of Justice."[5] I think he is parallel to or identical with Enoch. Christ obviously took up this idea, feeling that his task was to represent the role of the "Teacher of Justice" and thus of a Mediator; and he was up against an unpredictable and lawless God who would need a most drastic sacrifice to appease His wrath, viz. the slaughter of His own son. Curiously enough, as on the one hand his self-sacrifice means admission of the Father's amoral nature, he taught on the other hand a new image of God, namely that of a Loving Father in whom there is no darkness. This enormous antinomy needs some explanation. It needed the assertion that he was the Son of the Father, i.e., the incarnation of the Deity in man. As a consequence the sacrifice was a self-destruction of the amoral God, incarnated in a mortal body. Thus the sacrifice takes on the aspect of a highly moral deed, of a self-punishment, as it were.

Inasmuch as Christ is understood to be the second Person of the Trinity, the self-sacrifice is the evidence for God's goodness. At least so far as human beings are concerned. We don't know whether there are other inhabited worlds where the same divine evolution also has taken place. It is thinkable that there are many inhabited worlds in different stages of development where God has not yet undergone the transformation through incarnation. However that may be, for us earthly beings the incarnation has taken place and we have become participants in the divine nature and presumably heirs of the tendency towards goodness and at the same time subject to the inevitable self-punishment. As Job was not a mere spectator of divine unconsciousness but fell a victim to this momentous manifestation, in the case of incarnation we also become involved in the consequences of this transformation. Inasmuch as God proves His goodness through self-sacrifice He is incarnated, but in view of His infinity and the presumably different stages of cosmic development we don't know of, how much of God—if this is not too human an argument—has been transformed? In this case it can be expected that we are going to contact spheres of a not yet transformed God when our consciousness begins to extend into the sphere of the unconscious. There is at all events a definite expectation of this kind expressed in the "Evangelium Aeternum" of the Revelations containing the message: Fear God![6]

Although the divine incarnation is a cosmic and absolute event, it only manifests empirically in those relatively few individuals capable of enough consciousness to make ethical decisions, i.e., to decide for the Good. Therefore God can be called good only inasmuch as He is able to manifest His goodness in individuals. His moral quality depends upon individuals. That is why He incarnates. Individuation and individual existence are indispensable for the transformation of God the Creator.

The knowledge of what is good is not given a *priori*; it needs discriminating consciousness. That is already the problem in Genesis, where Adam and Eve have to be enlightened first in order to recognize the Good and discriminate it from Evil. There is no such thing as the "Good" in general, because something that is definitely good can be as definitely evil in another case. Individuals are different from each other, their values are different and their situations vary to such an extent that they cannot be judged by general values and principles. For instance generosity is certainly a virtue, but it instantly becomes a vice when applied to an individual that misunderstands it. In this case one needs conscious discrimination.

Your question concerning the relationship between the human being and an unconscious paradoxical God is indeed a major question, although we have the most impressive paradigm of Old Testament piety that could deal with the divine antinomy. The people of the Old Testament could address themselves to an unreliable God. By very overt attempts at propitiation I mean in particular the repeated assertion and invocation of God's justice and this in the face of indisputable injustice. They tried to avoid His wrath and to call forth His goodness. It is quite obvious that the old Hebrew theologians were continuously tormented by the fear of Yahweh's unpredictable acts of injustice.

For the Christian mentality, brought up in the conviction of an essentially good God, the situation is much more difficult. One cannot love and fear at the same time any more. Our consciousness has become too differentiated for such contradictions. We are therefore forced to take the fact of incarnation far more seriously than hitherto. We ought to remember that the Fathers of the Church have insisted upon the fact that God has given Himself to man's death on the Cross so that we may become gods. The Deity has taken its abode in man with the obvious intention of realizing Its Good in man. Thus we are the vessel or the children and the heirs of the Deity suffering in the body of the "slave."[7]

We are now in a position to understand the essential point of view of our brethren the Hindus. They are aware of the fact that the personal Atman is identical with the universal Atman and have evolved ways and means to express the psychological consequences of such a belief. In this respect we have to learn something from them. It saves us from spiritual pride when we humbly recognize that God can manifest Himself in many different ways.

Christianity has envisaged the religious problem as a sequence of dramatic events, whereas the East holds a thoroughly static view, i.e., a cyclic view. The thought of evolution is Christian and—as I think—in a way a better truth to express the dynamic aspect of the Deity, although the eternal immovability also forms an important aspect of the Deity (in Aristotle and in the old scholastic philosophy). The religious spirit of the West is characterized by a change of God's image in the course of ages. Its history begins with the plurality of the Elohim, then it comes to the paradoxical Oneness and personality of Yahweh, then to the good Father of Christianity, followed by the second Person in the Trinity, Christ, i.e., God incarnated in man. The allusion to the Holy Ghost is a third form appearing at the beginning of the second half of the Christian age (Gioacchino da Fiore),[8] and finally we are confronted with the aspect revealed through the manifestations of the unconscious. The significance of man is enhanced by the incarnation. We have become participants of the divine life and we have to assume a new responsibility, viz. the continuation of the divine self-realization, which expresses itself in the task of our individuation. Individuation does not only mean that man has become truly human as distinct from animal, but that he is to become partially divine as well. This means practically that he becomes adult, responsible for his existence, knowing that he does not only depend on God but that God also depends on man. Man's relation to God probably has to undergo a certain important change: Instead of the propitiating praise to an unpredictable king or the child's prayer to a loving father, the responsible living and fulfilling of the divine will in us will be our form of worship of and commerce with God. His goodness means grace and light and His dark side the terrible temptation of power. Man has already received so much knowledge that he can destroy his own planet. Let us hope that God's good spirit will guide him in his decisions, because it will depend upon man's decision whether God's creation will continue. Nothing shows more drastically than this possibility how much of divine power has come within the reach of man.

If anything of the above should not be clear to you, I am quite ready for further explanation.

Sincerely yours, C. G. JUNG

Notes

(*Letters* II, 312–16)
See also Jung's letter to Elined Kotschnig, 23 July 1934, in *Letters* I, 169–70.
1. Kotschnig asked for an answer to the problem of an unconscious, ignorant creator-god and if this did not imply "some principle, some Ground of Being, beyond such a demiurge."

2. Ezekiel 1:16ff.
3. Daniel 7:13ff.
4. Proverbs 8:22ff.
5. The Teacher of Justice, or of Righteousness, was the name given to the leader of a Jewish sect (probably the Essenes), parts of whose literature, the Dead Sea Scrolls, were found in 1947 (and after) near Qumran, northwest of the Dead Sea. The Essenes were an ascetic sect founded in the 2nd cent. B.C. living in communities in the Judaean desert.
6. Rev. 14:6–7
7. Or "servant." Cf. Phil. 2:6.
8. Cf. Jung's letter to Father Victor White, 24 November 1953, n. 10, in *Letters* II, 136.

To the Rev. Morton T. Kelsey

[ORIGINAL IN ENGLISH]

Dear Mr. Kelsey, 3 May 1958

Thank you very much for your kind letter.[1] I appreciate it indeed, since it is the first and only one I got from a Protestant theologian [in the U.S.A.] who has read *Job*. I can't help feeling that I am beneath consideration. All the more I value your kind effort to write to me. The psychology of the Book of Job seems to be of the highest importance concerning the inner motivation of Christianity. The fact that none—as far as I am able to see—of the existing commentaries has drawn the necessary conclusions has long since been a cause of wonder to me. Occasional outbursts of shortsighted wrath didn't surprise me. The almost total apathy and indifference of the theologians was more astonishing.

As you realize, I am discussing the admittedly anthropomorphic image of Yahweh and I do not apply metaphysical judgments. From this methodological standpoint I gain the necessary freedom of criticism. The absence of human morality in Yahweh is a stumbling block which cannot be overlooked, as little as the fact that Nature, i.e., God's creation, does not give us enough reason to believe it to be purposive or reasonable in the human sense. We miss reason and moral values, that is, two main characteristics of a mature human mind. It is therefore obvious that the Yahwistic image or conception of the deity is less than [that of] certain human specimens: the image of a personified brutal force and of an unethical and non-spiritual mind, yet inconsistent enough to exhibit traits of kindness and generosity besides a violent power-drive. It is the picture of a sort of nature-demon and at the same time of a primitive chieftain aggrandized to a colossal size, just the sort of conception one could expect of a more or less barbarous society *cum grano salis*.

This image owes its existence certainly not to an invention or intellectual formulation, but rather to a spontaneous manifestation, i.e., to religious experience of men like Samuel[2] and Job and thus it retains its validity to this day. People still ask: Is it possible that God allows such things? Even the Christian God may be asked: Why do you let your only son suffer for the imperfection of your creation?

The image of God corresponds to its manifestation, i.e., such religious experience produces such an image. There is no better image anywhere in the world. For this reason Buddha has placed the "enlightened" man higher than the highest Brahman gods.

This most shocking defectuosity of the God-image ought to be explained or understood. The nearest analogy to it is our experience of the unconscious: it is a psyche whose nature can only be described by paradoxes: it is personal as well as impersonal, moral and amoral, just and unjust, ethical and unethical, of cunning intelligence and at the same time blind, immensely strong and extremely weak, etc. This is the psychic foundation which produces the raw material for our conceptual structures. The unconscious is a piece of Nature our mind cannot comprehend. It can only sketch models of a possible and partial understanding. The result is most imperfect, although we pride ourselves on having "penetrated" the innermost secrets of Nature.

The real nature of the objects of human experience is still shrouded in darkness. The scientist cannot concede a higher intelligence to theology than to any other branch of human cognition. We know as little of a supreme being as of matter. But there is as little doubt of the existence of a supreme being as of matter. *The world beyond is a reality,* an experiential fact. We only don't understand it.[3]

Under these circumstances it is permissible to assume that the Summum Bonum is so good, so high, so perfect, but so remote that it is entirely beyond our grasp. But it is equally permissible to assume that the ultimate reality is a being representing all the qualities of its creation, virtue, reason, intelligence, kindness, consciousness, *and their opposites,* to our mind a complete paradox. The latter view fits the facts of human experience, whereas the former cannot explain away the obvious existence of evil and suffering. *[pothen to kakon];*[4]— this age-old question is not answered unless you assume the existence of a [supreme] being *who is in the main unconscious.* Such a model would explain why God has created a man gifted with consciousness and why He seeks His goal in him. In this the Old Testament, the New Testament, and Buddhism agree. Master Eckhart said it: "God is not blessed in His Godhead, He must be born in man forever."[5] This is what happens in Job: *The creator sees himself through the eyes of man's consciousness* and this is the reason why God had to become man, and why man is progressively gifted with the dangerous prerogative of the divine "mind." You have it in the saying: "Ye are gods,"[6] and man has not even begun yet to know himself. He would need it to be prepared to meet the dangers of the *incarnatio continua,*[7] which began with Christ and the distribution of the "Holy Ghost" to poor, almost unconscious beings. We are still looking back to the pentecostal events in a dazed way instead of looking forward to the goal the Spirit is leading us to. Therefore mankind is wholly unprepared for the things to come. Man is compelled by divine forces to go forward to increasing consciousness and cognition, developing further and further away from his religious background because he does not understand it any more.

His religious teachers and leaders are still hypnotized by the beginnings of a then new aeon of consciousness instead of understanding them and their implications. What one once called the "Holy Ghost" is an impelling force, creating wider consciousness and responsibility and thus enriched cognition. The real history of the world seems to be the progressive incarnation of the deity.

Here I must stop, although I should like to continue my argument. I feel tired and that means something in old age.

Thank you again for your kind letter!

Yours sincerely, C. G. JUNG

Notes

(*Letters* II, 434–36)

1. Kelsey, rector of St. Luke's Episcopal Church, Monrovia (near Los Angeles), California, wrote a highly appreciative letter about *Answer to Job*: "How can I thank you enough for this book? It has served as a catalyst enabling a fusion to take place between my theological thinking and the experience of life, which my analytical work has stimulated . . ."
2. Cf. I Sam. 3.
3. This paragraph is published in Kelsey, *Tongue Speaking: An Experiment in Spiritual Experience* (1964), 192f.
4. = Whence evil?
5. Cf. *Psychological Types*, CW 6, par. 418.
6. John 10:34.
7. Continuing incarnation, resulting from the past, present, and future indwelling of the Holy Ghost in man. Cf. Jung's letter to the Rev. Erastus Evans, 17 February 1954, n. 5, in *Letters* II, 155–57.

To Père William Lachat[1]

Dear Sir,   Küsnacht, 27 March 1954

It was very kind of you to send me your booklet[2] on the reception and action of the Holy Spirit. I have read it with special interest since the subject of the Holy Spirit seems to me one of current importance. I remember that the former Archbishop of York, Dr. Temple, admitted, in conversation with me, that the Church has not done all that it might to develop the idea of the Holy Spirit. It is not difficult to see why this is so, for [to pneuma pnei opou telei][3]—a fact which an institution may find very inconvenient! In the course of reading your little book a number of questions and thoughts have occurred to me, which I set out below, since my reactions may perhaps be of some interest to you.

I quite agree with your view that one pauses before entrusting oneself to the "unforeseeable action" of the Holy Spirit. One feels afraid of it, not, I think, without good reason. Since there is a marked difference between the God of the Old Testament and the God of the New, a definition is desirable. You nowhere explain your idea of God. Which God have you in mind: The New Testament God, or the Old? The latter is a paradox; good and demonlike, just and unjust at the same time, while the God of the New Testament is by definition perfect, good, the Summum Bonum even, without any element of the dark or the demon in him. But if you identify these two Gods, different as they are, the fear and resistance one feels in entrusting oneself unconditionally to the Holy Spirit are easy to understand. The divine action is so unforeseeable that it may well be really disastrous. That being so, the prudence of the serpent counsels us not to approach the Holy Spirit too closely.

If, on the other hand, it is the New Testament God you have in mind, one can be absolutely certain that the risk is more apparent than real since the end will always be good. In that event the experience loses its venturesome character; it is not really dangerous. It is then merely foolish not to give oneself up entirely to the action of the Holy Spirit. Rather one should seek him day by day, and one will easily lay hold of him, as Mr. Horton[4] assures us. In the absence of a formal statement on your part, I assume that you identify the two Gods. In that case the Holy Spirit would not be easy to apprehend; it would even be highly dangerous to attract the divine attention by specially pious behaviour (as in the case of Job and some others). In the Old Testament Satan still has the Father's ear, and can influence him even against the righteous. The Old Testament furnishes us with quite a number of instances of this kind, and they warn us to be very careful when we are dealing with the Holy Spirit. The man who is not particularly bold and adventurous will do well to bear these examples in mind and to thank God that the Holy Spirit does not concern himself with us over much. One feels much safer under the shadow of the Church, which serves as a fortress to protect us against God and his Spirit. It is very comforting to be assured by the Catholic Church that it "possesses" the Spirit, who assists regularly at its rites. Then one knows that he is well chained up. Protestantism is no less reassuring in that it represents the Spirit to us as something to be sought for, to be easily "drunk," even to be possessed. We get the impression that he is something passive, which cannot budge without us. He has lost his dangerous qualities, his fire, his autonomy, his power. He is represented as an innocuous, passive, and purely beneficent element, so that to be afraid of him would seem just stupid.

This characterization of the Holy Spirit leaves out of account the terrors of YHWH. It does not tell us what the Holy Spirit is, since it has failed to explain to us clearly what it has done with the *Deus absconditus*. Albert Schweitzer naïvely informs us that he takes the side of the ethical God and avoids the *absconditus*, as if a mortal man had the ability to hide himself when faced with an almighty God or to take the other, less risky side. God can implicate him in unrighteousness whenever he chooses.

I also fail to find a definition of Christ; one does not know whether he is identical with the Holy Spirit, or different from him. Everyone talks about Christ; but who is this Christ? When talking to a Catholic or Anglican priest, I am in no doubt. But when I am talking to a pastor of the Reformed Church, it may be that Christ is the Second Person of the Trinity and God in his entirety, or a divine man (the "supreme authority," as Schweitzer has it which doesn't go too well with the error of the parousia), or one of those great founders of ethical systems like Pythagoras, Confucius, and so on. It is the same with the idea of God. What is Martin Buber talking about when he discloses to us his intimate relations with "God"? YHWH? The olden Trinity, or the modern Trinity, which has become something more like a Quaternity since the Sponsa has been received into the Thalamus?[5] Or the rather misty God of Protestantism? Do you think that everyone who says that he is surrendering himself to Christ has really surrendered himself to Christ? Isn't it more likely that he has surrendered himself to the image of Christ which he has made for himself, or to that of God the Father or the Holy Spirit? Are they all the same Christ—the Christ of the Synoptics, of the *Exercitia Spiritualia*, of a mystic of Mount Athos, of Count Zinzendorf,[6] of the hundred sects, of Caux[7] and Rudolf Steiner, and—last but not least—of St. Paul? Do you really believe that anyone, be he who he may, can bring about the real presence of one of the Sacred Persons by an earnest utterance of their name? I can be certain only that someone has called up a psychic image, but it is impossible for me to confirm the real presence of the Being evoked. It is neither for us nor for others to decide who has been invoked by the holy name and to whom one has surrendered oneself. Has it not happened that the invocation of the Holy Spirit has brought the devil on the scene? What are invoked are in the first place images, and that is why images have a special importance. I do not for a moment deny that the deep emotion of a true prayer may reach transcendence, but it is above our heads. There would not even be any transcendence if our images and metaphors were more than anthropomorphism and the words themselves had a magical effect. The Catholic Church protects itself against this insinuation *expressis verbis*, insisting on its teaching that God cannot go back on his own institutions. He is morally obliged to maintain them by his Holy Spirit or his grace. All theological preaching is a mythologem, a series of archetypal images intended to give a more or less exact description of the unimaginable transcendence. It is a paradox, but it is justified. The totality of these archetypes corresponds to what I have called *the collective unconscious. We are concerned here with empirical facts, as I have proved.* (Incidentally, you don't seem to be well informed about either the nature of the unconscious or my psychology. The idea that the unconscious is the abyss of all the horrors is a bit out of date. The collective unconscious is neutral; it is only nature, both spiritual and chthonic. To impute to my psychology the idea that the Holy Spirit is "only a projection of the human soul" is false. He is a transcendental fact which presents itself to us under the guise of an archetypal image (e.g, [   ],⁸ or are we to believe that he is really "breathed forth" by the Father and the Son?). There is no guarantee that this image corresponds exactly to the transcendental entity.

The unconscious is ambivalent; it can produce both good and evil effects. So the image of God also has two sides, like YHWH or the God of Clement of Rome with two hands; the right is Christ, the left Satan, and it is with these two hands that he rules the world.⁹ Nicholas of Cusa calls God a *complexio oppositorum* (naturally under the apotropaic condition of the *privatio boni!*). YHWH's paradoxical qualities are continued in the New Testament. In these circumstances it becomes very difficult to know what to make of *prayer*. Can we address our prayer to the good God to the exclusion of the demon, as Schweitzer recommends? Have we the power of dissociating God like the countrywoman who said to the child Jesus, when he interrupted her prayer to the Virgin: "Shhh, child, I'm talking to your mother"? Can we really put on one side the God who is dangerous to us? Do we believe that God is so powerless that we can say to him: "Get out, I'm talking to your better half?" Or can we ignore the *absconditus*? Schweitzer invites us to do just this; we're going to have our bathe in the river, and never mind the crocodiles. One can, it seems, brush them aside. Who is there who can produce this "simple faith"?

Like God, then, the unconscious has two aspects; one good, favourable, beneficent, the other evil, malevolent, disastrous. The unconscious is the immediate source of our religious experiences. This psychic nature of all experience does not mean that the transcendental realities are also psychic; the physicist does not believe that the transcendental reality represented by his psychic model is also psychic. He calls it *matter*, and in the same way the psychologist in no wise attributes a psychic nature to his images or archetypes. He calls them "psychoids"[10] and is convinced that they represent transcendental realities. He even knows of "simple faith" as that *conviction which one cannot avoid*. It is vain to seek for it; it comes when it wills, for it is the gift of the Holy Spirit. There is only one divine spirit—an immediate presence, often terrifying and in no degree subject to our choice. There is no guarantee that it may not just as well be the devil, as happened to St. Ignatius Loyola in his vision of the *serpens oculatus*, interpreted at first as Christ or God and later as the devil.[11] Nicholas of Flüe had his terrifying vision of the *absconditus*, and transformed it later into the kindly Trinity of the parish church of Sachseln.[12]

Surrender to God is a formidable adventure, and as "simple" as any situation over which man has no control. He who can risk himself wholly to it finds himself directly in the hands of God, and is there confronted with a situation which makes "simple faith" a vital necessity; in other words, the situation becomes so full of risk or overtly dangerous that the deepest instincts are aroused. An experience of this kind is always numinous, for it unites all aspects of totality. All this is wonderfully expressed in Christian religious symbolism: the divine will incarnate in Christ urges towards the fatal issue, the catastrophe followed by the fact or hope of resurrection, while Christian faith insists on the deadly danger of the adventure; but the Churches assure us that God protects us against all danger and especially against the fatality of our character. Instead of taking up our cross, we are told to cast it on Christ. He will take on the burden of our anguish and we can enjoy our "simple faith" at Caux. We take flight into the Christian collectivity where we can forget even the will of God, for in society we lose the feeling of personal responsibility and can swim with the current. One feels safe in the multitude, and the Church does everything to reassure us against the fear of God, as if it did not believe that He could bring about a serious situation. On the other hand psychology is painted as black as possible, because it teaches, in full agreement with the Christian creed, that no man can ascend unless he has first descended. A professor of theology once accused me publicly that "in flagrant contradiction to the words of Christ" I had criticized as *childish* the man who remains an infant retaining his early beliefs. I had to remind him of the fact that Christ never said "remain children" but "become like children." This is one small example of the way in which Christian experience is falsified; it is prettied up, its sombre aspects are denied, its dangers are hidden. But the action of the Holy Spirit does not meet us in the atmosphere of a normal, bourgeois (or proletarian!), sheltered, regular life, but only in the insecurity outside the human economy, in the infinite spaces where one is alone with the *providentia Dei*. We must never forget that Christ was an innovator and revolutionary, *executed with criminals*. The reformers and great religious geniuses were *heretics*. It is there that you find the footprints of the Holy Spirit, and no one asks for him or receives him *without having to pay a high price*. The price is so high that no one today would dare to suggest that he possesses or is possessed by the Holy Spirit, or he would be too close to the psychiatric clinic. The danger of making oneself ridiculous is too real, not to mention the risk of offending our real god: *respectability*. There one even becomes very strict, and it would not be at all allowable for God and his Spirit to permit themselves to give advice or orders as in the Old Testament. Certainly everyone would lay his irregularities to the account of the unconscious. One would say: God is faithful, he does not forsake us, God does not lie, he will keep his word, and so on. We know it isn't true, but we go on repeating these lies ad infinitum. It is quite understandable that we should seek to hold the truth at arm's length, because it seems impossible to give oneself up to a God who doesn't even respect his own laws when he falls victim to one of his fits of rage or forgets his solemn oath. When I allow myself to mention these well-attested facts the theologians accuse me of blasphemy, unwilling as they are to admit the ambivalence of the divine nature, the demonic character of the God of the Bible and even of the Christian God. Why was that cruel immolation of the Son necessary if the anger of the "deus ultionum" is not hard to appease? One doesn't notice much of the Father's goodness and love during the tragic end of his Son.

True, we ought to abandon ourselves to the divine will as much as we can, but admit that to do so is difficult and dangerous, so dangerous indeed that I would not dare to advise one of my clients to "take" the Holy Spirit or to abandon himself to him until I had first made him realize the risks of such an enterprise.

Permit me here to make a few comments. On pp. 11f.: The Holy Spirit is to be feared. He is revolutionary *especially* in religious matters (not at all "perhaps even religious," p. 11 bottom). Ah, yes, one does well to refuse the Holy Spirit, because people would like to palm him off on us without telling us what this sacred fire is which killeth and maketh to live. One may get through a battle without being wounded, but there are some unfortunates who do not know how to avoid either mutilation or death. Perhaps one is among their number. One can hardly take the risk of that without the most convincing necessity. It is quite normal and reasonable to refuse oneself to the Holy Spirit. Has M. Boegner's[13] life been turned upside down? Has he taken the risk of breaking with convention (e.g., eating with Gentiles when one is an orthodox Jew, or even better with women of doubtful reputation), or been immersed in darkness like Hosea, making himself ridiculous, overturning the traditional order, etc.? It is deeds that are needed, not words.

p. 13. It is very civil to say that the Holy Spirit is "uncomfortable and sometimes upsetting," but very characteristic.

p. 16. It is clear that the Holy Spirit is concerned in the long run with the collectivity (*ecclesia*), but in the first place with the individual, and to create him he isolates him from his environment, just as Christ himself was thought mad by his own family.

p. 19. The Holy Spirit, "the accredited bearer of the holiness of God." But who will recognize him as such? Everyone will certainly say that he is drunk or a heretic or mad. To the description "bearer of the holiness" needs to be added the holiness which God himself sometimes sets on one side (Ps. 89).

p. 21. It is no use for Mr. Horton to believe that receiving the Holy Spirit is quite a simple business. It is so to the degree that we do not realize what is at issue. We are surrendering ourselves to a Spirit with two aspects. That is why we are not particularly ready to "drink" of him, or to "thirst" for him. We hope rather that God is going to pass us by, that we are protected against his injustice and his violence. Granted, the New Testament speaks otherwise, but when we get to the Apocalypse the style changes remarkably and approximates to that of older times. Christ's kingdom has been provisional; the world is left thereafter for another aeon to Antichrist and to all the horrors that can be envisaged by a pitiless and loveless imagination. This witness in favor of the god with two faces represents the last and tragic chapter of the New Testament which would like to have set up a god exclusively good and made only of love. This Apocalypse—was it a frightful gaffe on the part of those Fathers who drew up the canon? I don't think so. They were still too close to the hard reality of things and of religious traditions to share our mawkish interpretations and prettily falsified opinions.

p. 23. "Surrender without the least reserve." Would Mr. Horton advise us to cross the Avenue de l'Opéra blindfold? His belief in the good God is so strong that he has forgotten the fear of God. For Mr. Horton God is dangerous no longer. But in that case—what is the Apocalypse all about? He asks nevertheless, "To what interior dynamism is one surrendering oneself, natural or supernatural?" When he says, "I surrender myself wholly to God," how does he know what is "whole"? Our wholeness is an unconscious fact, whose extent we cannot establish. God alone can judge of human wholeness. We can only say humbly: "As wholly as possible."

There is no guarantee that it is really *God* when we say "god." It is perhaps a word concealing a demon or a void, or it is an act of grace coincident with our prayer.

This total surrender is disturbing. Nearly twenty years ago I gave a course at the Ecole Polytechnique Suisse for two semesters on the *Exercitia Spiritualia* of St. Ignatius.[14] On that occasion I received a profound impression of this total surrender, in relation to which one never knows whether one is dealing with sanctity or with spiritual pride. One sees too that the god to whom one surrenders oneself is a clear and well-defined prescription given by the director of the Exercises. This is particularly evident in the part called the "colloquium," where there is only one who speaks, and that is the initiated. One asks oneself what God or Christ would say if it were a real dialogue, but no one expects God to reply.

p. 26. The identity of Christ with the Holy Spirit seems to me to be questionable, since Christ made a very clear distinction between himself and the paraclete, even if the latter's function resembles Christ's. The near-identity of the Holy Spirit with Christ in St. John's Gospel is characteristic of the evangelist's Gnosticism. It seems to me important to insist on the chronological sequence of the Three Persons, for there is an evolution in three stages:

1. The Father. The opposites not yet differentiated; Satan is still numbered among the "sons of God." Christ then is only hinted at.

2. God is incarnated as the "Son of Man." Satan has fallen from heaven. He is the other "son." The opposites are differentiated.

3. The Holy Spirit is One, his prototype is the Ruach Elohim, an emanation, an active principle, which proceeds (as quintessence) *a Patre Filioque*. Inasmuch as he proceeds also from the Son he is different from the Ruach Elohim, who represents the active principle of Yahweh (not incarnate, with only angels in place of a son). The angels are called "sons," they are not begotten and there is no mother of the angels. Christ on the other hand shares in human nature, he is even man by definition. In this case it is evident that the Holy Spirit proceeding from the Son does not arise from the divine nature only, that is, from the second Person, but also from the human nature. Thanks to this fact, human nature is included in the mystery of the Trinity. Man forms part of it.

This "human nature" is only figuratively human, for it is exempt from original sin. This makes the "human" element definitely doubtful inasmuch as man without exception, save for Christ and his mother, is begotten and born bearing the stamp of the *macula peccati*. That is why Christ and his mother enjoy a nature divine rather than human. For the Protestant there is no reason to think of Mary as a goddess. Thus he can easily admit that on his mother's side Christ was contaminated by original sin; this makes him all the more human, at least so far as the *filioque* of the Protestant confession does not exclude the true man from the "human" nature of Christ. On the other hand it becomes evident that the Holy Spirit necessarily proceeds from the *two natures* of Christ, not only from the God in him, but also from the man in him.

There were very good reasons why the Catholic Church has carefully purified Christ and his mother from all contamination by the *peccatum originale*.

Protestantism was more courageous, even daring or—perhaps?—more oblivious of the consequences, in not denying—*expressis verbis*—the human nature (in part) of Christ and (wholly) of his mother. *Thus the ordinary man became a source of the Holy Spirit,* though certainly not the only one. It is like lightning, which issues not only from the clouds but also from the peaks of the mountains. This fact signifies the continued and progressive divine incarnation. Thus man is received and integrated into the divine drama. He seems destined to play a decisive part in it; that is why he must receive the Holy Spirit. I look upon the receiving of the Holy Spirit as a highly revolutionary fact which cannot take place until the ambivalent nature of the Father is recognized. If God is the *summum bonum,* the incarnation makes no sense, for a good god could never produce such hate and anger that his only son had to be sacrificed to appease it. A Midrash says that the Shofar is still sounded on the Day of Atonement to remind YHWH of his act of injustice towards Abraham (by compelling him to slay Isaac) and to prevent him from repeating it. A conscientious clarification of the idea of God would have consequences as upsetting as they are necessary. They would be indispensable for an interior development of the trinitarian drama and of the role of the Holy Spirit. The Spirit is destined to be incarnate in man or to choose him as a transitory dwelling-place. "Non habet nomen proprium," says St Thomas;[15] because he will receive the name of man. That is why he must not be identified with Christ. We cannot receive the Holy Spirit unless we have accepted our own individual life as Christ accepted his. Thus we become the "sons of god" fated to experience the conflict of the divine opposites, represented by the crucifixion.

Man seems indispensable to the divine drama. We shall understand this role of man's better if we consider the paradoxical nature of the Father. As the Apocalypse has alluded to it (*evangelium aeternum*) and Joachim of Flora[16] has expressed it, the Son would seem to be the intermediary between the Father and the Holy Spirit. We could repeat what Origen said of the Three Persons, that the Father is the greatest and the Holy Spirit the least. This is true inasmuch as the Father by descending from the cosmic immensity became the least by incarnating himself within the narrow bounds of the human soul (cult of the child-god, Angelus Silesius). Doubtless the presence of the Holy Spirit enlarges human nature by divine attributes. Human nature is the divine vessel and as such the union of the Three. This results in a kind of quaternity which always signifies *totality,* while the triad is rather a process, but never the natural division of the *circle,* the natural symbol of wholeness. The quaternity as union of the Three seems to be aimed at by the *Assumption of Mary.* This dogma adds the feminine element to the masculine Trinity, the terrestrial element (*virgo terra!*) to the spiritual, and thus sinful man to the Godhead. For Mary in her character of *omnium gratiarum mediatrix* intercedes for the sinner before the judge of the world. (She is his "paraclete.") She is [*philanthropos*] like her prefiguration, the Sophia of the Old Testament.[17] Protestant critics have completely overlooked the symbolic aspect of the new dogma and its emotional value, which is a capital fault.

The "littleness" of the Holy Spirit stems from the fact that God's pneuma dissolves into the form of little flames, remaining none the less intact and whole. His dwelling in a certain number of human individuals and their transformation into [uio ton theon] signifies a very important step forward beyond "Christocentrism." Anyone who takes up the question of the Holy Spirit seriously is faced with the question whether Christ is identical with the Holy Spirit or different from him. With dogma, I prefer the independence of the Holy Spirit. The Holy Spirit is one, a complexio oppositorum, in contrast to YHWH after the separation of the divine opposites symbolized by God's two sons, Christ and Satan. On the level of the Son there is no answer to the question of good and evil; there is only an incurable separation of the opposites. The annulling of evil by the privatio boni (declaring to be me on) is a petitio principii of the most flagrant kind and no solution whatever.[18] It seems to me to be the Holy Spirit's task and charge to reconcile and reunite the opposites in the human individual through a special development of the human soul. The soul is paradoxical like the Father; it is black and white, divine and demon-like, in its primitive and natural state. By the discriminative function of its conscious side it separates opposites of every kind, and especially those of the moral order personified in Christ and Devil. Thereby the soul's spiritual development creates an enormous tension, from which man can only suffer. Christ promised him redemption. But in what exactly does this consist? The imitatio Christi leads us to Calvary and to the annihilation of the "body," that is, of biological life, and if we take this death as symbolic it is a state of suspension between the opposites, That is to say, an unresolved conflict. That is exactly what Przywara has named the "rift,"[19] the gulf separating good from evil, the latent and apparently incurable dualism of Christianity, the eternity of the devil and of damnation. (Inasmuch as good is real so also is evil.)

To find the answer to this question we can but trust to our mental powers on the one hand and on the other to the functioning of the unconscious, that spirit which we cannot control. It can only be hoped that it is a "holy" spirit. The cooperation of conscious reasoning with the data of the unconscious is called the "transcendent function" (cf. Psychological Types, par. 828).[20] This function progressively unites the opposites. Psychotherapy makes use of it to heal neurotic dissociations, but this function had already served as the basis of Hermetic philosophy for seventeen centuries. Besides this, it is a natural and spontaneous phenomenon, part of the process of individuation. Psychology has no proof that this process does not unfold itself at the instigation of God's will.

The Holy Spirit will manifest himself in any case in the psychic sphere of man and will be presented as a psychic experience. He thus becomes the object of empirical psychology, which he will need in order to translate his symbolism into the possibilities of this world. Since his intention is the incarnation, that is, the realization of the divine being in human life, he cannot be a light which the darkness comprehendeth not. On the contrary, he needs the support of man and his understanding to comprehend the *mysterium iniquitatis* which began in paradise before man existed. (The serpent owes his existence to God and by no means to man. The idea: *omne bonum a Deo, omne malum ab homine* is an entirely false one.) YHWH is inclined to find the cause of evil in men, but he evidently represents a moral antinomy accompanied by an almost complete lack of reflection. For example, he seems to have forgotten that he created his son Satan and kept him among the other "sons of God" until the coming, of Christ—a strange oversight!

The data of the collective unconscious favour the hypothesis of a paradoxical creator such as YHWH. An entirely good Father seems to have very little probability; such a character is difficult to admit, seeing that Christ himself endeavoured to reform his Father. He didn't completely succeed, even in his own logia. Our unconscious resembles this paradoxical God. That is why man is faced with a psychological condition which does not let him differentiate himself from the image of God (YHWH). Naturally we can believe that God is different from the image of him that we possess, but it must be admitted on the other side that the Lord himself, while insisting on the Father's perfect goodness, has given him a picture of him which fits in badly with the idea of a perfectly moral being. (A father who tempts his children, who did not prevent the error of the immediate parousia, who is so full of wrath that the blood of his only son is necessary to appease him, who left the crucified one to despair, who proposes to devastate his own creation and slay the millions of mankind to save a very few of them, and who before the end of the world is going to replace his Son's covenant by another gospel and complement the love by the fear of God.) It is interesting, or rather tragic, that God undergoes a complete relapse in the last book of the New Testament. But in the case of an amtinomian being we could expect no other development. The opposites are kept in balance, and so the kingdom of Christ is followed by that of Antichrist. In the circumstances the Holy Spirit, the third form of God, becomes of extreme importance, for it is thanks to him that the man of good will is drawn towards the divine drama and mingled in it, and the Spirit is one. In him the opposites are separated no longer.

Begging you to excuse the somewhat heretical character of my thoughts as well as their imperfect presentation, I remain, dear monsieur, yours sincerely,

C. G. JUNG

Notes

(CW 18, pars. 1532–1557]
1. [(Translated from the French by A. S. B. Glover) See Jung's letters of 18 January and 29 June 1955 to Père William Lachat, in *Letters* II, 208–10, 267–68.]
2. [*La Réception et l'action du Saint-Esprit dans la vie personnelle et communautaire* (Neuchâtel, 1953).]
3. ["The Spirit bloweth where it listeth." John 3:8.]
4. [Unidentified.]
5. [*Apostolic Constitution* ("*Munificentissimus Deus*") of Pius XII (1950), sec. 33: ". . . on this day the Virgin Mother was taken up to her heavenly bridal-chamber." Cf. "Answer to Job," CW 11, par. 743, n. 4.]
6. [Count Nikolaus Ludwig von Zinzendorf (1700–60), founder of the Herrnhuter Brüdergemeinde, a community of Moravian Brethren.]
7. [Caux-sur-Montreux, Switzerland, a conference centre of the Moral Re-Armament movement. A World Assembly was held there in 1949.]
8. [Lacuna in the file copy of the letter.] [The intended word is likely *pneuma*. See CW 11, par. 240, where *pneuma* and Holy Ghost are equated].
9. [Cf. *Aion*, CW 9ii, pars. 99ff.]
10. [Cf. *Mysterium Coniunctionis*, CW 14, pars. 786f.]
11. [Cf. "On the Nature of the Psyche," CW 8, par. 395.]
12. [Cf. "Brother Klaus," CW 11; and "Archetypes of the Collective Unconscious," CW 9i, pars.12ff.]
13. [Unidentified.]
14. [Lectures at the Federal Polytechnic Institute (ETH), Zurich, June 1939 to March 1940. Privately issued.]
15. ["He has no proper name." *Summa Theologica*, I, xxvi, art. 1.]
16. [The "everlasting gospel" in Rev. 14:7 is "Fear God." For Joachim's view, see *Aion*, CW 9ii, pars. 137ff.]
17. [Cf. "Answer to Job," CW 11, pars. 613ff.]
18. [Cf. *Aion*, CW 9ii, pars. 89ff.]
19. [Erich Przywara, *Deus semper maior*, I.71f.]
20. [Cf. also "The Transcendent Function," CW 8.]

To the Rev. David Cox[1]

25 September 1957

The crux of this question is: "Within your own personality." "Christ" can be an external reality (historical and metaphysical) or an archetypal image or idea in the collective unconscious pointing to an unknown background. I would understand the former mainly as a projection, but not the latter, because it is immediately evident. It is not projected upon anything, therefore there is no projection. Only, "faith" in Christ is different from faith in anyone else, since in this case, "Christ" being immediately evident, the word "faith," including or alluding to the possibility of doubt, seems too feeble a word to characterize that powerful presence from which there is no escape. A general can say to his soldiers, "You must have faith in me," because one might doubt him. But you cannot say to a man lying wounded on the battlefield, "You ought to *believe* that this is a real battle," or "Be sure that you are up against the enemy." It is just too obvious. Even the historical Jesus began to speak of "faith" because he saw that his disciples had no immediate evidence. Instead they had to believe, while he himself being identical with God had no need to "have faith in God."

As one habitually identifies the "psyche" with what one knows of it, it is assumed that one can call certain (supposed or believed) metaphysical entities non-psychic. Being a responsible scientist I am unable to pass such a judgment, for all I know of regular religious phenomena seems to indicate that they are psychic events. Moreover I do not know the full reach of the psyche, because there is the limitless extent of the unconscious. "Christ" is definitely an archetypal image (I don't add "only") and that is all I actually know of him. As such he belongs to the (collective) foundations of the psyche. I identify him therefore with what I call the self. The self rules the whole of the psyche. I think our opinions do not differ essentially. You seem to have trouble only with the theological (and self-inflicted) devaluation of the psyche, which you apparently believe to be ultimately definable.

If my identification of Christ with the archetype of the self is valid, he is, or ought to be, a *complexio oppositorum*. Historically this is not so. Therefore I was profoundly surprised by your statement that Christ contains the opposites. Between my contention and historical Christianity there stretches that deep abyss of Christian dualism—Christ and the Devil, good and evil, God and Creation.

"Beyond good and evil" simply means: we pass no moral judgment. But in fact nothing is changed. The same is true when we state that whatever God is or does is *good*. Since God does everything (even man created by him is his instrument) everything is good, and the term "good" has lost its meaning. "Good" is a relative term. There is no good without bad.

I am afraid that even revealed truth has to evolve. Everything living changes. We should not be satisfied with unchangeable traditions. The great battle that began with the dawn of consciousness has not reached its climax with any particular interpretation, apostolic, Catholic, Protestant, or otherwise. Even the highly conservative Catholic Church has overstepped its ancient rule of apostolic authenticity with the *Assumptio Beatae Virginis*. According to what I hear from Catholic theologians, the next step would be the Coredemptrix. This obvious recognition of the female element is a very important step forward. It means psychologically the recognition of the unconscious, since the representative of the collective unconscious is the *anima*, the archetype of all divine mothers (at least in the masculine psyche).

The equivalent on the Protestant side would be a confrontation with the unconscious as the counterpart or consort of the masculine Logos. The hitherto valid symbol of the supreme spiritual structure was Trinity + Satan, the so-called 3 + 1 structure, corresponding to three conscious functions versus the one unconscious, so-called inferior function; or 1 + 3 if the conscious side is understood as one versus the co-called inferior or chthonic triad, mythologically characterized as three mother figures.[2] I suppose that the negative evaluation of the unconscious has something to do with the fact that it has been hitherto represented by Satan, while in reality it is the female aspect of man's psyche and thus not wholly evil in spite of the old saying: *Vir a Deo creatus, mulier a simia Dei*.

It seems to me of paramount importance that Protestantism should integrate psychological experience, as for instance Jacob Boehme did. With him God does not only contain love, but, on the other side and in the same measure, the fire of wrath, in which Lucifer himself dwells. Christ is a revelation of his love, but he can manifest his wrath in an Old Testament way just as well, i.e., in the form of evil. Inasmuch as out of evil good may come, and out of good evil, we do not know whether creation is ultimately good or a regrettable mistake and God's suffering. It is an ineffable mystery. At any rate we are not doing justice either to nature in general or to our own human nature when we deny the immensity of evil and suffering and turn our eyes from the cruel aspect of creation. Evil should be recognized and one should not attribute the existence of evil to man's sinfulness. Yahweh is not offended by being feared.

It is quite understandable why it was an [*Euaggelon*] [evangel, "good tidings"] to learn of the *bonitas Dei* and of his son. It was known to the ancients that the *cognitio sui ipsius* [self-knowledge][3] was a prerequisite for this, not only in the Graeco-Roman world but also in the Far East. It is to the individual aptitude that the man Jesus owes his apotheosis: he became the symbol of the self under the aspect of the infinite goodness, which was certainly the symbol most needed in ancient civilization (as it is still needed today).

It can be considered a fact that the dogmatic figure of Christ is the result of a condensation process from various sources. One of the main origins is the age old god-man of Egypt: Osiris-Horus and his four sons. It was a remodeling of the unconscious archetype hitherto projected upon a divine non-human being. By embodying itself in a historical man it came nearer to consciousness, but in keeping with the mental capacity of the time it remained as if suspended between God and man, between the need for good and the fear of evil. Any doubt about the absolute *bonitas Dei* would have led to an immediate regression to the former pagan state, i.e., to the amorality of the metaphysical principle.

Since then two thousand years have passed. In this time we have learned that good and evil are categories of our moral judgment, therefore relative to man. Thus the way was opened for a new model of the self. Moral judgment is a necessity of the human mind. The Christ ([*o Christos*]) is the Christian model that expresses the self, as the [*Anthropos*] is the corresponding Egypto-Judaic formula. Moral qualification is withdrawn from the deity. The Catholic Church has almost succeeded in adding femininity to the masculine Trinity. Protestantism is confronted with the psychological problem of the unconscious.

It is, as far as I can see, a peculiar process extending over at least four thousand years of mental evolution. It can be contemplated in a "euhemeristic" way as a development of man's understanding of the supreme powers beyond his control. [The process consists of the following stages:] (1) Gods. (2) A supreme Deity ruling the gods and demons. (3) God shares our human fate, is betrayed, killed or dies, and is resurrected again. There is a feminine counterpart dramatically involved in God's fate. (4) God becomes a man in the flesh and thus historical. He is identified with the abstract idea of the Summum Bonum and loses the feminine counterpart. The female deity is degraded to an ancillary position (Church). Consciousness begins to prevail against the unconscious. This is an enormously important step forward in the emancipation of consciousness and in the liberation of thought from its involvement in things. Thus the foundation of science is laid, but on the other hand, that of atheism and materialism. Both are inevitable consequences of the basic split between spirit and matter in Christian philosophy, which proclaimed the redemption of the spirit from the body and its fetters. (5) The whole metaphysical world is understood as a psychic structure projected into the sphere of the unknown.

The danger of this viewpoint is exaggerated skepticism and rationalism, since the original "supreme powers" are reduced to mere representations over which one assumes one has complete control. This leads to a complete negation of the supreme powers (scientific materialism).

The other way of looking at it is from the standpoint of the archetype. The original chaos of multiple gods evolves into a sort of monarchy, and the archetype of the self slowly asserts its central position as the archetype of order in chaos. One God rules supreme but apart from man. It begins to show a tendency to relate itself to consciousness through a process of penetration: the humanizing effect of a feminine intercession, expressed for instance by the Isis intrigue. In the Christian myth the Deity, the self, penetrates consciousness almost completely, without any visible loss of power and prestige. But in time it becomes obvious that the Incarnation has caused a loss among the supreme powers: the indispensable dark side has been left behind or stripped off, and the feminine aspect is missing. Thus a further act of incarnation becomes necessary. Through atheism, materialism, and agnosticism, the powerful yet one-sided aspect of the Summum Bonum is weakened, so that it cannot keep out the dark side, and incidentally the feminine factor, any more. "Antichrist" and "Devil" gain the ascendancy: God asserts his power through the revelation of his darkness and destructiveness. Man is merely instrumental in carrying out the divine plan. Obviously he does not want his own destruction but is forced to it by his own inventions. He is entirely unfree in his actions because he does not yet understand that he is a mere instrument of a destructive superior will. From this paradox he could learn that—*nolens volens*—he serves a supreme power, and that supreme powers exist in spite of his denial. As God lives in everybody in the form of the *scintilla* of the self, man could see his "daemonic," i.e., ambivalent, nature in himself and thus he could understand how he is penetrated by God or how God incarnates in man.

Through his further incarnation God becomes a fearful task for man, who must now find ways and means to unite the divine opposites in himself. He is summoned and can no longer leave his sorrows to somebody else, not even to Christ, because it was Christ that has left him the almost impossible task of his cross. Christ has shown how everybody will be crucified upon his destiny, i.e., upon his self, as he was. He did not carry his cross and suffer crucifixion so that we could escape. The bill of the Christian era is presented to us: we are living in a world rent in two from top to bottom; we are confronted with the H-bomb and we have to face our own shadows. Obviously God does not want us to remain little children looking out for a parent who will do their job for them. We are cornered by the supreme power of the incarnating Will. God really wants to become man, even if he rends him asunder. This is so no matter what we say. One cannot talk the H-bomb or Communism out of the world. We are in the soup that is going to be cooked for us, whether we claim to have invented it or not. Christ said to his disciples "Ye are gods." This word becomes painfully true. If God incarnates in the empirical man, man is confronted with the divine problem. Being and remaining man he has to find an answer. It is the question of the opposites, raised at the moment when God was declared to be good only. Where then is his dark side? Christ is the model for the human answers and his symbol is the *cross*, the union of the opposites. This will be the fate of man, and this he must understand if he is to survive at all. We are threatened with universal genocide if we cannot work out the way of salvation by a symbolic death.

In order to accomplish his task, man is inspired by the Holy Ghost in such a way that he is apt to identify him with his own mind. He even runs the grave risk of believing he has a Messianic mission, and forces tyrannous doctrines upon his fellow-beings. He would do better to dis-identify his mind from the small voice within, from dreams and fantasies through which the divine spirit manifests itself. One should listen to the inner voice attentively, intelligently and critically (*Probate spiritus!*), because the voice one hears is the *influxus divinus* consisting, as the *Acts of John* aptly state, of "right" and "left" streams, i.e., of opposites.[4] They have to be clearly separated so that their positive and negative aspects become visible. Only thus can we take up a middle position and discover a middle way. That is the task left to man, and that is the reason why man is so important to God that he decided to become a man himself.

I must apologize for the length of this exposition. Please do not think that I am stating a truth. I am merely trying to present a hypothesis which might explain the bewildering conclusions resulting from the clash of traditional symbols and psychological experiences. I thought it best to put my cards on the table, so that you get a clear picture of my ideas.

Although all this sounds as if it were a sort of theological speculation, it is in reality modern man's perplexity expressed in symbolic terms. It is the problem I so often had to deal with in treating the neuroses of intelligent patients. It can be expressed in a more scientific, psychological language; for instance, instead of using the term God you say "unconscious," instead of Christ "self," instead of incarnation "integration of the unconscious," instead of salvation or redemption "individuation," instead of crucifixion or sacrifice on the Cross "realization of the four functions or of "wholeness" [sic]. I think it is no disadvantage to religious tradition if we can see how far it coincides with psychological experience. On the contrary it seems to me a most welcome aid in understanding religious traditions.

A myth remains a myth even if certain people believe it to be the literal revelation of an eternal truth, but it becomes moribund if the living truth it contains ceases to be an object of belief. It is therefore necessary to renew its life from time to time through a *new interpretation*. This means re-adapting it to the changing spirit of the times. What the Church calls "prefigurations" refer to the original state of the myth, while the Christian doctrine represents a new interpretation and re-adaptation to a Hellenized world. A most interesting attempt at re-interpretation began in the eleventh century,[5] leading up to the schism in the sixteenth century. The Renaissance was no more a rejuvenation of antiquity than Protestantism was a return to the primitive Christianity: it was a new interpretation necessitated by the devitalization of the Catholic Church.

Today Christianity is devitalized by its remoteness from the spirit of the times. It stands in need of a new union with, or relation to, the atomic age, which is a unique novelty in history. The myth needs to be retold in a new spiritual language, for the new wine can no more be poured into the old bottles than it could in the Hellenistic age. Even conservative Jewry had to produce an entirely new version of the myth in its Cabalistic Gnosis. It is my practical experience that psychological understanding immediately revivifies the essential Christian ideas and fills them with the breath of life. This is because our worldly light, i.e., scientific knowledge and understanding, coincides with the symbolic statement of the myth, whereas previously we were unable to bridge the gulf between knowing and believing.

Coming back to your letter (pp. 2–3, 25 September) I must say that I could accept your definition of the Summum Bonum, "Whatever God is, that is good," if it did not interfere with or twist our sense of good. In dealing with the moral nature of an act of God, we have either to suspend our moral judgment and blindly follow the dictates of this superior will, or we have to judge in a human fashion and call white white and black black. In spite of the fact that we sometimes obey the superior will blindly and almost heroically, I do not think that this is the usual thing, nor is it commendable on the whole to act blindly, because we are surely expected to act with conscious moral reflection. It is too dangerously easy to avoid responsibility by deluding ourselves that our will is the will of God. We can be forcibly overcome by the latter, but if we are not we must use our judgment, and then we are faced with the inexorable fact that humanly speaking some acts of God are good and some bad, so much so that the assumption of a Summum Bonun becomes almost an act of hubris.

If God can be understood as the perfect *complexio oppositorum*, so can Christ. I can agree with your view about Christ completely, only it is not the traditional but a very modern conception which is on the way to the desired new interpretation. I also agree with your understanding of Tao and its contrast to Christ, who is indeed the paradigm of the reconciliation of the divine opposites in man brought about in the process of individuation. Thus Christ stands for the treasure and the supreme "good." (In German "good" = *gut*, but the noun *Gut* also means "property" and "treasure.")

When theology makes metaphysical assertions the conscience of the scientist cannot back it up. Since Christ never meant more to me than what I could understand of him, and since this understanding coincides with my empirical knowledge of the self, I have to admit that I mean the self in dealing with the idea of Christ. As a matter of fact I have no other access to Christ but the self, and since I do not know anything beyond the self I cling to his archetype. I say, "Here is the living and perceptible archetype which has been projected upon the man Jesus or has historically manifested itself in him." If this collective archetype had not been associated with Jesus he would have remained a nameless Zaddik. I actually prefer the term "self" because I am talking to Hindus as well as Christians, and I do not want to divide but to unite.

Since I am putting my cards on the table, I must confess that I cannot detach a certain feeling of dishonesty from any metaphysical assertion—one may speculate but not assert. One cannot reach beyond oneself, and if somebody assures you he can reach beyond himself and his natural limitations, he overreaches himself and becomes immodest and untrue.

This may be a *deformation professionelle*, the prejudice of a scientific conscience. Science is an honest-to-God attempt to get at the truth and its rule is never to assert more than one can prove within reasonable and defensible limits. This is my attitude in approaching the problem of religious experience.

I am unable to envisage anything beyond the self, since it is—by definition—a borderline concept designating the unknown totality of man: there are no known limits to the unconscious. There is no reason whatsoever why you should or should not call the beyond-self Christ or Buddha or Purusha or Tao or Khidr or Tifereth. All these terms are recognizable formulations of what I call the "self." Moreover I dislike the insistence upon a special name, since my human brethren are as good and as valid as I am. Why should their name-giving be less valid than mine?

It is not easy for a layman to get the desired theological information, because even the Church is not at one with herself in this respect. *Who* represents authentic Christianity? Thus the layman whether he likes it or not has to quote Protestant or Catholic statements *pêle-mêle* as Christian views because they are backed up by some authority. In my case I believe I have been careful in quoting my sources.

You as a theologian are naturally interested in the best possible view or explanation, while the psychologist is interested in all sorts of opinions because he wants to acquire some understanding of mental phenomenology and cares little for even the best possible metaphysical assertion, which is beyond human reach anyhow. The various creeds are just so many phenomena to him, and he has no means of deciding about the truth or the ultimate validity of any metaphysical statement. I cannot select the "best" or the "ultimate" opinions because I do not know which kind of opinion to choose from which Church. Also I do not care particularly where such opinions come from, and it is quite beyond my capacity to find out whether they are erroneous or not.

I would be wrong only if I attributed, for instance, the idea of the *conceptio immaculata* to Protestantism or the *sola fide* standpoint to Catholicism. The many misunderstandings attributed to me come into this category. In either case it is plain to see that someone has been careless in his assumptions. But if I attribute Ritschl's christological views to Protestantism, it is no error in spite of the fact that the Church of England does not subscribe to the opinions of Mr. Ritschl or of Mr. Barth.[6] I hope I have not inadvertently been guilty of some misquotation.

I can illustrate the problem by a typical instance. My little essay on Eastern Meditation[7] deals with the popular tract *Amitāyur Dhyāna Sūtra*, which is a relatively late and not very valuable Mahāyāna text. A critic objected to my choice: he could not see why I should take such an inconspicuous tract instead of a genuinely Buddhist and classical Pāli text in order to present Buddhist thought. He entirely overlooked the fact that I had no intention whatever of expounding classical Buddhism, but that my aim was to analyse the psychology of this particular text. Why should I not deal with Jacob Boehme or Angelus Silesius as Christian writers, even though they are not classical representatives either of Catholicism or of Protestantism?

A similar misunderstanding appears in your view that I am not doing justice to the *ideal* of community. Whenever possible I avoid *ideals* and much prefer *realities*. I have never found a community which would allow "full expression to the individual within it." Suppose the individual is going to speak the truth regardless of the feelings of everybody else: he would not only be the most abominable enfant terrible but might equally well cause a major catastrophe. Edifying examples of this can be observed at the meetings of Buchman's so-called Oxford Group Movement. At the expense of truth the individual has to "behave," i.e., suppress his reaction merely for the sake of Christian charity. What if I should get up after a sermon about ideals and ask the parson how much he himself is able to live up to his admonitions? In my own case the mere fact that I am seriously interested in psychology has created a peculiar hostility or fear in certain circles. What has happened to those people in the Church, that is in a Christian community, who ventured to have a new idea? No community can escape the laws of mass psychology. I am critical of the community in the same way as I suspect the individual who builds his castles in Spain while anxiously avoiding the expression of his own convictions. I am shy of ideals which one preaches and never lives up to, simply because one cannot. I want to know rather what we *can* live. I want to build up a possible human life which carries through God's experiment and does not invent an ideal scheme knowing that it will *never* be fulfilled.

To the Rev. David Cox

A Later Letter[8], 12 November 1957

I am much obliged to you for telling me exactly what you think and for criticizing my blunt ways of thinking and writing (also of talking, I am afraid). It seems, however, to be the style of natural scientists: we simply state our proposition, assuming that nobody will think it to be more than a disputable hypothesis. We are so imbued with doubts concerning our assumptions that skepticism is taken for granted. We are therefore apt to omit the conventional *captatio benevolentiae lectoris* with its "With hesitation I submit . . . ," "I consider it a daring hypothesis . . . ," etc. We even forget the preamble: "This is the way I look at it. . . ."

The case of the Jesuit[9] was that he put the direct question to me: "How on earth can you suggest that Christ was not human?" The discussion was naturally on the *dogmatic level*, as there is no other basis on which this question can be answered. It is not a question of *truth*, because the problem itself is far beyond human judgment. My "Answer to Job" is merely a reconstruction of the psychology discernible in this and other Old Testament texts for the interested layman. He knows very little of Higher Criticism, which is historical and philological in the main, and it is but little concerned with the layman's reactions to the paradoxes and moral horrors of the Old Testament. He knows his Bible and hears the sermons of his parson or priest. As a Catholic he has had a dogmatic education.

When talking of "Job" you must always remember that I am dealing with the psychology of an archetypal and anthropomorphic image of God and not with a metaphysical entity. As far as we can see, the archetype is a psychic structure with a life of its own to a certain extent.

God in the Old Testament is a guardian of law and morality, yet is himself unjust. He is a moral paradox, unreflecting in an ethical sense. We can perceive God in an infinite variety of images, yet all of them are anthropomorphic, otherwise they would not get into our heads. The divine paradox is the source of unending suffering to man. Job cannot avoid seeing it and thus he sees more than God himself. This explains why the God-image has to come down "into the flesh." The paradox, expressed of course with many hesitations in the particularities of the myth and in the Catholic dogma, is clearly discernible in the fact that the "Suffering Righteous man" is, historically speaking, an erroneous conception, not identical with the suffering God, because he is Jesus Christ, worshipped as a separate God (he is a mere prefiguration, painfully included in a trinity) and not an ordinary man who is forced to accept the suffering of intolerable opposites he has not invented. They were preordained. He is the victim, because he is capable of three-dimensional consciousness and ethical decision. (This is a bit condensed. Unlike Yahweh, man has self-reflection.)

I don't know what Job is supposed to have seen. But it seems possible that he unconsciously anticipated the historical future, namely the evolution of the God-image. God had to become man. Man's suffering does not derive from his sins but from the maker of his imperfections, the paradoxical God. The righteous man is the instrument into which God enters in order to attain self-reflection and thus consciousness and rebirth as a divine child trusted to the care of adult man.

Now this is not the statement of a truth, but the psychological reading of a mythological text—a model constructed for the purpose of establishing the psychological linking together of its contents. My aim is to show what the results are when you apply modern psychology to such a text. Higher Criticism and Hebrew philology are obviously superfluous, because it is simply a question of the text which the layman has under his eyes. The Christian religion has not been shaped by Higher Criticism.

The trouble I have with my academic reader is that he cannot see a psychic structure as a relatively autonomous entity, because he is under the illusion that he is dealing with a concept. But in reality it is a living thing. The archetype, all have a life of their own which follows a biological pattern. A Church that has evolved a masculine Trinity will follow the old pattern: 3 + 1, where 1 is a female and, if 3 = good, 1 as a woman will mediate between good and evil, the latter being the devil and the shadow of the trinity. The woman will inevitably be the Mother-Sister of the Son-God, with whom she will be united *in thalamo*, i.e., in the [*hieros gamos*], *quod est demonstratum* by the second Encyclical concerning the Assumption.[10]

A passionate discourse between the man Job and God will logically lead to a mutual rapprochement: God will be humanized, man will be "divinized." Thus Job will be followed by the idea of the Incarnation of God and the redemption and apotheosis of man. This development, however, is seriously impeded by the fact that the "woman," as always, inevitably brings in the problem of the shadow. Therefore *mulier taceat in ecclesia*. The arch-sin the Catholic Church is ever after is sexuality, and the ideal *par excellence* virginity, which puts a definite stop to life. But if life should insist on going on, the shadow steps in and sin becomes a serious problem, because the shadow cannot be left to eternal damnation any more. Consequently, at the end of the first millennium of the Christian aeon, as predicted in the Apocalypse, the world was suspected of being created by the devil.[11] The impressive and still living myth of the

Holy Grail came to life with its two significant figures of Parsifal and Merlin. At the same time we observe an extraordinary development of alchemical philosophy with its central figure of the *filius macrocosmi*, a chthonic equivalent of Christ.

This was followed by the great and seemingly incurable schism of the Christian Church, and last but not least by the still greater and more formidable schism of the world towards the end of the second millennium.

A psychological reading of the dominant archetypal images reveals a continuous series of psychological transformations, depicting the autonomous life of archetypes behind the scenes of consciousness. This hypothesis has been worked out to clarify and make comprehensible our religious history. The treatment of psychological troubles and the inability of my patients to understand theological interpretations and terminology have given me my motive. The necessities of psychotherapy have proved to me the immense importance of a religious attitude, which cannot be achieved without a thorough understanding of religious tradition, just as an individual's troubles cannot be understood and cured without a basic knowledge of their biographical antecedents. I have applied to the God-image what I have learned from the reconstruction of so many human lives through a knowledge of their unconscious. All this is empirical and may have nothing to do with theology, if theology says so. But if theology should come to the conclusion that its tenets have something to do with the empirical human psyche, I establish a claim. I think that in those circumstances my opinion should be given a hearing. It cannot be argued on the level of metaphysical assertions. It can be criticized only on its own psychological level, regardless of whether it is a psychologically satisfactory interpretation of the facts or not. The "facts" are the documented historical manifestations of the archetype, however "erroneous" they may be.

I have stated my point of view bluntly (for which I must ask your forgiveness!) in order to give you a fair chance to see it as clearly as possible. The end of your letter, where you deal with Christ, leaves me with a doubt. It looks to me as if you were trying to explain the empirical man Jesus, while I am envisaging the archetype of the Anthropos and its very general interpretation as a collective phenomenon and not as the best possible interpretation of an individual and historical person. Christianity as a whole is less concerned with the historical man Jesus and his somewhat doubtful biography than with the mythological Anthropos or God-Son figure. It would be rather hazardous to attempt to analyse the historical Jesus as a human person. "Christ" appears from a much safer (because mythological) background, which invites psychological elucidation. Moreover it is not the Jewish rabbi and reformer Jesus, but the archetypal Christ who touches upon the archetype of the Redeemer in everybody and carries conviction.

My approach is certainly not theological and cannot be treated as a theologoumenon. It is essentially a psychological attempt based upon the archetypal, amoral God-image, which is not a concept but rather an irrational and phenomenal experience, an *Urbild*. But in so far as theologians are also concerned with the adult human psyche (perhaps not as much as medical psychology), I am convinced that it would be of advantage to them to become acquainted with the psychological aspects of the Christian religion. I will not conceal the fact that theological thinking is very difficult for me, from which I conclude that psychological thinking must be an equally laborious undertaking for the theologian. This may explain why I inundate you with such a long letter.

When I see how China (and soon India) will lose her old culture under the impact of materialistic rationalism, I grow afraid that the Christian West will succumb to the same malady, simply because the old symbolic language is no longer understood and people cannot see any more where and how it applies. In Catholic countries anyone leaving the Church becomes frankly atheistic. In Protestant countries a small number become sectarians, and the others avoid the churches for their cruelly boring and empty sermons. Not a few begin to believe in the State—not even knowing that they themselves are the State. The recent broadcasts of the B.B.C.[12] give a good picture of the educated layman's mind with regard to religion. What an understanding! All due to the lack of a psychological standpoint, or so it seems to me.

I am sorry that I am apparently a *petra scandali*. I do not mean to offend. Please accept my apologies for my bluntness. I am sincerely grateful to you for giving me your attention.

Faithfully yours, C. G. JUNG

Notes

(*CW* 18, pars. 1648–1690)
 1. [Extracts from H. L. Philp, *Jung and the Problem of Evil* (London, 1958), 239–50. The book consists of correspondance between the author [Philp] and Jung in the form of questions and answers (in English), and an extended critical attack of 175 pages on Jung's writings on religion, with particular reference to *Answer to Job*. It concludes with Jung's answers to questions sent by another correspondent, the Rev. David Cox (author of *Jung and St. Paul*, 1959). Jung's answers to Cox's letters are reproduced here by permission of the Princeton University Press).]
 2. [Cf. "The Phenomenology of the Spirit in Fairytales," *CW* 9i, pars. 425f., 436ff.; *Aion*, *CW* 9ii, par. 351; and "The Spirit Mercurius," *CW* 13, pars. 270ff.]

3. [Cf. "The Spirit Mercurius," *CW* 13, par. 301.]
4. [James, *The Aprocryphal New Testament*, 255: "The Acts of Peter." Cf. "Transformation Symbolism in the Mass" *CW* 11, par. 429.]
5. [Cf. *Aion*, *CW* 9ii, pars. 139ff.]
6. [Albrecht Ritschl (1822–1889) and Karl Barth (1886–1968), resp. German and Swiss Protestant theologians.]
7. ["The Psychology of Eastern Meditation," *CW* 11.]
8. [H. L. Philp, 250–54.]
9. [Cf. *CW* 18, par. 1645.]
10. [*Apostolic Constitution* ("*Munificentissimus Deus*") of Pius XII, sec. 22: "The place of the bride whom the Father had espoused was in the heavenly courts." Sec. 33: ". . . on this day the Virgin Mother was taken up to her heavenly bridal chamber."]
11. [*Aion*,*CW* 9ii, pars. 225ff.]
12. [Probably a series of five talks on "Religion and Philosophy," by Robert C. Walton, J. D. Mabbott, Alasdair MacIntyre, and the Rev. F. A. Cockin, broadcast in Sept.–Oct. 1957, according to information from the B.B.C.]

WORKS CITED

Arnold, Matthew. 1965. *The Poems of Matthew Arnold.* Ed. Kenneth Allot. London: Longman.

Bultmann, Rudolf. 1953. New testament and mythology. In *Kerygma and Myth: A Theological Debate.* Ed. Hans Werner Bartsch. Trans. Reginald H. Fuller. Vol. 1. Published in two volumes. 2d ed. London: S. P. C. K., 1962–64.

Buber, Martin. 1952. *Eclipse of God: Studies in the Relationship Between Religion and Philosophy.* New York: Harper and Brothers.

Campbell, Joseph. 1974. *The Mythic Image.* Bollingen Series 100. Princeton: Princeton University Press.

Cassirer, Ernst, et al., eds. 1948. *The Renaissance Philosophy of Man.* Chicago: University of Chicago Press.

Charles, R. H., ed. 1913. *The Apocrypha and Pseudepigrapha of the Old Testament.* In 2 vols. Oxford: Clarendon. Vol. 2. Enoch I, 46:1–3.

de Chardin, Teilhard. 1965. *The Phenomenon of Man.* Trans. Bernard Wall. Intro. Julian Huxley. New York: Harper Colophon.

Descartes, René. 1966. *Meditations.* Trans. John Veitch. Intro. L. Lévi-Bruhl. La Salle, Illinois: Open Court.

Edinger, Edward F. 1987a. *The Christian Archetype.* Toronto: Inner City Books.

———. 1987b. *Ego and Archetype.* Repr. New York: Pelican.

———. 1985. *Anatomy of the Psyche: Alchemical Symbolism in Psychotherapy.* La Salle, Illinois: Open Court.

———. 1984. *The Creation of Consciousness.* Toronto: Inner City Books.

Ellenberger, Henri F. 1970. *The Discovery of the Unconscious: The History and Evolution of Dynamic Psychiatry.* New York: Basic Books.

Evans, Richard I. 1964. *Conversations with C. G. Jung and Reactions from Ernest Jones.* Princeton, New Jersey: Van Nostrand Reinhold Co.

Frankl, Viktor. 1962. *Man's Search for Meaning: An Introduction to Logotherapy.* Trans. Ilse Lasch. Boston: Beacon.

Jaffé, Aniela. 1971. *The Myth of Meaning.* New York: G. P. Putnam's Sons.

Jung, C. G. 1988. *Nietzsche's Zarathustra: Notes of the seminar given in 1934–1939.* In two volumes. Ed. James L. Jarrett. Bollingen Series XCIX. Princeton: Princeton University Press.

———. 1983. *The Zofingia Lectures.* Trans. Jan Von Heinck. Ed. William McGuire. Intro. Marie Louise Von Franz. CW Supplementary Volume A. Bollingen Series XX. Princeton: Princeton University Press.

———. 1977. *C. G. Jung Speaking: Interviews and Encounters.* Ed. William McGuire and R. F. C. Hull. Bollingen Series XCVII. Princeton: Princeton University Press.

———. 1975a. *Letters*. In two volumes. Vol. 2. Selected and edited by Gerhard Adler, in collaboration with Aniela Jaffé. Bollingen Series XCV. Princeton: Princeton University Press.

———. 1975b. *The Symbolic Life: Miscellaneous Writings*. Posthumous and other miscellaneous works. *CW* 18. Bollingen Series XX. Princeton: Princeton University Press.

———. 1973. *Letters*. In two volumes. Vol. 1. Selected and edited by Gerhard Adler, in collaboration with Aniela Jaffé. Bollingen Series XCV. Princeton: Princeton University Press.

———. 1971. *Psychological Types*. *CW* 6. Bollingen Series XX. Princeton: Princeton University Press.

———. 1969a. *Psychology and Religion: West and East*. *CW* 11. 2d ed. Bollingen Series XX. Princeton: Princeton University Press.

———. 1969b. *The Structure and Dynamics of the Psyche*. *CW* 8. 2d ed. Bollingen Series XX. Princeton: Princeton University Press.

———. 1966. *Two Essays in Analytical Psychology*. *CW* 7. 2d ed. Bollingen Series XX. Princeton: Princeton University Press.

———, and C. Kerényi. 1963a. *Essays on a Science of Mythology: The Myths of the Divine Child and the Divine Maiden*. Trans. R. F. C. Hull. New York: Harper & Row (1949).

———. 1963b. *Memories, Dreams, Reflections*. Recorded and edited by Aniela Jaffé. Trans. Richard and Clara Winston. New York: Pantheon.

———. 1955. *Mysterium Coniunctionis*. *CW* 14. Bollingen Series XX. Princeton: Princeton University Press, 1970.

———. 1952. Answer to Job. In *CW* 11. 2nd. ed. Bollingen Series XX. Princeton: Princeton University Press, 1969.

———. 1951. *Aion: Researches into the Phenomenology of the Self*. *CW* 9ii. Bollingen Series XX. Princeton: Princeton University Press, 1959.

———. 1950a. Concerning mandala symbolism. In *CW* 9i. Bollingen Series XX. Princeton: Princeton University Press, 1959.

———. 1950b. 1934. A study in the process of individuation. In *CW* 9i. Bollingen Series XX. Princeton: Princeton University Press, 1959.

———. 1948. 1942. A psychological approach to the dogma of the trinity. In *CW* 11. 2d ed. Bollingen Series XX. Princeton: Princeton University Press, 1969.

———. 1933. *Modern Man in Search of a Soul*. New York: Harcourt Brace.

Kant, Immanuel. 1965. *Critique of Pure Reason*. Trans. Norman Kemp Smith. New York: St. Martins Press.

Livy. 1960. *The Early History of Rome*, Books I–V. Harmondsworth, Middlesex: Penguin Books.

Melville, Herman. 1970. *White Jacket*. Vol. 5. *The Writings of Herman Melville*. Evanston, Illinois: Northwestern University Press.

Nietzsche, Friedrich. 1982. *The Gay Science*. Trans. Walter Kaufman. New York: Random House.

———. 1964. *Thus Spake Zarathustra*. Trans. Thomas Common. New York: Thistle Press.

Ostrowski-Sachs, Margaret, 1971. *From Conversations with C. G. Jung*, Juris Druck and Verlag Zürich (limited circulation).

Rolfe, Eugene. 1989. *Encounter with Jung*. Boston: Sigo Press.

Schneemelcher, Wilhelm, ed. 1964. *New Testament Apocrypha*. Philadelphia: Westminster Press. Original German edition edited by Edgar Hennecke.

Serrano, Miguel. 1966. *C. G. Jung and Hermann Hesse: A Record of Two Friendships*. Trans. Frank MacShane. New York: Schocken Books.

Sophocles. 1954. *Oedipus at Colonus*. Trans. Robert Fitzgerald. Chicago: University of Chicago Press.

Thomas à Kempis. 1894. *Imitation of Christ*. Philadelphia: Altemus.

von Franz, Marie-Louise. 1991. *Dreams*. Boston: Shambhala.

———. 1975. *C. G. Jung: His Myth in Our Time*. New York: Putnam.

———. n.d. The dream of Nicholas von der Flüe. Unpublished ms.

Whitehead, Alfred North. 1956. *Science and the Modern World*. New York: Mentor.

INDEX

A

Abraham, 37, 52, 113, 179
Achaeans, *xviii*
Achilles, *xviii*
Adonai, 133
Aion, *xxi*, 52–53, 134, 146, 151, 157, 182, 194–195
ajna, in Tantric yoga, 133–134
Al Chadir, 139
alchemy, 45
Allah, 30, 52
Amalekites, *xx*
anahata, in Tantric yoga, 133
anchorite as image, Jung on, 144
animism, discussion of, *xvi–xvii*
Annunciation, 100–102
Answer to Job, *xiii*, *xix*, *xxi*, 25, 38, 51, 78–80, 112, 131–132, 157, 171, 182, 191, 194
anthropomorphism, *anthropos*, 24, 131, 174
Aphrodite, *xviii*
apperception, in Jung, 27–28, 135
Aquarius, Age of, 156–157
archetypal psyche, 18, 21, 40
Ares, *xviii*
Arnold, Matthew, 15–16, 42
assumptio beatae virginis, 105
Assumption of Mary, *assumptio*, 102, 179
Athena, *xviii*
Athi Plains, in Jung, 90
Attis, *xvii*, 139, 155, 158
augurs, in Ancient Rome, 29, 36, 47, 104
Augustine, 35, 141, 146

B

baptism, 53–55, 61, 94, 104, 151
Barth, Karl, 190, 195
Basel Cathedral, 18
Behemoth, 25, 73
Bernet, Pastor Walter, 15, 21, 23, 25, 66, 128–134
Binah, in Jewish Kabbalah, 105, 107
Boehme, Jacob, 11, 125, 184, 190
Bohr, Niels, 139
Bonhoeffer, Dietrich, 146
Book of Job, *xiii*, 25, 70, 141, 162, 165, 169
Brooke, Valentine, 27, 30, 135–137
Brother Klaus, 126–127, 182
Buber, Martin, 3, 31–33, 51, 123–125, 138–140, 173
Buddhist world view, 71–75, 118, 124, 134, 149, 156, 162, 170, 189–190
Bultmann, Rudolf, 41–42, 51, 131, 142

C

Campbell, Joseph, 72
Carus, Carl Gustav, 13, 146
Cathars, discussion of, 61–62, 151
causality, 28–29, 69, 135
    Kant *vs.* Aristotle, 28, 160
Caux–sur–Montreux, 173, 175, 182
Charles, R. H., 79–80
Christ, *xx*, *xxi*, 41, 51–61, 65–66, 71, 73, 75, 79–81, 86–89, 93–95, 98–100, 103–105, 111, 115–124, 130–132, 139–143, 147–193

Christian Church, *xxi*, 3, 5, 19,
    37–41, 52–54, 57–60, 91–109,
    141–156, 169, 175, 183–194
Cicero, 141, 146
Clement of Rome, 51–52, 96, 147,
    174
Cockin, The Rev. F. A., 195
Codex Jung, 151
collective psyche, *xiv*, 19, 112–113
collective Self, *xiv*
coniunctio, 58–61, 106, 111–113
consciousness, of the divinity, 89
consolamentum, 60–62, 118, 148,
    150–151
continuing incarnation, *xxii*, 86, 99,
    100–102, 110–111, 115
    part 3, 75–120
Copernicus, world view of, 4, 9, 32
Council of Nicaea, 151
covenant, 37
Cox, Rev. David, 109, 183–195
creation as consciousness, in Jung,
    89, 117, 145

D
Daniel, Book of, 79, 141, 165, 168
demiurge, 25, 167
Descartes, René, 4–6, 9
determinism, *contra* free will, 74
Deucalion, 52
Deus absconditus, 94–95, 173
Deus Pater, 55, 147
dia, 23
diabolos, 20
dialectic, 23
divine drama, xiii, 80, 99, 120, 179–181
donum spiritus sancti, 40

E
Edinger, Edward F., *xv*, 20, 51, 93,
    103–104
Eleusis, mysteries of, 47
empty centre, 22–23
Enoch, 79–80, 141, 165

Entwicklungswege, xiii
episteme, 3
epistemological premises
    part 1, 1–47
Esau, 53
ethics, psychological, 84–86
Etruscans, 104
evangelium aeternum, 60, 148, 179
evolution. *See* God–image, stages of.
Evans, Richard I., 134, 171
Ezekiel, 79, 97, 164, 168

F
faith, *xxii*, 11, 15–17, 19, 36–41, 97,
    116, 124–128, 132, 141, 146,
    151, 174–175, 183
filius macrocosmi, 193
Flora, Joachim of Gioacchino, 60,
    93, 148–151, 167, 179
Flournoy, Henri, 137
Frankl, Viktor, 85
Frau N., 68, 151, 162–163
Freeman, John, 27, 30, 137
Freud, Sigmund, 81, 85, 132

G
Gabriel, the Angel, 100–101
Gioacchino. *See* Flora, Joachim of.
Gnosticism, in Buber–Jung
    controversy, 138, 150, 178
Godhead, 53, 55, 88, 102, 147, 170,
    179
God–image, *xiii–xxii*, 3, 6, 16,
    20–31, 51–52, 55–56, 59–64,
    77–78, 81, 84, 91, 98–99, 102,
    105, 109, 110–115, 130–131,
    133, 136, 139, 170, 191–194
    stages of evolution, *xv–xxii*

H
Harding, Esther, 59
Heidegger, Martin, 31
Hermetic philosophy, 139, 180

hierarchical polytheism, discussion
of, *xviii–xix*
Hitler, Adolf, in Jung, 137
Hokhmah, in Jewish Kabbalah, 105,
107
Holy Spirit, 40, 53, 57, 59–61,
91–105, 119–120, 148–151,
172–181
Homer, *xviii*, 23, 134
Homer's *Iliad, xviii*, 23
Hosea, 146, 177
hubris, 44, 188
human subjectivity, 3, 6

I
I Ching, 29, 37, 97
imitatio Christi, 57–58, 149–149, 180
Incarnatio, 65, 89, 159–161, 170
incarnation. *See* continuing
incarnation.
individuation, *xv, xxii*, 24, 45, 56, 87,
113, 117, 129–130, 148, 167,
180, 187–188
as religious development,
xxi–xxii
Ishmael, 52
Ixion, the wheel of, 73

J
Jaffé, Aniela, 63, 137, 159, 161
Job. *See Answer to Job* and Book of Job.
John, First Letter, 38
Judaism, 35–38, 46
Jung, Carl
Jung's epistemology, 9, 26, 31
Jung's letters, selections from,
121–195

K
Kabbalah, Jewish, 105, 139
Kant, Immanuel, 1, 3–4, 6–9, 12, 26,
28, 40, 96, 116, 123, 126, 140
Kelipoth, in Jewish Kaballah, 105
Kelsey, Rev. Morton T., 88, 169–171

kenosis, 87
Kerényi, Karl, 157
Kotschnig, Elined, 56, 66, 77–80,
134, 164–168
Krishna, 139

L
Lachat, Père William, 91, 94,
172–182
Lang, Bernhard, 3, 8, 39, 115,
123–127
Lapis Philosophorum, 139
Lateran Council, 92, 151
legein, 23
Leviathan, 25, 73
ligare, 35
Livy, 104
logos, 3
logotherapy, 85
Lucretius, 141, 146
Luke, Book of, 53, 85, 100, 151, 157,
171

M
Mabbott, J. D., 195
MacIntyre, Alasdair, 195
Maeder, Alphonse, 140
Malkhuth, in Jewish Kabbalah,
105–107
mana, 8
mandala, as symbol, 22, 72, 129, 159
Marcion, *xxi*, 44–45
Mars, *xviii*
Mary, the Virgin, 53, 94, 100–102,
178–179
Materia, 42, 143
matriarchy, discussion of, *xvii–xviii*
Melville, Herman, 82–84
Memories, Dreams, Reflections, 90, 102,
134, 158, 161
Mithras, 139
moira, 69
monotheism. *See* tribal monotheism
and universal monotheism.

morphe, 24
Mussolini, Benito, in Jung, 137
Mysterium Coniunctionis, xxi, 58, 69,
    105–106, 157–158, 182
mythologem, in Jung, 41, 132,
    142–143, 154, 174

N
Neumann, Erich, xvii, 63–67, 89,
    140, 158, 159–161
New Testament, xxi, 41, 44, 51–53,
    88, 94, 132, 170–177, 181, 195
Nidhana–chain of Suffering, 71–72,
    118, 151, 162
Nietzsche, Friedrich, 12, 15, 31
nolens volens, 139, 186
noumenon, 7, 11, 15, 29, 33, 44–46,
    55, 60, 66–67, 70, 73, 82, 101,
    117, 125, 140–143, 180, 193
nous, 7
numina, 36, 141
numinosum, 40, 42, 146

O
Odin, 139
Old Testament, xxi, 44, 88, 94, 98,
    113–115, 131, 151, 166,
    170–172, 176, 180, 184, 191

P
Paraclete, 60–61, 150–151
paradoxical God, xxii, 49, 52–53, 61,
    111–115, 120, 166, 181, 192
    part 2, 49–74
Patre Filoque, 98, 178
Paul, St., 16–17, 32, 39, 86, 116,
    125–128, 157, 173, 194
pentecostal, in Jung, 89, 170
perfecti, 61–62
Perseus, 101
phanein, 7
Pharisaism, 156
phrenes, 133–134

phylogeny, compared to ontogeny,
    xv
pistis, 39–40, 116, 125, 127
polytheism. *See* hierarchical
    polytheism.
Probate spiritus, 113–114, 187
Protestantism, 94, 131, 143, 173,
    179, 184–185, 188, 190
Przywara, Erich, 180, 182
psyche, discovery of, xv. *See also*
    individuation.
psychological maturity, in Jung, 87

R
Radin, Paul, 153, 157
religare, etymology, 35, 141
religere, etymology, 35, 37, 39, 141
religio, etymology, 39, 40, 141–142,
    146
religious realities, 15, 18, 20–21, 23,
    117, 128
Richardson, Maurice, 135, 137
Ritschl, Albert, 190, 195
Ruach Elohim, 98, 178

S
S. Joannes à Cruce, 55, 147
Sachseln, the vision at, 11, 125–127,
    175
Sartre, Jean–Paul, 31
Satan, xx, 42, 53–58, 62, 98, 118,
    148–150, 153, 155, 172–174,
    178, 180–184
Schneelmelcher, Wilhelm, 53
Schopenhauer, Arthur, 12–13
Schweitzer, Albert, 96, 173–174
Sefirothic Tree, diagram, 107
Self, conceived in Jungian terms, xiv,
    xix, 36–39, 47, 53, 56, 64–65, 70,
    72–73, 80–81, 84–85, 87–88, 97,
    111, 114, 138
self–consciousness of God, 63–65,
    118, 159

shadow, 53, 56–58, 85, 102, 118,
148–149, 155–156, 173, 192
Shekinah, in Jewish Kabbalah, 106
Sinclair, Upton, 146, 163
Smith, Robert C., 31, 138–140
Sophia, 79, 165, 180
Sophocles, 47
Summum Bonum, 11, 109–110, 125,
142, 170, 172, 179, 185, 186, 188
sunyata, in Tantric yoga, 134

T
Tanner, Pastor, 35, 41, 89, 141–146
Tantric Yoga, 133
Tao, 22, 129, 188–189
Tarquin, Lucumo (Lucius Tarquin
Priscius), 104
Terry lectures, Jung's, 19
Thomas à Kempis, 57
Tifereth, in Jewish Kabbalah,
105–107, 139, 189
tribal monotheism, discussion of,
xix–xx
Trinitarian belief, 30, 59, 93, 99, 102
Trinity image, 11, 22, 57, 59, 72,
91–93, 102, 125, 143, 165–167,
173, 178
Trinity, archetype of, 72

U
unconsciousness, 64–66, 72–73, 77,
119, 159, 162–165

unio mentalis, 58
universal monotheism, discussion of,
xx–xxi

V
virgo terra, 102, 179
vision of Nicholas of Flüe, 11
vision of St. Paul, 16–17, 116, 128
visuddba, in Tantric yoga, 133–134
von der Flüe, Nicholas, 10–11, 22,
125, 127, 174–175
von Franz, Marie–Louise, 11, 93
von Hartmann, Eduard, 12

W
Walton, Robert C., 195
White, Father Victor, 51, 59, 140,
147–158, 168
Whitehead, Alfred North, 5, 6
Whitmont, Edward, 146

Y
Yahweh, xix–xxi, 25, 30, 37, 52–55,
70, 73, 80, 97–98, 113, 115, 132,
141, 147, 154, 162, 165–167,
169, 173–174, 178–184, 192

Z
Zacharias, Gerhard, 153, 157
Zofingia Lectures, 8